An Unsung Soldier

D D E

THE WHITE HOUSE

December 20, 1960

Dear Andy:

At the end of each of the past seven years, I have tried, by
individual letters, to express my gratitude to my close associates in the Administration for their unfailing dedication
and selflessness in the service of the nation. In these final
days of this Administration and the last holiday season we
shall spend together, I strive once more to find the words
to express the depth of my indebtedness to you. Personally
and officially your counsel, assistance and your very presence have meant much to me.

Let me thank you once again for your invaluable contribution
to the people of our country, and at the same time urge you
to keep the ranks closed and colors flying.

With best wishes to you and Dossy for a Merry Christmas
and warm personal regard,

As ever,

D.E.

Brigadier General Andrew J. Goodpaster, USA
The White House

An Unsung Soldier

The Life of Gen. Andrew J. Goodpaster

ROBERT S. JORDAN

NAVAL INSTITUTE PRESS
ANNAPOLIS, MARYLAND

Naval Institute Press
291 Wood Road
Annapolis, MD 21402

Library of Congress Cataloging-in-Publication Data

Jordan, Robert S.,
  An unsung soldier : the life of Gen. Andrew J. Goodpaster / Robert S. Jordan.
    pages cm
  Includes bibliographical references and index.
  ISBN 978-1-61251-278-5 (hardcover : alk. paper) — ISBN 978-1-61251-279-2
(ebook) 1. Goodpaster, Andrew Jackson, 1915–2005. 2. Generals—United States—
Biography. 3. Eisenhower, Dwight D. (Dwight David), 1890–1969—Friends and
associates. 4. National security—United States—Decision making—History—
20th century. 5. United States. Army—Biography. 6. North Atlantic Treaty
Organization—Biography. 7. United States—History, Military—20th century. 8.
United States Military Academy—Biography. 9. Cold War. I. Title. II. Title: Life of
Gen. Andrew J. Goodpaster.
  E745.G66J67 2013
  355.0092—dc23
  [B]
                              2013018691

Photos courtesy of the George C. Marshall Foundation, Lexington, Virginia.

∞ Print editions meet the requirements of ANSI/NISO z39.48-1992 (Permanence
of Paper).
Printed in the United States of America.

21 20 19 18 17 16 15 14 13   9 8 7 6 5 4 3 2 1
First printing

This book is dedicated to the memories of
Dr. Norman H. Gibbs
Chichele Professor of the History of War, All Souls College, Oxford University

and

Dr. Edgar S. Furniss Jr.
Professor of Politics, Princeton University; Director, The Mershon Program,
The Ohio State University

Mentors to many students and scholars—especially to a young student who
found himself in awesomely unfamiliar academic environments

Contents

Foreword

I am happy to have this opportunity to say a word about my dear friend and sometime colleague, Gen. Andrew Goodpaster. I do this having in mind that I was honored with the Goodpaster Award of the George C. Marshall Foundation. In addition, I was invited to dedicate "Goodpaster Hall" on the campus of St. Mary's College, in nearby Maryland.

I first met General Goodpaster when he became commandant of the National War College—the military's highest institution of professional military education—and I became a student there shortly thereafter. General Goodpaster took me "under his wing" and provided me with invaluable perspectives on leadership, policy and strategy development, and war prevention. While I confess to receiving somewhat special treatment, General Goodpaster so endeared himself to my entire class that they elected him an honorary member of the class at the end of the year. That was an initiation of an increasingly close association, which grew until his unfortunate passing in 2005.

There never is a poor time for a career military person to bring up the subject of leadership. In 1981, when General Goodpaster was superintendent at West Point, he described his concept of leadership: "I thought that the framework [for the Department of Behavioral Sciences and Leadership] had to be leadership, but a deep and broad understanding of leadership. I think that has been the case. And the related disciplines—psychology, for example, and some elements of sociology—would fall within the framework of a sense of how you should give leadership. How does an officer give leadership at the various echelons of responsibility?"[1]

This observation had been earlier reframed thus: "If we wish to know the meaning of behavior, we must know the meanings of the behaver [*sic*]; to remain outside his frame of experience is simply to remain in the dark."[2]

With warfare today relying more and more on high technology, it is noteworthy that General Goodpaster's Princeton doctoral dissertation, written in 1950, anticipated this significant trend before it had become such a dominant aspect of both strategy and tactics. For him, knowledge of engineering (he was commissioned in the Corps of Engineers from West Point) had to be linked to, or partnered with, knowledge of the social and behavioral sciences. He also was convinced that, as the United States had entered the world political-military arena to stay after the great victory of World War II, military officers should obtain a thorough grounding in history and international affairs. I watched him put his ideas into practice when we were both at the National War College.

General Goodpaster's leadership style was understated and quietly focused—he led by persuasion, by rational discourse, and by unfailing courtesy and consideration for others. These traits made him both a successful Supreme Allied Commander in NATO and an essential White House assistant and confidante to President Dwight D. Eisenhower.

In a completely different vein, General Goodpaster joined the board of St. Mary's College of Maryland in 1987. He devoted twelve years to a substantial overhaul of the college's overall progress, curriculum procedures, and faculty compensation to lift St. Mary's to the first tier of liberal arts colleges in the nation.

Policy was as much a part of him as command and combat; in the Army an officer who was outstanding in both was a marked man. This is why Goodpaster rose quickly through the ranks, always being called back into a policy role even as he desired command assignments. He invariably wanted to know *why*, as well as *what* and *how*, when confronted with a policy dilemma. Also, he shared President Eisenhower's insistence on considering the various alternatives when arriving at a decision. Not only was he not a "yes-man," he did not want to be associated with them as he advanced up the career ladder.

Professor Jordan has written a painstakingly researched, yet eminently readable, account of the career and accomplishments of General Goodpaster, for which I, for one, am very grateful.

Lt. Gen. Brent Scowcroft, USAF (Ret.)
National Security Advisor to President Gerald Ford and
President G. H. W. Bush

Preface

> "It is absurd to make out that the means ever became
> more important than the end."
>   —GRAHAM GREENE, *The Lost Childhood and Other Essays*

Few military men of his generation have been both "warriors" and "think-ers," yet Gen. Andrew Jackson Goodpaster Jr. qualifies to be among that select company. To write about so-called action generals who more often than not possessed vivid personalities, although still a challenge, pales against the challenge of writing about a contemplative general who also could be an operational commander in combat or near-combat situations.

General Goodpaster was a dedicated cold warrior throughout his active-duty military career of nearly forty years. He was also a sophisti-cated observer and commentator on the foreign policy and national secu-rity scene for nearly a quarter-century thereafter. In fact, it was said that during the course of his professional and post-military career, "he contin-ued to receive calls from agencies involved with national security affairs for a variety of assignments at the highest and, in the Cold War, most impor-tant level of policy—the three-way intersection of presidential politics, mil-itary planning, and international relations."[1]

It is difficult to speak of a nonconformist when discussing a very senior military man, but the more Goodpaster's personality is examined, the more difficult it is to simply consider him the consummate "insider." Although he was notably successful at playing by the rules at each level of his career, nonetheless he managed to retain his distinct character and personality. This was true for many of the general officers who came to the peak of their careers either near the end of World War II or during the early Cold War years—Lyman Lemnitzer, Lauris Norstad, and Matthew Ridgway come to mind. Yet none of them in their earlier years came to the attention of the "movers and shakers" who controlled their professional futures in quite the same manner as Goodpaster. Two persons stand out as his mentors: George "Abe" Lincoln, and Dwight D. Eisenhower. George C. Marshall was his model of the "complete officer."

As his career unfolded, Goodpaster could retain the aspect of a detached observer even as—by extension—he was able to relate successfully to those around him within a largely closed yet supportive hierarchical professional environment. From his relatively humble origins, he achieved the highest international military command assignment possible—as the supreme allied commander, Europe (SACEUR), of the North Atlantic Treaty Organization (NATO).

Thereafter, he earned the gratitude of the Army as a whole when he returned to West Point as its superintendent from 1977 to 1981 to help restore integrity to its reputation, which had been sullied by a widespread cadet cheating scandal involving engineering examinations. Along the way, he became one of the first serving Army officers to obtain a doctoral degree in an Ivy League university. He also, of course, became an essential part of the Eisenhower White House entourage relatively early in his military career, often performing essentially civilian responsibilities informally, as well as becoming through his presence not only a trusted aide but also a counselor and friend to the president.

Not resting on his laurels, upon his final retirement and for over a quarter-century thereafter, he was actively involved in both the formal and informal worlds of Washington policy-making, making his mark repeatedly as a respected participant. He identified himself with organizations as diverse at St. Mary's College of Maryland and the Atlantic Council, serving as an officer in both, along with contributing his time and presence to many other worthwhile activities.

Robert S. Jordan
Woodbridge, Virginia
December 2012

Acknowledgments

The Eisenhower Presidential Library in Abilene, Kansas, and the George C. Marshall Foundation in Lexington, Virginia (wherein are the Goodpaster Papers), underwrote travel and maintenance costs, and their staffs have been unfailingly supportive. In particular, tribute must be paid to David Haight and to Christopher Abraham of the Eisenhower Presidential Library and to Joanne Hartog for monitoring my research progress, and especially to archivist and assistant librarian Jeffrey Kozak, both of the Marshall Foundation. Jehanne Moharram for the Naval Institute Press painstakingly and patiently copyedited the manuscript. Thanks also to the Association of the United States Army for providing a last-minute subvention.

The late Dr. Stephen Ambrose, an Eisenhower biographer, should also be remembered both as a friend and as a professional colleague in the Eisenhower Center at the University of New Orleans. Dr. J. Kenneth McDonald has consistently supported this endeavor, both as a constructive critic and as a valued friend and former colleague.

Individuals who were encouraging and helpful in a practical sense are David Acheson, Roger Axtell, Stephen Benedict, Edwin A. Deagle Jr., Jay Gatlin, Christian Graff, Matthew Graff, Dr. Gregory Granger, Ambassador Martin Hillenbrand, Ambassador Aubrey Hooks, Ambassador Robert E. Hunter, Brig. Gen. Amos A. Jordan, Dr. Lawrence S. Kaplan, Max Lawver, Caleb Leming, C. Richard Nelson, Professor Robert O'Neill, Dr. Gregory Pedlow, Dr. Wayne Rasmussen and Susan Rasmussen (for both logistic and moral support), Dr. Steven Rearden, Lt. Gen. Brent Scowcroft, Professor John Shy, Dr. Lewis "Bob" Sorley, Nicholas Stratton, Roger Sullivan, Ambassador George Vest, Andrew Ward, Kenneth Weisbrode, and especially my wife, Jane Hatch Jordan.

Responsibility for the outcome rests, of course, with the author.

Terms and Abbreviations

Note: All agencies listed are U.S. agencies unless otherwise noted.

ACDA	Arms Control and Disarmament Agency
ACE	Allied Command Europe (NATO)
AEC	Atomic Energy Commission
APGA	Association of Princeton Graduate Alumni (Princeton University)
ARPA	Advanced Research Projects Agency
CE	Corps of Engineers (U.S. Army)
CIA	Central Intelligence Agency
CID	Committee of Imperial Defense (UK)
CINCEUR	Commander-in-chief, U.S. forces, Europe
CMH	Center of Military History
COMUSMACV	Commander, U.S. Military Assistance Command, Vietnam
CORONA	Code word for a program of strategic reconnaissance satellites
DCI	Director of central intelligence
DDCI	Deputy director of central intelligence
DDP	Deputy director for plans, CIA Operations
DOD	Department of Defense
ELINT-COMINT	Electronic Intelligence-Communications Intelligence
IISS	International Institute for Strategic Studies
JASC	Joint Advanced Study Committee
JCS	Joint Chiefs of Staff
JWPC	Joint War Plans Committee
MBFR	Mutual and balanced force reductions
Memcon	Memorandum of conversation
NATO	North Atlantic Treaty Organization
NCO	Noncommissioned officer
NSC	National Security Council
OCB	Operations Coordinating Board (NSC)
OPD	Operations and Plans Division (of the War Department)

OSD	Office of the Secretary of Defense
PfP	Partnership for Peace
PPS	Policy Planning Staff
PROVN	Program for the Pacification and Long-Term Development of Vietnam
PSAC	President's Science Advisory Committee
S&P	Strategy and Policy Group
SAC	Strategic Air Command
SACEUR	Supreme allied commander, Europe (NATO)
SALT	Strategic Arms Limitation Talks
SCS	Screening and Costing Staff
SHAPE	Supreme Headquarters Allied Powers Europe (NATO)
START	Strategic Arms Reduction Talks
SWNCC	State-War-Navy Coordinating Committee
TCC	Temporary Council Committee (NATO)
TCP	Technological Capabilities Panel
USAF	U.S. Air Force
USCINCEUR	U.S. commander-in-chief, European Command
USMA	U.S. Military Academy (at West Point)
USSR	Union of Soviet Socialist Republics
WH	White House
WPD	War Plans Division (later renamed OPD)
WUDO	Western Union Defense Organization

Part I
A Career in Preparation and Execution

Chapter One

The Professional Foundation

"During our first two years, my first two years at West Point, we knew about the war in China. We knew that there was war in the world and we knew that the situation in Europe was unstable and becoming more and more dangerous."

—GEN. ANDREW J. GOODPASTER

In demeanor, Andrew Goodpaster was described as being austere yet approachable in a no-nonsense way. He dressed neatly but not stylishly. He smiled readily, was courteous but not obsequious, usually waited for others to speak before interjecting his own thoughts, and except perhaps because of his height, could easily be missed in a crowd.

The Eisenhower historian Stephen Ambrose had this to say: "General Andrew Goodpaster, in Ike's opinion, was not only the best officer in the U.S. Army, but also one of the two or three smartest men in the country. Well over six feet tall, ramrod straight, impeccable in his perfectly pressed uniform, with rugged features, broad shoulders, and a powerful chest, he was graceful in his movements, polite yet firm in his attitude."[1] He seemed more at ease with himself than self-regarding.

An important personality trait that Goodpaster possessed was trust-worthiness. He took seriously this observation: "The elements that go into inspiring trust are a style that is not offensive to the majority, a transcending honesty, a high level of intelligence, a willingness to deal with problems that immediately touch people's lives, a sense of patriotism, and public confidence in those to whom presidents lend their prestige and authority."[2]

In sum, he came across as quietly self-confident, not seeking the lime-light but not shirking it either. His understated personality enhanced his rapid progression in staff as well as command assignments. Although much his own man, his aptitude as a "facilitator" for the success of others gained him respect and the early attention of important career mentors. Put in sociological terms: "Among leaders there is self-advertising, in which the leader's self-image is advanced by his own posturing; and there are fame-makers, others who advance the leader's image."[3]

Specifically, from his days at West Point to his service as President Eisenhower's staff secretary and defense liaison officer, Goodpaster was an excellent illustration of the second—he left the first type to others. Contributing to this was his gift of influencing others in a way that drew them to him—a personality trait that is not learned.

As befitting an ambitious graduate of West Point, he was determined to conduct himself professionally so that opportunities for advancement would be there for him. When command assignments came to him, he grasped them enthusiastically and effectively. In fact, he continually sought them out.

"Abe" Lincoln and West Point

Goodpaster's origins were modest. He was born in Granite City, Illinois, in 1915 to Andrew Jackson and Teresa Mrovka Goodpaster. His father owned a small farm, and occasionally worked as a streetcar conductor in St. Louis, Missouri. After wending his way through the public schools of Granite City, with parental encouragement he entered McKendree College in Lebanon, Illinois, where he stayed for only two and a half years, preparing for a career teaching high school mathematics (in those days, he was known as "Jack"). For financial reasons, he dropped out in order to go to St. Louis to work in a meatpacking plant, where he was elected the first president of the company's labor union. The kind of employment opportunities in the St. Louis area that suited his temperament and ambitions were obviously scarce, but even then he showed leadership qualities.

At that juncture, in 1935, upon the nomination of Rep. E. M. Schaefer of the 22nd District of Illinois and after a competitive examination, Goodpaster obtained an appointment to West Point (he was unsuccessful in obtaining an appointment to the Naval Academy). When asked how he adjusted to being a plebe (first-year cadet) at West Point, Goodpaster answered, "I had a vague notion of what it was. It was still quite a shock to go in there. But they left no doubt as to what was expected of you, and I very soon concluded that it was well within my capabilities to do what had to be done."[4]

In this respect, Goodpaster reflected this definition of adulthood: "If the term 'adult' means anything, its meaning must be social. One does not declare oneself adult: one is perceived to be. Unavoidably, the qualities we call adult are on the side of 'sanity,' 'normality,' rationality, continuity, sobriety, responsibility, wisdom, conduct as opposed to mere behavior, the good of the family or group or species as distinct from the desires of the individual."[5]

Goodpaster himself put it well, when he commented on his initial experience at West Point: "When we went into West Point, it was with a four-year commitment to serve after graduation. We didn't think too much about that; but as time went on the whole atmosphere was that this was a calling. That this was one of the great fields of service and then duty, honor, country began to take hold of us and a . . . a feeling that to serve your country in the military was one of the worthiest things that we could do. . . . We saw the officers there, they were fine people."[6]

As the members of the class of 1939 moved through their undergraduate experience, "we had that sense that the world was headed toward war and it was a sobering thought because we had the feeling that we would be drawn into it. The cadets all talked about it."[7] Stephen Ambrose summarized the situation confronting Goodpaster and his West Point contemporaries: "In 1939, on the eve of World War II, the United States had an Army of 185,000 men with an annual budget of less than $500 million. America had no military alliances and no American troops were stationed in any foreign country. The dominant political mood was isolationism."[8]

In fact, Goodpaster's class had been made larger than its predecessors—nearly eight hundred—to accommodate for the expected growth of the officer corps in anticipation of the exigencies of war: "We are the class of 1939, first and largest of the large classes—fledglings untried in the larger game for which we have been preparing. Humbly we hope we may be worthy tools, may carry the Spirit of the Corps out with us into the Service, and yet may leave behind the Corps itself, better than we found it."[9]

Mentoring is a widespread human activity, and especially so within a military setting in which continuity of management is an essential—indeed obligatory—aspect of successful leadership. In Goodpaster's case, the pivotal mentor for him throughout his career was then-captain George "Abe" Lincoln, an instructor in the Department of Economics, Government, and History. During his years on the faculty at West Point, Lincoln was to redefine the role of the officer to conform more closely to the needs of modern and ever-changing warfare. Lincoln had graduated from West Point in 1929 and had proceeded from there to Oxford University as a Rhodes scholar, thus setting the stage for generations of talented West Pointers who went on to win the coveted scholarship.[10] Doubtless conditioned by his own experience at Oxford, Lincoln introduced into the curriculum more courses in the humanities and social sciences. Engineering, for him, could not play its proper role in preparing the cadets for what lay before them without partnering with these other disciplines.

Lincoln was the person who had the greatest influence on Goodpaster while he was at West Point, and this beneficial relationship continued for the rest of their lives. For Lincoln, Goodpaster was emblematic of the type of officer that he envisioned would hold the future of the Army in their grasp. Early on, this mentoring relationship brought an invaluable opportunity to Goodpaster in the late winter of 1939, when Lincoln nominated him to represent West Point in a Council on Foreign Relations–sponsored student conference. This was the first time the academy had sent a delegate.

Goodpaster recalled: "I was sent down from West Point as our delegate to that enterprise. . . . We engaged in three days of debate. . . . At the end of it, three of us were voted to set out our respective views: one, I think from Harvard, supported the continuation of the Neutrality Act. . . . I had taken the position that we should disengage from the Act but maintain, as I put it, freedom of action depending on the course of events without commitment to any particular group or side at that time."[11]

Undoubtedly to Lincoln's satisfaction, Goodpaster left this impression:

> The outstanding man of the sixteen [university seniors] was Andrew Goodpaster. This became increasingly apparent as the conference progressed. He was a frequent contributor to the general discussion, never in the sense of talking too much but of speaking up at the right time and in the right way. . . . He thinks clearly and can express his ideas simply and directly. . . . He was one of the three spokesmen for the university men at the Friday night dinner. This in itself is a sign of his ability, for the spokesmen are chosen from the outstanding men of the group. His "speech"—for lack of a better term—was a fifteen-minute description of what he considered to be the most effective foreign policy for the United States during the next half year. It brought a salvo of applause from the Council members present.[12]

Goodpaster also was brigade adjutant, served on the debate team that won a national championship, and served on the Honor Committee, in addition to playing football and swimming. When Goodpaster graduated second in his class, he was already marked as a "comer" possessing natural leadership.

To seal his commitment to an Army career, when Goodpaster was about to enter his first assignment, he married Dorothy "Dossy" Anderson, whom he had met during his first year, when she had been working in the West Point Library, on 28 August 1939. Dossy was the daughter of the academy's executive officer, Lt. Col. (later Maj. Gen.) Jonathan Waverly Anderson. The Goodpasters had two daughters, Susan and Anne, in the course of a satisfying marriage coupled with highly successful military service—not so easily accomplished.[13]

Later on, Goodpaster addressed the question of leadership development at the academy as follows: "The idea of progressive development on which we built the duty concept—it's obedience for the Plebe; it's self-discipline for the Yearling; it's a sense of responsibility and a commitment to the mission as the cadet progresses in his duty sense as he goes through the Military Academy. . . . It is the objective of West Point to nurture both these elements of duty—1) the ability to assess and decide what ought to be done, and 2) the desire to do it. Both rest on well-recognized legal, moral, and social underpinnings."[14]

All of these feelings and attitudes were present in the psychic makeup of this young midwesterner in the early years of a vocation that, to him, seemed selfless as well as self-justified.[15] Put in another context: "It's true it isn't easy to be young in these times. . . . An ethical system based on universal values, you can try to impose it on others. But the meaning one gives to one's own life is another story."[16]

Early Career Unfolds

In September 1939, not long after Goodpaster graduated, Germany invaded Poland, and three days later Britain and France had declared war. "In a 'fireside chat' radio broadcast [President Franklin D. Roosevelt] said: 'I cannot ask that every American remain neutral in thought. Even a neutral cannot be asked to close his mind or conscience.'"[17] Goodpaster would have agreed with this presidential observation. He clearly understood that combat would be inevitable; what he did not foresee at that stage of his life and career was that a decade or so later he would occupy a place at or near the seats of political/military power.

After commissioning in the Corps of Engineers, Goodpaster's first assignment was with the 11th Combat Engineers Regiment in Panama, considered at the time a high-priority duty station (under the Neutrality Act, armed forces could only be deployed in defense of the Western Hemisphere).[18] There were few, if any, areas of more hemispheric strategic significance than the Panama Canal. This made the port city of Balboa and its surrounding territory a prime assignment for Goodpaster. At that time, the Pacific side of the Canal Zone was designated the defense priority. The official war-fighting doctrine of the Army was built around holding on to the so-called strategic triangle of Alaska-Hawaii-Panama, along with planning for a war with Japan in the Pacific.[19] To the planners of that time, there was more at stake in the triangle than in Europe, as difficult as it may seem in retrospect. The Pearl Harbor disaster seemed to confirm this planning priority.

Nonetheless, the Panama Canal area was not Goodpaster's first choice: "First of all, the word was around that service overseas had special value, special interest. . . . If I couldn't get the Philippines, then Panama, 'cause I knew about the construction of the canal. . . . The vacancy came the next year in the Philippines and the number one man in the class of 1940 chose the Philippines, went out there, served on Bataan, and died on Bataan."[20]

Goodpaster's unit was charged with building cantonments for the Army ground and air units that were being sent down for training and to assist in the zone's defense. He observed, "When we got to Panama and I joined the Eleventh Engineers, I soon discovered that the ruling requirement was speed and resourcefulness in getting the job done."[21] Here is how Goodpaster described the task: "The cantonment that we built in Panama was about . . . four acres in size. We enclosed it with barbed wire, we put towers at the corners, and then within it, the cantonment included screened-in tents, with wooden floors, screen barracks, screened mess halls, and screen latrines. And this now was a living area for the 1,800 people that we had been instructed to care for. That was a cantonment."[22]

When the post library was being disbanded, Goodpaster related, "one of [the books] turned out to be one of my prized possessions. Its title was *Infantry in Battle*. The author of the book was George C. Marshall, who was then a colonel at Fort Benning. And he had a lot in this book about instances of good command procedure and instances of poor command procedure. . . . I found Marshall's book, and the book on combat orders, extremely helpful in elaborating the process of command decision. . . . This turned out to be, for me, quite a fundamental lead into how to exercise command."[23]

Marshall had already become Goodpaster's model of an officer who could command the respect of those around him by virtue of his force of character.[24] At some point in his career, Marshall had composed his "Rules of Leadership." They are worth recalling, because these rules could apply to Goodpaster as he was just embarking on his career: "1) Learn and benefit from early childhood experiences; 2) Experiment with a variety of challenging life experiences to gain self-confidence; 3) Have a vision for your life and a plan for achieving your vision; 4) Develop close lifelong friendships with people you can trust; 5) Become the 'master of the situation'; 6) Learn the value of self-discipline."[25]

Goodpaster understood by then that getting the job done meant understanding what needed doing and then accomplishing it as speedily as possible. To do this, he acknowledged that the official "specs" for his construction project had to be adapted to the circumstances on the ground without contravening standing orders. By the completion of his tour of duty in Panama, Goodpaster felt he had "earned his spurs" as an Army engineer.

In 1942 Captain Goodpaster was sent to Camp Claiborne, Louisiana, where his task was to help train African-American inductees in the ways of the combat engineers: "They did not want to take instruction from other [African-Americans] . . . they were termed then colored NCOs [noncommissioned officers] that were sent down to form the cadre of our regiment. But we really moved out quickly. We trained them as bulldozer operators, heavy equipment operators, gave them training in the placement of mines, the clearing of mines, demolitions, building hasty bridges, all the things that engineers were involved in."[26]

After only a few months, then-major Goodpaster was assigned to Fort Leavenworth to take the Command and General Staff College course, but in only nine weeks, instead of the usual nine months. From there he took command of the 48th Combat Engineer Battalion at Camp Gruber, Oklahoma.[27] While his battalion was participating in maneuvers in Louisiana, "I got one little piece of experience, unsought, that in going out forward of the general troop area to do a little personal reconnaissance I got captured by the enemy, and I learned what it was like all of a sudden, to be gone from the unit and to be under the control of somebody else."[28] The battalion was scheduled for overseas duty, having been assigned on 1 November 1943 to the 1108th Engineer Combat Group, II Corps, Fifth Army in Italy. The group consisted of the 48th and 235th Combat Engineer Battalions. Concomitantly, in the late spring of 1943 Goodpaster was promoted to lieutenant colonel.

Initially, the Allies had thought that the Italian campaign would be short—especially after the Italian army and government had changed sides. This proved to be wishful thinking because Hitler had ordered his commanders to fight as long and as hard as possible. The mountainous regions of the Italian peninsula north of Rome "had been organized into a series of defensive positions. . . . The Italian campaign is . . . a doughboy's war and an engineer's war and they are the ones who will win it, mile by mile."[29]

Goodpaster recounted his first experience under fire: "As we moved up to the Volturno River, we were charged with building and then the maintenance of a pontoon bridge across the Volturno. And it was at that particular point that I learned what artillery fire was like on the receiving end. I was not damaged, but we began to lose some of our troops. . . . Finally, in early December, we got the mission for which the 48th became rather famous. That was the conversion of what had been a mainline railroad that the Germans had destroyed between Naples and Rome. . . . I think we put in more than a dozen major bridges and a lot of culverts. . . . There we came under quite frequent artillery fire. We had to work both at night and day to get our job done."[30]

The possibilities for incurring heavy casualties were very great. The German general Kesselring had anticipated the Allies' plan: "They were now dug in along the steep escarpment of Monte Cassino. . . . The Germans could kill the British, Americans, and Canadians as easily as if they were shooting fish in a barrel."[31] This put a premium on personal leadership skills, not only to perceive what to do, but also in doing it under withering fire.

Inescapably, the casualty rates were high and the goal proved beyond reach. The Rapido operation was one of the worst battlefield failures of the Italian campaign, which meant that early in his career Goodpaster was exposed to the inglorious aspects of war.[32] One company commander in the 148th infantry reported: "I had 184 men. Forty-eight hours later, I had 17. If that's not mass murder, I don't know what is."[33]

Service as infantry was a second mission of engineers; as the attack unfolded, instead of pulling back, they would convert themselves into ground troops and participate openly in the hostilities.[34] As a result, Goodpaster learned firsthand what it felt like to see troops blown up or strafed. He remarked that he "developed the practice on Sundays of getting a list of where my troops were and going back to see them in the hospitals. That . . . hit [me] harder in a way than when I learned that troops had been killed because this was an actual visit to see how they were, and what their prospects were."[35]

Goodpaster recalled the situation that confronted him and his troops:

> To the north side of Route 6 as it went on into Cassino, there
> was a wide open plain, and the north branch of the Rapido had
> been diverted [by the Germans] to flood that plain, which was

very soft soil. They did quite a job of flooding it. As a result, it was not possible to get tanks up to the area of the stream itself. In this area, the stream must have been about thirty feet to forty feet wide, with very steep banks. Many of the banks had been built with masonry to channel the stream and direct its flow. . . .

I talked to a couple of officers who had reconnoitered up there, and they had come up with the idea that if we could get the tanks down into the streambed, which was gravel and rock bottom because of the speed of the flow of the water, it was now dry or essentially dry. . . .

A small group of us went up and removed the mines that the Germans had put around the obstruction that they had put in, and opened up a way so the tanks could get down into the stream. . . . As we were coming back up the stream the tank battalion commander was leading his tanks down, and he told me later he was never more amazed in his life to see this engineering lieutenant colonel walking up the streambed toward him, and telling him that he could get his tanks into the stream and down the dry streambed, and up the other side. He did that.[36]

Ever mindful of his troops, Goodpaster very graciously sent the following message to them:

During the six days which ended at noon Dec. 21, 1943, this battalion completed the mission of opening up for two-way passage of class 40 motor traffic a five-mile stretch of railroad containing twelve major obstacles, all under observed enemy artillery fire from German "Winter Line" prepared positions, the forward end being under automatic weapons fire. . . . I have served in and with some of the finest units in the army. You men who constitute this battalion can take your place among them; your performance of the last six days, though many of you probably do not realize it yet, matches the proudest accomplishment of the Corps of Engineers throughout its brilliant century and a half history. . . . I am proud to share with you the privilege of serving in this battalion. /s/ Andrew Goodpaster, Lt. Col., 48th Engr Combat Battalion Commanding.[37]

Although at this point, it is very unlikely that Eisenhower would have been aware of Goodpaster, he nonetheless embodied a quality that

Eisenhower prized: "I must have those [commanders] who appreciated the importance of morale and had demonstrated a capacity to develop and maintain it."[38]

Afterward, Goodpaster's battalion received a Distinguished Unit Citation for "outstanding performance of duty in action against the enemy, during the period 15 December to 21 December 1943." The citation read:

> This unit was assigned the mission of converting the railroad . . . into a two-way highway. The road contained twelve obstacles ranging from craters to destroyed bridges and constituted a high exposed defile. Open throughout to direct German observation and observed artillery fire, which was accurate, continuing, and concentrated, on all work parties and equipment. Obstacle sites, not accessible by road, were reached by routes opened and constructed through mine and trip-wire fields flanking the railroad. . . . The performance of the 48th Engineer Combat Battalion was an inspiration to other units and reflects the highest traditions of the Corp of Engineers.[39]

It was not long thereafter that Goodpaster suffered sufficiently severe wounds to justify his return to the United States for treatment. He took a shell fragment in the upper arm and shoulder. For this, he received the Silver Star. The commendation read:

> ANDREW J. GOODPASTER, 021739, Lieutenant Colonel, CE, Headquarters, 48th Engineer Combat Battalion, for gallantry in action. . . . While engaged in this mission, he and one of the Infantry Battalions' Commanders were wounded by the same shell. Lieutenant Colonel Goodpaster rendered first aid to the Infantry Officer and saw to his evacuation, then, in spite of his wound, searched for and found the next in command, and spent several hours with him going over the defensive situation before he made his way back for treatment. His action was above and beyond the call of duty and was in the finest tradition of the Corps of Engineers and of the military service. Entered service from Granite City, Illinois. By command of Major General KEYES.[40]

Chapter Two

Professional Planning

"A hard precipitating factor, encouraging the militarization of policy . . . has been the emergence of a new class of professional warriors."
—ARTHUR M. SCHLESINGER JR., *The Cycles of American History*

In late 1944 the Lincoln-Goodpaster relationship resumed when Lincoln, learning that Goodpaster was in Washington at Walter Reed Hospital recovering from combat, recruited him for the new Operations and Plans Division (OPD) of the General Staff of the War Department. Goodpaster had thought that he was headed into civilian life for medical reasons. Lincoln was chief of the Strategy and Policy Group (S&P), which was established in 1943 within OPD. This placed Goodpaster in the center of Allied wartime strategic planning for Europe and the Far East. Goodpaster recounted: "I was back in the States on convalescence at the time. I joined the Army Staff here in the Pentagon in August of 1944, and a good many of my duties in the Strategy Section of the Operations Division, OPD, involved staff work connected with the conduct of the operations in Europe."[1] Significantly for Goodpaster's future, the Operations Division was known as General Marshall's Command Post.[2]

This was his earliest direct involvement with Eisenhower. "Lincoln's wartime relations with George Marshall, Dwight Eisenhower, and John McCloy enabled him to engage Goodpaster in the new National Security Council (NSC) policy planning for what became the four-decade strategy for the Cold War."[3] What other early career Army officer of those times could claim to be the recipient of such patronage—well earned as it was?

Because Lincoln played such a continuously significant role in Goodpaster's career, it is useful here to trace his own career trajectory.[4] Promoted to brigadier general in November 1944 at the age of thirty-eight, Lincoln formed the "Lincoln Brigade," to which he actively recruited fellow Rhodes scholars to a new unit in S&P, the Strategic Policy Section. The S&P's purpose was to support the work of the State-War-Navy Coordinating Committee (SWNCC), which served as the coordinating agency for the president with respect to national security and foreign policy in World War II.

Lincoln considered a Rhodes scholarship to Oxford University to be a premier recognition of all-around personal excellence. He believed strongly that combining the sharply contrasting educational philosophies and traditions of West Point and Oxford provided officers with an intellectual breadth that would serve them well in senior planning assignments. Goodpaster had aspired to a Rhodes scholarship while at West Point, and would have been considered were it not that he was by then over the age limit. Even so, "[Lincoln's] experience with his first soldier-scholar, Andrew Goodpaster, USMA Class of 1939, from 1944 to 1947, proved to him that his role as mentor could produce very talented soldier-scholars capable of dealing with demands comparable to those [Lincoln] faced as Marshall's strategic planner in World War II."[5]

An example of Goodpaster's usefulness was his inclusion in the early summer of 1945—before Japan's capitulation—in the last long wartime planning trip of OPD to the Pacific. The party visited various places over the course of several weeks. Goodpaster wrote the report. "[Goodpaster] ended with a reminder of the principles that should guide [OPD] in dealing with overseas commands—to give 'every consideration' to theater requests for trained personnel and other stated needs, to 'avoid arguments over generalities,' and, if correspondence failed to 'get down to the specific cases on a complicated subject,' to send out a party of staff officers to talk things over 'before blood pressures begin to rise.'"[6]

Planning and Planners

Marshall understood that "plans are useless, but planning is indispensable." An informed observer went further in explaining this catchphrase: "Thinking carefully and deeply about the future does not provide a charted course for policy; the variables and the contingencies are far too numerous. The act of planning does, however, prepare the decision maker to maintain coherence and adjust effectively rather than sink in a sea of chaotic pressures."[7]

Within this context, whereas the Americans brought industrial and logistical expertise to the Anglo-American wartime relationship, Marshall understood that his British ally brought something equally important: how to organize the planning and operational components of the largest international wartime endeavor in history. Specifically, as part of Marshall's reorganization of his planning machinery, he copied important aspects of the British style of administration, known as the cabinet secretariat system. The exigencies of war and the running of an empire during the late nineteenth and early twentieth centuries had been the motivating force for Britain, and it had become likewise for the United States when it entered the world arena during and after World War II. This meant that on the U.S. national side, Marshall created "joint" committees of the services (including the Army Air Force) and, for the Allies, a "combined" chiefs-of-staff committee.[8]

To support this arrangement, one of the first things that Marshall did after Pearl Harbor was to shake up his headquarters staff. On 9 March 1942, "having seen his General Staff grow imperceptibly from 122 to nearly 700, Marshall massively slimmed down the operation, with all the changes coming into effect immediately. . . . Within two months no fewer than six hundred officers had come off the Staff. . . . One of the senior Planners who survived the mass cull, Lawrence Lincoln ["Abe" Lincoln's brother], was to call it 'a matter of evolution, or perhaps almost revolution, effected by necessity.'"[9]

Directly relating to this bureaucratic arrangement, the War Plans Division (WPD)—soon to be renamed the OPD—was given the role of a central command post inside the War Department. "Accordingly, the reorganization assigned to WPD those General Staff duties relating both to the 'formulation of plans and the strategic direction of military forces in the theaters of war.' . . . OPD was itself virtually a complete general staff." Its mandate involved "the recognized primary interest of OPD in regard to all matters affecting overseas operations."[10] For a rising young officer fresh from combat, there could not be a better place for Goodpaster to gain insight into the upper reaches of the higher command functions.

Goodpaster served in OPD until mid-1947, which included a one-year tour with the Joint War Plans Committee (JWPC) of the Joint Chiefs of Staff (JCS). This was an excellent assignment for a "teachable officer," for "the JWPC planning process was very efficient in linking the operational and strategic levels of war. It consisted of formulating a strategic concept . . . [that] then led to a campaign plan for each theater of war."[11] In June 1944—just before Goodpaster arrived—"the JWPC finished its inquiry into Pacific strategy and issued a comprehensive study, JPS 476, entitled 'Operations against Japan, Subsequent to Formosa.' It incorporated the essential point made by OPD's Strategy Section officers about the necessity to develop plans for an early invasion of Japan proper."[12]

Goodpaster's "first duty there was to participate in finalizing a plan for the occupation of Japan. . . . The Joint War Plans Committee considered it, passed it up to the Joint Staff Planners, who passed it up to the Joint Chiefs of Staff. . . . This was the plan that contemplated the division of Japan into four occupation zones. . . . Years later when the Japanese scholars discovered this plan in our archives, they were absolutely appalled."[13]

It was in this assignment that Goodpaster first came officially to Eisenhower's attention: "I suppose the first time I met him was in 1946. The war had ended. He was back as chief of staff of the Army and I was then serving on the Joint War Plans Committee of the Joint Chiefs of Staff and was of course quite familiar with the positions that he and the other chiefs were taking on the flow of business that came before the Joint Chiefs at that time, particularly everything that involved planning and operations for the period immediately following the close of the war."[14]

Goodpaster was assigned to the Political-Military Survey Section: "I worked on a number of things there. One project brought me into contact with General Eisenhower and that was to set up an advance study board of young officers who, on Eisenhower's request, would try to project themselves forward five years, ten years, to look at what the future shape of the Army might be and ought to be."[15] Goodpaster was at the center of this enormous and enormously important undertaking, which gave him valuable staff experience at the highest level.

Life as a Washington Planner

In 1950, after three years away at Princeton, Goodpaster was assigned as the Army member to the Joint Advanced Study Committee (JASC), located within the JCS. The JASC was carrying on the work of the JWPC:

General Dwight D. Eisenhower formed the original group in January 1947 with the idea that the unprecedented technological developments of the recent past and near future may have necessitated a thorough re-thinking of all major phases of military activity. He envisioned that a group of officers would be freed from all current demands and would endeavor to develop a basic philosophy of national security and a modern theory of war, determine the nature of a possible future war, what the requirements would be to win that war, and the proper course to attain those requirements. He suggested a time lead of from 10 to 15 years, and emphasized objectivity and imagination as essential to the group's efforts.[16]

It is obvious that the three officers (Army, Navy, Air Force) who were assigned would be of the very highest caliber. They chose to examine how the "bomb" would affect military thinking in the future. Significantly, given the perilous situation then existing in Korea, Goodpaster reported: "An outstanding point which has emerged from a two months' survey of all U.S. atomic weapons activities 'from mine to target' is that the United States is not now in position for immediate atomic action against a class of targets which is of major present importance to U.S. security. Further, current actions to improve this situation are far too slow and incomplete."[17]

He had in mind the conventional thinking that the Chinese entry into Korea represented a "dynamic surge of Soviet Communism."[18] Obviously, therefore, serious consideration as to the employment of tactical nuclear weapons in Korea was on the table. Goodpaster, in fact, recommended to Gen. Alfred Gruenther, then the Army vice chief of staff for plans, "facilitation of the placing of our highest forms of technological power behind our military forces engaged in the UN opposition to Soviet-Communist aggrandizement."[19] He added, "It is apparent that action is urgently required: 1. To facilitate the effective use of atomic weapons against this class of targets. . . . This much must be done regardless of the question of actual authorization of the use of the bombs for this purpose. 2. To develop the necessary psychological readiness to use this weapon where such is indicated on a military basis."[20]

One interesting side effect of this preoccupation with how to use (and therefore justify) the stockpiling of nuclear weapons was speculation as to how these weapons had changed the nature of leadership decision-making—unless they were to be regarded as simply a new form of artillery or aerial bombardment. Not only were there such new considerations as alliance obligations and homeland destructiveness, there were also considerations as to whether there had been an alteration of the very nature of war-making and war-winning decision-making. If this were so, then what about the balance between civilian leadership and military necessity in a democracy?[21] Goodpaster noted, for example, that effective planning for the employment of tactical nuclear weapons would enhance the perceived power of the Presidency in war.[22]

To someone as thoughtful as Goodpaster, the quandary of how to address the nature of atomic/nuclear weapons both strategically and tactically, and from there how to relate this growing weapons arsenal to the nature of representative government, would have been troubling. Could almost instantaneous decision-making on their use be reconciled with the need, in a democracy, to rely as much if not more on persuasion than on compulsion? Indeed, nuclear leadership "must justify itself by its detachment, moderation, and power of analysis."[23] These traits personified Goodpaster.

Goodpaster seemed to have relished conceptual thinking: "I have been undertaking to develop a better understanding of the military component of a nation's life as a system of actions, a system of decisions, and a system of relationships. I am not sure whether this should be an extra-curricular activity or not and have therefore done about half of my work on it in the office and half at home. . . . The reason for reaching for such a framework comes from the fact the whole structure of military activity has been disturbed in a very fundamental way by the introduction of atomic explosives."[24]

Goodpaster remained in this assignment for only the latter six months of 1950. His efficiency report for this period concluded: "His wide knowledge of political matters, his clear understanding of military organization, concepts, procedures, plans, and actions render him particularly well fitted for staff assignments at high command levels. It is quite unusual to find an officer with the exceptional qualifications of Lt. Colonel Goodpaster."[25]

A Soldier at Princeton

In 1947 Goodpaster went to Princeton University for graduate study in engineering. As he recounted: "After I and my associates had been in OPD for about three years, the Chief of Engineers renewed his claim on us and said that it was time for two of my colleagues and myself to go get our graduate education in engineering. Lincoln, our boss, said that he would not agree to that, that he wanted us to go to graduate school, but it should be for the study of international relations. . . . We would go and we would get our engineering degrees, to establish our credentials in our branch, and in addition would be able to pursue the kind of broader planning against a broader perspective that we had been engaged in, in OPD."[26]

At that time, it was not at all usual to assign a serving officer full-time to a civilian institution for graduate study in the social sciences (or the arts, for that matter). It is thus noteworthy that Goodpaster himself recognized the desirability of a broader educational experience. For example, he wrote to Dr. Bernard Brodie of Yale University's Institute of International Studies in January 1947: "I am interested both in broader studies of history and political affairs fitted to plans and policy work on the War Department Staff and elsewhere, and in other broad and basic studies which do not have specific application. As a result, I seem to be riding two or maybe three horses at once. . . . There is a need for understanding of the forum in which these matters are determined and for an awareness of the fundamental elements of history, philosophy, and social forces which orient national policies."[27]

Along with Goodpaster, Stanley Joulwan was assigned to Columbia University and Edward L. Rowny went to Yale. Goodpaster summarized: "After I'd been there two years and had completed the studies for a Master of Science degree in Engineering and a Master of Arts degree in International Relations, [his academic mentors] Professor Harold H. Sprout [of the Department of Politics] and Dr. Edward Meade Earle [of the nearby Institute of Advanced Study] proposed to the Army that I stay for the third year. I had done all my course work for a PhD, and all I would have to do is prepare the dissertation during that third year."[28] It was almost a precondition for Goodpaster and his faculty sponsors to aim for the doctorate after he had passed his "Generals." The Princeton doctoral program in politics (which included international relations) was based on the premise that the candidate, although earning a master's degree at the General Examinations stage, was expected to go on to complete the doctorate. Goodpaster was fortunate in having Professor Sprout as his dissertation supervisor, as the latter was famous for going out of his way with students to be helpful.[29]

It is quite clear that Goodpaster adapted readily to the "cloistered" environment of Princeton, and that he earned from the faculty not only the respect that goes to the better students but also their friendship.[30] An example is an exchange in 1955 between Professor Sprout, while he was spending a year at Oxford, and Goodpaster, who was then serving in the White House. Sprout brought to Goodpaster's attention the situation of the recipients of the British-sponsored Marshall scholarships (named for General Marshall and the Marshall Plan) who were in the commissioned reserve but were not given an exemption from their service in order to complete their scholarship years. This was in distinction to the policy for the Rhodes, Fulbright, and Rotary scholarship holders. As Sprout put it, "As you will surmise, I have no personal stake in this issue at all beyond the stake that every American has in promoting cordial relations with Britain and in doing whatever he can to reciprocate the warm welcome which one receives here these days."[31] Through this exchange of letters, an inequality was rectified.

In 1976 the Association of Princeton Graduate Alumni (APGA) awarded Goodpaster its James Madison Medal. The medal's purpose is "to recognize the distinction of alumni of the Graduate School. . . . The Madison Medal recognizes an alumnus or alumna of the Graduate School who has had a distinguished career, advanced the cause of graduate education or achieved a record of outstanding public service." Foreshadowing the writing of this biography, the author, as president at the time of APGA, described Goodpaster as "Soldier, Statesman, Scholar."[32]

National Technology and International Politics

Although the "Internet age" has overtaken the "technology age," Goodpaster's dissertation, whose title is above, is worth recalling because the general outlines of what he proposed to examine remain relevant today.[33] He managed to combine in a single topic information and analysis that was both academically sound and professionally relevant.

He recognized the importance of a nation's technology as a component of national power. It was not lost on him, of course, how America's overwhelming industrial strength played such a key role in the victory of World War II. As he wrote: "A nation's technology is one of the factors bearing most strongly upon the domestic and international well-being of its citizenry. A nation's welfare, its internal prosperity, its external security are strongly influenced by the kind and size of its productive activities. From an international standpoint, the role that a nation plays in the world family of nations—the influence that it wields, the pressures and problems that it faces, its powers and limitations, its relative advantages and disadvantages—stem in good part from the processes, the facilities, and the input and output of its own industries and those of other nations. The analyst of international politics, however he defines his field, must take into account the manifold, pervasive influence of technology."[34]

It is interesting to note that in a sense Goodpaster's dissertation presages the pervasive influence of the technology of the Internet and of the various related industries that have been spawned, and how they are transforming the manner in which virtually the entire world arranges its affairs. For an officer who was at that time still just embarking on what would be a lengthy and notable career at the forefront of public affairs, his insights formed while a graduate student served him well. As he put it: "The ever-changing nature of technology has extensive consequences. The products of a particular period, in kind and in quantity, are the *implements*

[Goodpaster's emphasis] with which international action is conducted. The radio, the telephone, and other communication devices tell much as to the tempo of diplomacy, the methods and scale of cultural penetration."[35]

Goodpaster was especially interested in how technology affects international affairs, not surprising since the Cold War was just about to shape every other aspect of American national life. He made this clear at the outset of his dissertation: "The proposition to be investigated might be framed as follows: The characteristics of a nation's technology changes as the result of the interworking of physical, social, and psychological factors external to technology; and these characteristics, and the changes in them that occur, produce the impact which technology has upon international politics."[36]

Technology can, of course, have both good and bad aspects, as the rearmament of Germany prior to World War II revealed. Goodpaster waxed almost poetic in discussing this point: "[Technology] destroys in one place as it builds in another; it weakens here as it strengthens elsewhere; . . . while it raises problems, it provides means by which a capable government can devote to solving them."[37]

Likewise, Goodpaster was wise to note throughout his dissertation that technological innovation can lead to greater or lesser benefits for humankind. In fact, many of the technologies that are transforming society at an increasingly rapid pace had either their inspiration or their applications generated because of perceived military needs or aspirations. The sophisticated means of communication that exist today—including the use of drones—would not have particularly surprised Goodpaster, but he would have cautioned that they cannot substitute for human judgment both in the abstract and in day-to-day decision-making.

Goodpaster concluded thus:

> Upon national capabilities, the products of technology have a rather direct influence; they are the material sustenance of programs of national action. Also, as implements of action, they tend to set the character and tempo—whether in warfare, diplomacy, psychological appeal and subversion or economic action. . . . [Yet] technology is itself but a single, passive factor in the resolution of such problems; the resolution can only be achieved through the efforts of analysis and statesmanship.[38]

After the successful oral defense of his dissertation, Goodpaster gossiped about it like any graduate student would, concluding in a letter to a friend: "All in all the experience gave meaning to the old adage about the professors knifing each other through their students."[39] Likewise, he also appraised his experience, concluding, for example: "I was embarrassed to admit that my fundamental ideas on technology did not change very much as a result of the year's work. I do feel, however, that my understanding of what was implied in those general ideas was considerably improved."[40]

Chapter Three

Goodpaster and the Creation of NATO/SHAPE

"The willingness of proud sovereign states to entrust their precious armed forces to the command of a foreigner in time of peace was a measure of their willingness to subordinate their national interests to the common weal."
— Lord Hastings Ismay, *The Memoirs of General Lord Ismay*

It is easy, almost facile, to claim that the treaty commitment of 1949 to create the North Atlantic Treaty Organization (NATO) was only a restoration of the World War II winning coalition.[1] In fact, this represented the first time in American history that the United States had committed itself formally in this way while not actually at war. Although in retrospect it seems almost ineluctable that the democratic states of Western Europe, along with those in Scandinavia and the Mediterranean, would be linked through the formation of the broader "Atlantic" concept, this was not assured at the time. Visionary leadership combined with hard-boiled intra-Washington and cross-Atlantic bargaining accompanied every stage of this historic realignment of Euro-Atlantic relationships.[2]

After the outbreak of the Korean War in 1950, there was widespread fear that the Korean "feint" was a preliminary to full-scale war in Europe. As it was put: "Rather than retreat from Europe, American policymakers envisioned the North Korean invasion of South Korea as part of the global Communist assault against the West. . . . The United States embraced the alliance and intended to fortify it and reshape it as a military organization."[3] This was Eisenhower's challenge when he was invited by President Truman with the concurrence of the North Atlantic Council to become the first supreme allied commander, Europe (SACEUR), charged with creating a multinational force-in-being.

Goodpaster played a central role in swiftly bringing about this "militarization" of the erstwhile political alliance. In fairness, Goodpaster and his colleagues benefited greatly from the plans, headquarters, and personnel of the pre-existing Western Union Defense Organization (WUDO), which was created in 1948 and was the military arm of the Brussels Treaty. WUDO was incorporated directly into the newly formed Allied Command Europe (ACE). Thus, it was possible within only a few months for Goodpaster and his colleagues to lay down the basic structure of ACE.

Although it seems in retrospect to be only a footnote in American history, at the time the transformation of the alliance from being primarily political in nature to possessing a military component was a dramatic departure from the manner in which the United States had conducted itself politically and militarily since its emergence on the global stage.

Creating a Multinational Headquarters

Goodpaster's career took an unexpected but very exciting turn when, after six months back in Washington, where he had been enmeshed in the intellectual as well as the practical aspects of defensive nuclear war, he found himself alongside Eisenhower, who became the central figure in the creation of the military structure of NATO.

Initially, Eisenhower considered morale to be his biggest problem. Europeans just did not want to think about fighting—or building the forces to fight—another war.[4] Goodpaster put it retrospectively: "A militarily denuded Europe stood momentarily transfixed by the fear of a Soviet invasion."[5] Eisenhower, as the symbol of victory, was well equipped both actually and symbolically to counter this attitude, understandable as it was. The appointment of Eisenhower and the formation almost immediately of his supporting staff gave tangible evidence that the United States was firmly committed to resist what was perceived at the time as a "clear and present danger" from the Soviet-dominated East.

Eisenhower's insistence on an integrated command structure—in distinction to one "international" in form—reassured all of the member nations that they would have a "presence" in the headquarters.[6] It was very important, therefore, that the American supporting staff officers, such as Goodpaster, possess the ability to work effectively alongside officers from a different linguistic and cultural, as well as military, tradition. Goodpaster said, "Eisenhower gave us very clear instructions, working through Gruenther. And both of them of course, had had experience with this— that the headquarters would be . . . completely integrated so far as services were concerned . . . [and] that the headquarters itself would operate on a completely international basis."[7]

Eisenhower once exclaimed in frustration that "devising an organization that satisfies the nationalistic aspirations of twelve different countries or the personal ambitions of affected individuals is a very laborious and irksome business."[8] It was obvious that "[Eisenhower] and members of the SHAPE [Supreme Headquarters Allied Powers Europe] Planning Group could not draw up an organization solely based on military considerations. Of equal importance were questions of personalities, politics, and national prestige."[9] Goodpaster recalled:

> My first connection with NATO came on 16 December 1950. It came at a time when the world situation seemed to be deteriorating rapidly. . . . Then serving in Washington, I received a request from Col. R. J. Wood, until then an instructor at the National War College, later to be the Staff Secretary at SHAPE, to leave for Paris at noon the next day. . . . I found [myself] late on 18 December comprising the initial contingent of what was to become the European headquarters of the NATO Allied Forces. Gen. Alfred M. Gruenther . . . had instructed us to establish an Advanced Planning Group and to develop plans and proposals for the organization and buildup of the headquarters and the command structure of the Allied forces.[10]

Eisenhower came over just three weeks later.[11] The abruptness that accompanied this new assignment is exemplified in this exchange between General Gruenther, who had moved from Army vice chief of staff to deputy supreme allied commander, and Goodpaster's JCS superior, Admiral A. C. Davis: "General Eisenhower asked me to check with you to ascertain whether or not it would be agreeable to you to have Lt. Colonel Andrew J. Goodpaster assigned to him on a period of 30 days temporary duty to assist in studying problems incident to the establishment of SHAPE. I recognize that there is the danger of losing Goodpaster, and I do not want to promise that he would not be kept on permanently at the end of the 30-day period."[12]

For a rising officer who possessed skills both in battlefield leadership and in staff planning, this newly created cockpit of the Cold War seemed made to order. As events were to prove, for both Goodpaster and Eisenhower, such indeed became the case.

When Eisenhower arrived in Paris, he quickly set to work with the Advanced Planning Group to devise a structure for the new command,

ACE, and its new headquarters, SHAPE. There could be no more convincing example of Goodpaster's identification with SHAPE than the fact that he was the staff officer who drafted General Order Number 1, which activated the headquarters.[13]

Suffice it to say, Goodpaster worked in close proximity to Eisenhower during these eventful weeks. As he recalled: "I had been a staff officer at SHAPE when then-General Eisenhower set up the headquarters. I had worked very, very closely with him on matters of security policy, of course with the direct relation to military planning, but in the context of what were then called the political and economic capabilities of the member nations."[14]

One of Goodpaster's tasks was to assist Eisenhower in forming the political and military guidelines for the new treaty organization, and thus, he was Eisenhower's liaison to the various national diplomatic and political personalities who were closely involved. He recalled that between January and April "[we were] getting quite close to the point now of actually operating the apparatus we have constructed with the end in view of increasing our military capability through creation of forces improved in quality, quantity, and readiness, and development of improved ideas on how they might be employed."[15] Fortunately, many, if not most, of the senior officers at SHAPE had been with Eisenhower in World War II, so their working relationships fell more easily in place.

As to his personal staff, Eisenhower said to Gruenther: "By having an American staff [that reported directly to him], it is solely for the good of the NATO organization (give them the example of a Congressional committee). After all, there are relatively few American officers engaged in this kind of thing. . . . Goodpaster and one or two others are the principal ones."[16] This was not an idle observation, for those officers were hand-picked. Gruenther implied as much in a speech at West Point, during which he referred to several officers who were academy graduates as making "a very fine impression on everyone with whom they come in contact. We have . . . a lieutenant colonel who is probably the most brilliant and most respected officer in the entire headquarters."[17]

Goodpaster, of course, phrased the relationship differently:

> [General Gruenther] would take the broad principles and the main lines of effort that General Eisenhower laid down on how to solve or resolve or satisfactorily meet the defense need, the security need there in Europe, and he then would convert that into proposals for our staff organization, for the organization of our command and so

on. I was invited to come over as one of the initial planners. And in those early days I would work on the plan for the organization of our headquarters and the plan for the organization of the command, the terms of command authority, and things of that kind, submit them to General Gruenther and he would then take them up with General Eisenhower. We would have the guidance from Eisenhower to go on and, of course, he drew very heavily on his experience as the Supreme Commander during World War II.[18]

Goodpaster also assisted in establishing SACEUR's parallel command structure for the American national military contingents assigned to NATO. Eisenhower's national role was titled U.S. commander-in-chief, European command (USCINCEUR). Under his successor, Gen. Matthew Ridgway, this other (and perhaps militarily more important) responsibility increased in importance. In this other "hat," as an American commander, CINCEUR would report directly to the JCS, bypassing the NATO chain of command. In reality, on most matters the deputy USCINCEUR would primarily be involved.[19]

A good illustration of Goodpaster's being at the center of not only the military but also the formation of the civilian side of the alliance was his being delegated to represent the SACEUR in the work of the so-called Temporary Council Committee (TCC). This high-level committee of national representatives of the North Atlantic Council was created in September 1951 "to reconcile the military needs of the Alliance with the member nations' capacity and/or willingness to support these needs with money and material."[20] Here is how the situation was described:

> As the military side of NATO grew, it became increasingly apparent that the administrative organs of the alliance were unable to handle effectively the attendant military, political, and financial problems; further reorganization was necessary. . . . At the Ottawa Conference in September 1951, the council created the Temporary Council Committee (TCC). The TCC, although primarily concerned with the preparation of a comprehensive plan for production rates of military equipment and for force buildups, also examined the structure of the alliance. The TCC's report in December 1951 offered specific proposals for force targets and military standards for adoption by the alliance. It also underlined the need for improving and strengthening the nonmilitary structure of NATO.[21]

The committee—known as the "Twelve Apostles"—was asked to render a report to the North Atlantic Council at the Rome Council meeting, scheduled for the end of November. From the larger committee, an executive bureau—known as the "Three Wise Men"—was composed of the chairman, W. Averill Harriman of the United States, with Sir Edwin Plowden of the United Kingdom and Jean Monnet of France as vice chairmen. The TCC's actual work was delegated to these three men.[22]

Goodpaster observed: "I went over and was a staff officer, assistant to the chief of staff, General Gruenther, but I worked very closely with General Eisenhower particularly on something called the 'Three Wise Men Report' . . . a study which would correlate military needs with political-economic capabilities of the member nations and come up with a force program. . . . In this I was General Eisenhower's representative to the committee and its supporting staff, part of which [the Screening and Costing Staff (SCS)] was headed by General [Joseph] McNarney and again General [Abe] Lincoln was detailed from West Point to come over and work with us."[23]

There could be no other assignment that could prepare Goodpaster, as a mid-level serving officer, for higher alliance command because it not only gave him a broad cross-alliance sense of needs and wants, it also brought him into contact with the major political-military figures of the other member-states as well as his own. For example, "as the replies [to the questionnaires] came in, the staff of the Executive Bureau studied them and assembled them into a form useful for further individual and comparative study. Then each country had its reply appraised by a committee of experts and by the Bureau. When a particular country's programme was considered, the representative of that country on the TCC sat with the Executive Bureau. . . . This examination was characterized by a frankness on the part of the delegations which was unusual in such delicate matters, invading as they did the innermost recesses of a nation's national existence."[24]

This was so because the report also dealt with the civilian structure of the alliance. Goodpaster had, perforce, stayed in close touch with Eisenhower during this time "because that was kind of a make or break operation. And he was determined it would be a make operation."[25] That Goodpaster contributed effectively to the jointness of the TCC enterprise is attested by this note from Ambassador Harriman to Eisenhower: "It has been my good fortune, and the good fortune of the U.S. Delegation and the Executive Bureau to work closely with Lt. Colonel Andrew Goodpaster. We have all been impressed by his wide knowledge, his fine judgment in the difficult areas of international security in which we have been dealing, and the depth and precision of [his] thinking, which has many times assisted us in moving forward with our work. You were good enough to lend him full time to assist in the preparation of the final report and his contribution thereto was substantial."[26]

Goodpaster wrote to his friend "Abe" Lincoln, commenting on how to deal with wrapping-up the work of the TCC: "[W]e have done a little preparatory work toward the final action on the reports contemplated for the Lisbon ministerial meeting of the North Atlantic Council. In addition, I started some work ten days or so ago aimed at outlining a course of action in connection with the FY '53 aid program, and working out some of the relationships and assignments both for us and the U.S. agencies concerned."[27]

Goodpaster's appraisal of the whole TCC enterprise was thus:

> The TCC operation wound up somewhat above the minimum standard I had set for it. The minimum standard was simply that it should avoid doing any real harm. Above that, everything would be velvet. In actual fact, it will have one or two accomplishments to its credit—some progress on the further infrastructure development, and a firmer statement of exactly what we will wind up the year with in the way of forces, budgets, etc. The operation has been extremely interesting to me in showing in what elements of our over-all problem representatives of military, economic, political, etc., lines of thought can (and frequently cannot) make a contribution.[28]

SHAPE chief of staff Gruenther added this note, commenting specifically on Goodpaster's role: "I cannot let this occasion go by without expressing my gratitude for the tremendous help you were to SHAPE in reporting so faithfully the details of progress of the [TCC] meetings you attended. I am confident that this important project would not have turned out as well had you not done so much to be in two places at once, giving advice both to them and to us. General Eisenhower and I are both grateful for this invaluable assistance."[29]

Goodpaster's mind had ranged over virtually the entire gamut of SHAPE's organizational effectiveness; he thus displayed a capacity for analysis that few officers possessed. Goodpaster could both be intimately involved in some daily problem-solving activity and at the same time be able to step back and view the problem analytically, which probably was an important reason why he stood out from his contemporaries and had captured the attention of his superiors.

An example of this trait is his lengthy commentary to a correspondent from the RAND Corporation—Goodpaster was by this time firmly ensconced in the "think tank" world:

> As you know, I am very much interested in this question of the timing of decision-making. I think you have something quite fundamental in this point. I have a small collection of observations regarding the view of this matter taken by some people whose abilities in this field I respect very highly. Mr. Churchill says he follows the line of "keeping options open" for future choice whenever possible. Marshall was quite vigorous in his views at one time on "post-war planning," which was reaching and implementing a host of firm conclusions at a time when major, basic elements of information were still unknown. Colonel Lincoln has the expression "let us temporize until we see how events develop." General Gruenther has a more operational technique, which he calls exposing oneself to the pressures of a given problem. I think I discern in General Eisenhower a tendency to put problems in the broadest possible frames of reference, recognizing that uncertainty and flexibility must be (and can be) introduced. While I don't count myself in this galaxy, I have a little rule which I at least consider from time to time and that is to reach no decision before it is necessary if it significantly limits future choices.[30]

In virtually all of his staff assignments, he seemed to have been left alone to do his analytic best, while also helping solve the day-to-day problems connected with guiding the postwar United States into uncharted waters. Already by this point in his career, Goodpaster had established a network of friends—both personal and professional—that any officer of his rank would have envied.

Looking back over a span of over thirty years, Goodpaster commented in 1971 that "as we note the achievements of Allied Command Europe—a vital arm of the military instrument of NATO—we must view those achievements in relation to the objectives of the Alliance which NATO's military instrument is charged to serve." The objectives of deterrence and defense had been recognized, but in his estimation, solidarity and détente remained elusive. Goodpaster went on:

The traditional objective of deterrence—preventing war and making peace secure—must be today, as it was in 1951, the paramount route by which we provide for our security while maintaining our freedom. . . . The second traditional objective is defense. For deterrence to be effective, we must make unmistakably clear to any potential aggressor that the peoples of the Atlantic Community have the collective will and means to defend their territories and to make aggression unprofitable. . . . The third objective of our military instrument is solidarity—collective action and unity in the Alliance.

This has proved to be a strikingly successful means for the NATO nations to rise above the quarrels and conflicts of the past which have exhausted them and twice this century nearly destroyed them. . . . A final objective in the military instrument of NATO is détente—a relaxation of tensions. To be meaningful and durable, a détente must be based upon reducing and removing the *causes* of tension—rather than merely the *symptoms* of tension [Goodpaster's emphasis].[31]

Goodpaster came out of this earlier NATO assignment with a reputation as "an honest broker, a man to be trusted, one who was fair and discreet and enjoyed Eisenhower's total confidence."[32] He was already providing the high level of performance, in staff work and dealing with political as well as senior military figures from throughout the alliance, which was to be a hallmark of his entire career, and which subsequently led him to service in the White House.

His next assignment, in July–October 1954, was as chief of the San Francisco Engineer District. As he said: "Well, I went out to San Francisco, and at the end of two months, a man who had served with me in SHAPE, General Paul T. Carroll, who was serving in the White House as Eisenhower's Staff Secretary and Defense Liaison Officer, died of a heart attack. And General Eisenhower, by then President, asked that I come into the White House to take up that duty. . . . And my stay in the White House with General Eisenhower and then for two months with President Kennedy was to last for six and a half years."[33]

A minor-appearing matter is worthy of note because it illustrates how carefully rank and status is calibrated at the most senior levels of the government. Goodpaster was impelled to write the following memorandum at the ascension to power of the Kennedy entourage: "I will need some kind of designation by President Kennedy to cover my status while I continue here, since the previous designation has terminated. I mentioned to the President this morning that, with Ralph Dungan as Staff Secretary, I could have some designation like 'Staff Assistant to the President' and he thought that would be fine."[34]

A Brief Foray into Nobel Speechwriting

While at NATO, Goodpaster experienced an unusual opportunity to be of direct service to General Marshall. This occurred in 1953, when Marshall was en route to Oslo, Norway, to receive the Nobel Peace Prize. He fell sick and had to interrupt his travel to stay briefly with General Gruenther (who was by then the SACEUR) at SHAPE. Goodpaster recounted the episode in 2003: "[Marshall] landed in Europe with a few central ideas in his head but nothing on paper. . . . I knew his thinking, however, having worked with him previously, and by our third meeting, his health had improved greatly—and his speech was all but finished."[35]

In the speech, Marshall acknowledged the place of military strength in world politics, but he also inserted a caveat: "The maintenance of peace in the present hazardous world does depend in very large measure on military power, together with allied cohesion. But the maintenance of large armies for an indefinite period is not a practical or a promising basis for policy. We must stand together strongly for these present years . . . but we must, I repeat, must find another solution."[36]

What Goodpaster did not mention was that "Colonel Andrew Goodpaster . . . got down on the floor in Marshall's bedroom and put the various sections of the dictated bits together."[37] It is doubtful that Goodpaster would have been drawn into this writing crisis if his own credentials in written composition were not already well established. Goodpaster's reputation in this respect had doubtless already spread throughout the headquarters.

By the same token, Eisenhower would not have been tapped for similar staff positions if he had not possessed similar skills. For example, during the invasion period of liberating Europe, Eisenhower had written to Marshall: "Dear General: Please do not look upon any communication I send you as a defensive explanation. Not only do I refuse to indulge in alibis but frankly, I feel that you have given such evidence of confidence in me that I never experience the feeling of having to defend my actions. My communications, therefore, whether in letter or in telegraphic form, spring simply from my belief that in higher echelons the common understanding of problems is the most certain way to insure smooth functioning."[38]

Chapter Four

Solarium: The Articulation of a National Posture

"Out of the crooked timber of humanity nothing straight was ever made."

—Immanuel Kant

An indication of Eisenhower's regard for Goodpaster can be seen at the very outset of his presidency, before Goodpaster joined the White House staff. The occasion was Eisenhower's desire to examine the parameters and possibilities of refashioning the Truman administration's foreign and national security policies to suit the existing global situation. This was distinct from Eisenhower's campaign promise to "go to Korea." Rather, it was an attempt to discern what the situation would be after a settlement in Korea and after the death of Stalin. The main adversary was still the Soviet Union, and the main hostile ideology was still the Soviet version of the Communist state.[1]

Thus, the basic "strategic dilemma" was the same for both Truman and Eisenhower—in spite of nominal disagreement. As it was put: "The clear determination of the Soviet Union to reject American proposals for a new world order, to defy American demands for liberalization in Eastern Europe, and to insist on the [United Nations] Security Council veto gradually pushed the Truman Administration toward the realization that international control was pointless and unattainable in any event as long as the two postwar great powers were unwilling to collaborate."[2]

Goodpaster described the setting: "You had the death of Stalin in early 1953. And there were a lot of ideas back then about what should be done. People around the president, high up in the government, wanted to capitalize on it. A lot of people brought a lot of agendas to this issue and tried to push them on the president. He didn't take too well to that kind of pressure, and he did not want to get swept up in a political wave."[3] He wanted a grand strategy that "called for, not so much the emotional and transitory sacrifices of a crisis, but rather those which enable us to carry forward, steadily, surely, and without complaint the burdens of a prolonged and complex struggle—with liberty at stake."[4] The nuclear dimension came into sharp and alarming focus when, at this same time, the Soviet Union detonated its own nuclear bomb.

Truman's Containment: A Cold War Antidote?

Before the outbreak of the Korean hostilities in 1950, the JCS had come to share Ambassador George Kennan's view of the Cold War as being "a state of international tension, wherein political, economic, technological, sociological, psychological, paramilitary, and military measures short of overt armed conflict involving regular military forces are employed to achieve national objectives."[5] How to define and refine this broad generalization was the de facto primary policy debate as between the Truman and Eisenhower administrations. Certainly one of the dilemmas in that search for definitions was that in the mind of some, Kennan's own view of what he meant by containment was initially over-generalized and, as will be seen, thereafter shifting in emphasis.

An observation of the Oxford social historian Theodore Zeldin is apropos: "When, in the past, people have not known what they wanted, when they have lost their sense of direction, and everything appeared to be falling apart, they have generally found relief by changing the focus of their vision, switching their attention. What once seemed all-important is suddenly hardly noticed any more. . . . In the course of history, humans have repeatedly changed the spectacles through which they have looked at the world and themselves."[6]

Kennan resigned as director of the State Department's Policy Planning Staff (PPS) in 1949 to be replaced by his deputy, Paul Nitze. This presaged a "harder" line toward the Soviet Union as America's chief adversary and a greater emphasis on military force to counteract the perceived Soviet threat. Nitze had been the principal author of the famous (or infamous) National Security Council report NSC-68, which advocated a more aggressively militant stand toward the presumed threats posed by the Soviet Union to a weak and divided Europe.

Kennan recalled: "One of the reasons for my leaving the staff at the end of 1949 was my disagreement with NSC-68. I had the very strong feeling that the Russians were not going to attack us, but that on the other hand the strength of their armed forces, the disparity between theirs and ours, was a reality and would not go away; it would remain a reality for an indefinite time; and that our plans ought not be laid toward an ostensible 'peak of maximum danger'; they ought to be laid, in the military sense, in such a way as to endure for many, many years into the future as a permanent fixture of our policy."[7]

"A central issue in the postwar debate over service roles and missions was the question of how future wars would be fought, and, in particular, the role of atomic weapons in military strategy. . . . In an age becoming accustomed to rapid advances in military technology, nuclear weapons loomed far larger and more ominous than all other instruments of warfare. . . . For the majority of military planners, nuclear weapons represented chiefly a dramatic enlargement of existing military capabilities that might or might not eventually revolutionize warfare."[8]

The story of this unusual document, NSC-68, is thus worth recounting at some length:

> In April 1950, the secretariat received a seventy-page typescript from the Department of State stamped TOP SECRET and given the label NSC-68. It was distributed to the president and the council's statutory members and advisors, the vice president, the secretaries of state and defense, the chairman of the National Security Resources Board, the chairman of the Joint Chiefs of Staff, and the director of Central Intelligence.
>
> Entitled "United States Objectives and Programs for National Security," the paper analyzed the ongoing cold war and courses of action open to the United States. After reviewing arguments for continuing on the current course, turning to isolation, or deliberating opening war on the Soviet Union, NSC-68 made a case for an alternative, described in its table of contents as "A Rapid Buildup of Political, Economic, and Military Strength in the Free World." To appreciate this document, you should keep in mind that the cold war was still new. . . . The cold war had come as a surprise.[9]

NSC-68, in spite of Kennan's forebodings, had not attracted much attention until the outbreak of war in Korea. Goodpaster recalled: "What it called for was a major upgrading of American military forces. . . . It was then pulled off the shelf and used as the framework of the expanded military program."[10] He also suggested that NSC-68 was used as a budgetary ploy to convince Truman to raise the defense budget.[11]

Another point of departure from Truman to Eisenhower was the idea of a period of "maximum danger," which the Truman administration had placed at 1954–1956. This served as a guidepost for planning the rapid buildup of countervailing military forces. Instead, Eisenhower favored Kennan's notion of the "long haul"—the stretched-out notion of an almost interminable situation of threat and counterthreat. Eisenhower seemed to agree that "containment meant you were counting on forces of change, natural forces, nationalism, internal social change, and the like."[12]

Whether Goodpaster agreed that the Truman administration "militarized" Kennan's notion of containment by pushing more rapid rearmament is probably irrelevant, because Goodpaster would have been more concerned, in his career assignment, in carrying out whatever conception of the Soviet threat that Eisenhower adopted.[13] Nonetheless, Goodpaster found himself involved in the debate over what should become the guiding policy prescription for those troubled and dangerous times.

The journalist Barton Gellman summarized: "The broad strategy of containment had three ends: to restore a balance of power and build up war-stricken allies, to exploit tensions in the then-monolithic Communist International and thereby to reduce Moscow's means of projecting power, and (in the long run) to moderate and to negotiate Soviet global behavior."[14]

The Solarium Initiative

Goodpaster's Princeton friend, Edward Meade Earle, put the situation thus: "Strategy is the art of controlling and utilizing the resources of a nation—or a coalition of nations—including its armed forces, to the end that its vital interests shall be effectively promoted and secured against enemies, actual, potential, or merely presumed. The highest type of strategy—sometimes called grand strategy—is that which so integrates the policies and armaments of the nation that the resort to war is either rendered unnecessary or is undertaken with the maximum chance of victory."[15]

Reflecting this concept, Eisenhower, with Secretary of State John Foster Dulles' agreement, decided to initiate a systematic overview of the possible courses of action that the United States might take in response to the sharply changing circumstances of the Cold War. This was especially important given that both superpowers were arming themselves with nuclear weapons of all sorts. It was widely known that Eisenhower was preoccupied with the nightmare of a Soviet nuclear surprise attack on the United States or its allies. This, to his way of thinking, was the primary threat against which America's scientific resources should be devoted.

The first reassessment step was taken on 8 May 1953, when

Eisenhower held an off-the-record meeting from 5:00 to 6:45 in the afternoon with the Dulles brothers, [Secretary of the Treasury George] Humphrey, [Under Secretary of State Gen. Walter Bedell] Smith, [publicist and speech writer] C. D. Jackson, and [National Security Advisor Robert "Bobby"] Cutler in the White House solarium for the purpose of generally discussing the state of East-West relations. "It is difficult to conclude that time is working in our favor," the secretary of state began the discussion. . . . It was evident that the "course" mapped out by Truman is "a fatal one for us and the free world." Unless "we change this policy, or get some break, we will lose bit by bit the free world, and break ourselves financially."[16]

Viewed from this rather dramatic angle, the eresult was not so much a radical departure as an updating and refining of the Truman administration's notion of containment. Therefore, the story as to how Eisenhower's idea—which was dubbed the "New Look," even if it was not entirely new—was implemented is worth recounting in detail, especially as the listing of the participants reads like a Who's Who of Washington's power brokers:

A working committee comprising Cutler, Smith, and Allen Dulles supervised the organization, which included the appointment of a panel, chaired by General James Doolittle and including Robert Amory, Lt. General Lyman Lemnitzer, Dean Rusk, and Admiral Leslie C. Stevens . . . to draft "precise and detailed terms of reference for each alternative." Among the factors each task force would be asked to consider were: "forces needed, costs in manpower, dollars, casualties, world relations, intelligence estimates; time-table; tactics in every other part of the world while actions were being taken in a specific area; relations with the UN and our Allies; disposition of an area after gaining a victory therein; influencing world opinion; Congressional action required."[17]

The criteria for selecting the task force participants were as follows:

Members of Task Force A were to have an "intimate understanding of the past policies and actions of the United States, the rest of the free world, and of the USSR, and broad-gauge political, military, economic, and psychological planning for the future." The requirements for inclusion on Task Force B were an "intimate knowledge of Communist reactions and methods; sound political and military judgment both regarding the Communist orbit and the free world; knowledge of United States military capabilities to wage general war, including the use of unconventional [i.e., nuclear] weapons; [and] ability to evaluate the economic capabilities of the United States and the rest of the free world to support the alternative." The qualifications for working on Alternative C included "imaginative military, political, psychological and subversive planning experience; profound experience on Soviet-Communist actions and reactions; knowledge of the military situation in Korea and Soviet satellite areas; and ability to evaluate the economic resources required to follow such a course."[18]

Kennan, the leader of Task Force A, commented later: "I was very fortunate in the [task force members] that I had around me. They were drawn from different departments of the government, and some of them were even outsiders. . . . It is my impression that we were not asked to take that [working] paper as something that had been approved and that we had to recognize as valid. We were, however, to approach it critically ourselves. But we were to take off from that paper; where we disagreed with it, to say that we disagreed; or where we were in accord with it, to say so and to base our paper accordingly."[19]

The Process

Robert "Bobby" Cutler, the special assistant for national security affairs, also described what the goal and process were:

> The solarium was a small penthouse on the White House roof. . . . General Smith's earnest positive voice explained our one-page proposal of three task forces, each with a leader. . . . The President began suggesting names for members of the task forces (each with seven men of varied backgrounds under a chairman). "Put Andy Goodpaster on your list, and be sure to get him." . . . The leaders were General Lemnitzer, later chairman of the Joint Chiefs of Staff and Supreme NATO Commander; Major General

James McCormack, later Administrative Vice President of the Massachusetts Institute of Technology; and George Kennan, former United States Ambassador to the USSR. . . . The Council assembled an elite group.[20]

Goodpaster described Eisenhower's method: "The three teams were: a) To provide the argument for the existing policy of containment to prevent Soviet expansion in Europe, hopefully without engaging in a general war; b) Within containment, to move from an essentially passive stance to one more actively responsive to any Soviet aggression which would lead to general war, emphasizing American and allied retaliation with all means at their disposal; c) To confront Soviet military expansion, and to force the Red Army to withdraw from the occupied territories of Eastern Europe in particular. . . . Eisenhower put each of these men in charge of a group of seven or eight people, each charged with making the very best case they could for that particular line of policy. I was still serving with NATO in Europe at the time and he brought me back to participate in the 'rollback' group. And he told me later, he said, 'Well, I wanted to be sure that I had one man that I could at least hope had some common sense participating in the rollback study.'"[21]

Later, Goodpaster recounted:

I had occasion to come back to the States with General Gruenther who was testifying before the Congress and seeing then-President Eisenhower in it would have been April, perhaps early May, of 1953. While I was there, I went around to the White House to visit with some of my friends who had been at SHAPE, General Paul Carroll in particular who was a staff assistant to Eisenhower at that time. I had lunch with him. And joining our table was Brigadier General Bobby Cutler, a Boston lawyer and banker who by that time was serving as Eisenhower's special assistant for national security affairs.

The moment Pete Carroll introduced me to Bobby Cutler, Cutler's eyes opened up and I could tell there was really something on his mind. We had an interesting conversation but he did not reveal what was on his mind. He told me in June when I came back to participate in the Solarium exercise, that at the time of the luncheon he had just come from a talk with Eisenhower, who was assigning individuals to each of these task forces by name and giving his reasons for doing so. And as Bobby Cutler told me: President Eisenhower had put me on Task Force C.[22]

As it turned out, Goodpaster must have followed through as desired, for later on he commented wryly: "The rollback option . . . 'sank without a trace except for propaganda and covert operations.'"[23] Goodpaster identified more specifically Eisenhower's motives:

> At the end of it, I would say that it was very clear that rollback was dead and that something in the area of containment or areas of interest would be pursued. Rollback sank, it was finished as of that day. It had been very much in the rhetoric of the campaign and, to some degree, in the early months of the Eisenhower administration. But he used this, and in my belief he did it very intentionally and deliberately, as a means of forging a single controlling idea that would dominate his administration. Having done that, it was no longer necessary for him then to try to influence every particular decision, every particular action that was taken. He could look then to the Secretary of State, to the Secretary of Defense, to others to act within that broad, defined policy.[24]

Eisenhower used the Solarium method—which came to be considered as an exercise unique in the history of U.S. national security policymaking—for several purposes: (1) to demark his outlook on how to deal with the Soviet threat; (2) to use this method to "bring on board" his newly assembled national security configuration; (3) to ensure that a coherent argument could be made for both the American public and the NATO allies that the United States knew what it wanted to accomplish to avoid both a superpower nuclear exchange and a conventional war in Europe.[25]

Another aspect of Eisenhower's attitude toward the nonmilitary features of the Cold War was his consistent interest in psychological warfare, disinformation, and liberation (or "rollback") propaganda. Without going into detail, it can be safely noted, for example, that "Eisenhower's staff secretary, Colonel Andrew J. Goodpaster, later recalled that the president had 'never ridded himself of some feeling that our government, elements in our government—and specifically the CIA—had gone beyond their authority and in fact had carried out a line of propaganda of their own which was not in accord with his policy.'"[26]After the Hungarian uprising of October 1956, much of these efforts were left to die a slow bureaucratic death.[27] By 1958 the administration had embraced a less didactic evolution strategy.[28]

On a more pragmatic level, one of Eisenhower's purposes in organizing this review was to widen the circle of participants in the exercise, thus enabling them, at its conclusion, to "buy in" to what Eisenhower had wanted in the first place. Goodpaster later speculated as to why Eisenhower took such a personal interest in the project: "I'm sure, from later discussions, that one of his purposes was to deepen the understanding of these matters on the part of the principal advisors, some of whom had had very limited experience in these fields."[29]

As to the efficacy of the position papers, Kennan observed: "I cannot judge from this distance how useful [my] paper was or how useless. It probably had less importance than we thought at the time; perhaps greater importance today historically. . . . What emerged in the end was something not too different from what had existed before we came into the picture, but with a greater stamp of presidential approval than had existed before."[30]

All of these considerations lend some credence to the view that Eisenhower knew all along what he wanted the outcome to be. "Whether Eisenhower actually altered his own thinking as a result of these deliberations is impossible to determine. Goodpaster says Project Solarium did not tell Eisenhower 'anything that he hadn't thought through before.'"[31] If Goodpaster understood what was afoot as far as Eisenhower's motives were concerned, it is very likely many—if not most—of the other participants did as well.

The new administration wanted to emphasize an intellectual departure from the Truman legacy as well as create a strategic synthesis. Solarium effectively laid to rest any lingering sentiments for Truman's strategy for dealing with the Soviet threat; it also justified Eisenhower's (and John Foster Dulles') concept of how to adapt America's Cold War stance to the rapidly changing circumstances, both domestically and abroad, which confronted Eisenhower at the outset of his presidency.

As will be described shortly, this synthesis was to last for only a limited time because of the changing nature of warfare as ever-more lethal new weapons were being introduced, along with the political and psychological needs of coalition warfare. The pressures of decision-making—both tactically and opportunistically—had begun to sink in. Just as the so-called limited Korean conflict had, by the early 1950s, come to overhang all other political/military considerations—and budgetary, as well—so indeed did the increasingly ever-present "brush wars" of the latter 1950s that accompanied decolonization (Suez being the linchpin), even if they did not necessarily directly involve the United States militarily. They began to take on a life of their own—Vietnam, of course, was the overarching example, but not the only one.

To summarize:

> Debate over whether or how the United States won the Cold War will continue for decades, but it is certain that Eisenhower's [Solarium] synthesis made survival possible. He transformed an ambivalent doctrine of containment into a workable policy of deterrence. Kennan's preference for propaganda, covert action, and political pressure was insufficient. Nitze's plan was too risky and inexact. The two approaches required a synthesis that deterred Soviet aggression while maintaining a common front with U.S. allies and limiting the domestic costs of a long and expensive struggle. The strategy put forth in NSC-162/2 struck such a balance and proved enduring, not least because the diverse Solarium participants took part in a process designed for "each," as Eisenhower liked to say from his days at NATO, "in the presence of all."[32]

This unique example of presidential leadership foretold one of the techniques that Eisenhower employed throughout his presidency to get things done—stand back, set the tone and define the issue, and then let others step into the limelight. This was, equally, Goodpaster's natural instinct, which is one important reason why he was consistently successful as he moved from one staff assignment to another.

Chapter Five

The "New Look"

"[The New Look] fundamentally I think came from the conviction on Eisenhower's part that we were in the nuclear age and that the nuclear complement of war had really already, even then, become a dominant component—we're talking large-scale war."
— Gen. Andrew J. Goodpaster

On 29 October 1953, Eisenhower approved NSC-162/2, and thus the "New Look," which "called for development and maintenance of:

1. A strong military posture, with emphasis on the capability of inflicting massive retaliatory damage by offensive striking power;
2. U.S. and allied forces in readiness to move rapidly, initially to counter aggression by Soviet bloc forces and to hold vital areas and lines of communication;
3. A mobilization base and its protection against crippling damage adequate to insure victory in the event of general war."
Of equal importance, it is worth noting, NSC 162/2 stressed the need for "a sound, strong and growing economy."[1]

The term "New Look" is attributed to Eisenhower's chairman of the JCS, Adm. Arthur W. Radford. Eisenhower himself—and presumably Goodpaster—did not intend to imply an abrupt change from the Truman notion of containment. Nonetheless, it was no secret that the administration was seeking for a way to reduce the military budget by minimizing conventional forces and by maximizing nuclear forces. Accompanying this was more reliance on covert operations against unfriendly regimes. Thus, by placing maximum reliance on nuclear weapons, the budgetary emphasis benefited the Strategic Air Command (SAC), at the expense (or so the Army thought) of the ground conventional forces.

This meant that all was not well between the senior Army leadership and the White House. Eisenhower's "New Look" strategy depended on the concept of "massive [nuclear] retaliation" if there was a direct and immediate threat either to the NATO area or to the continental United States, thus reducing the need for maintaining large conventional ground forces. Eisenhower recognized that the United States' capacity to fend off a real or imagined nuclear threat amounted to the same thing, which required preparing to act on the worst threat assumption.

This was interpreted by the senior Army leadership as reducing the role (and hence the budget) of the forces that the Army felt were still needed to fend off a Soviet ground attack in Europe. Admiral Radford summarized it thus: "The logical thing to do was to emphasize America's nuclear striking power and to rely on indigenous ground forces as a first line of defense against local aggression. American forces should be redeployed to the United States where they would be reorganized to form a small, highly mobile strategic reserve that could come to the aid of our allies in the event of a war."[2]

Goodpaster interpreted it this way:

> Now the institution, the Pentagon and its major component elements, were far from having made the adjustment to that kind of a concept. But he had no doubt in his mind. [Eisenhower] expressed it in highly simplified terms that, for example, any major war in Europe was bound to become an all-out war and a nuclear war. There were many for whom that was too simple, and that was very harsh medicine, but that was a conviction on his part, and the attempts to preserve forces as they had existed in a previous time simply cut very little ice with him.[3]

The Distribution of Administrative Influence

PPS director Paul Nitze's major contribution in 1949 was to link Kennan's essentially pessimistic view of the Soviet Union's peaceful intentions to a more aggressive notion as to how to win should conflict erupt between the two nuclear-armed powers.[4]

> A Report to the National Security Council by the Executive Secretary on United States Objectives and Programs for National Security, April 14, 1950. This celebrated study, which remained classified until 1975, was the first major project that Nitze supervised after becoming director of the State Department's Policy Planning Staff on January 1, 1950. Coauthored by Nitze and members of a joint State-Defense study team, NSC-68 proposed

a course of action that followed logically in the wake of earlier efforts to contain Soviet expansion. However, it differed from most previous assessments in that it viewed the Soviet threat as not only political but increasingly military in nature. . . . NSC-68 urged significantly increased U.S. military preparedness, especially in nonstrategic and nonnuclear capabilities.[5]

We should note, however, that for Eisenhower the use of nuclear weapons would govern the use of all other weapons systems.[6] "By 1957, the United States had nearly six thousand nuclear bombs and over two thousand medium- and long-range bombers. This destructive capability, coupled with research programs to develop new weapons technologies, seemed more than sufficient to the president."[7] This is why Eisenhower's notion of deterrence could be summarized as prepare for a war so terrible that it should never be fought.[8]

The phrase "massive retaliation" was introduced by John Foster Dulles as a counter to the Truman administration's use of the term "containment." The latter was criticized as being too passive to sloganize a credible deterrent, yet when it came time to retaliate "at times and places of our own choosing" (to paraphrase Dulles), the Eisenhower administration was no less willing to engage in warfare on such a scale than was its predecessor. As explained:

> The possibility that the United States might convert local wars into a general nuclear war alarmed U.S. and allied opinion, and this in turn led Dulles into a series of efforts to clarify his meaning in a more specific and moderate direction. He was not entirely successful in this respect, and indeed could not afford to be. For massive retaliation was primarily a declaratory policy intended to deter various kinds of aggression against members of the free world. Dulles and Eisenhower used the threat of massive retaliation as a means of warning a would-be Soviet or Chinese Communist aggressor that the United States would not allow it the choice of conditions for combat.[9]

By the end of the Eisenhower years, it was evident that the New Look doctrine of massive retaliation was either not credible or had achieved its purpose. As Eisenhower proudly pointed out in his final State of the Union address: "For the first time in our nation's history we have consistently maintained in peacetime, military forces of a magnitude sufficient to deter and if need be to destroy predatory forces in the world."[10] In addition, of course, and in the meantime, countering nuclear war with nuclear war—strike-counterstrike—therefore seemed to Eisenhower the most reassuring way to allay his surprise-attack anxiety.

He went on to list the various types of weaponry that had been either developed or introduced during his presidency. For example, Eisenhower cited the following: "Today we spend ten times as much each day on these [long-range ballistic missile] programs as was spent in all of 1952. . . . The explosive power of our weapons systems for all purposes is almost inconceivable . . . and either our B-58 Medium Range Jet Bomber or our B-52 Long Range Jet Bomber can carry more explosive power than was used by all the combatants in World War II—Allies and Axis combined. . . . Sea warfare has been revolutionized, and the United States is far and away the leader."[11] Therefore, for the future, conventional forces would need building up to address low-level or non-European conflicts that might or might not involve either of the two Communist powers.

In fact, arguing that there existed in the late 1950s and early 1960s a "Sino-Soviet bloc" carried the concept way beyond any notion of its reality. This resulted in a misdiagnosis of the nature of the Communist threat in Indochina, and this led eventually to the disaster of Vietnam. As Kennan observed, "The Chinese would, in the normal course of things, become more and more nationalistic and less and less available as a puppet for the Soviet Union."[12] So much for the so-called domino theory, which was gaining policy credence.

There is no doubt, however, that Eisenhower brandished the prospect of using nonconventional weapons in a "battlefield" sense, if the Soviet Union tried to invade Europe. Goodpaster recalled that when Eisenhower was SACEUR, he drew attention to the so-called

> nuclear cannon, a 280-mm gun bearing an atomic projectile; it was very clumsy, cumbersome, very difficult to handle on roads over in Germany. . . . But it still represented a capability, a devastating capability, insofar as the other side was concerned. The thought of their troops being hit by an atomic round would be very sobering, and I think Eisenhower was well aware of the way that the Soviet Union would think about the possibility of this being used against them. It was a deterrent in his mind, and not just a deterrent to war of their initiation, but a deterrent also to

their attempting to use pressure tactics or threats to force conces-
sions. They faced the problem that if they tried to back that up
with military action, they could very well have a nuclear attack
against them, against their forces in the field or against their air-
fields, and so on.[13]

Contributing to this preoccupation, Eisenhower had been carrying in
his mind a strong dread, his so-called Pearl Harbor nightmare, that if the
conditions seemed favorable, the Soviet Union would mount a nuclear surprise attack on the American homeland or on the allies. "[Eisenhower] was
convinced . . . that modern weapons had increased the danger of such a surprise attack on the nation and wanted [the newly appointed Technological
Capabilities Panel (TCP)] to suggest measures through which science and
technology might reduce the peril."[14] This panel was dubbed the "surprise attack panel" and was led by Dr. James R. Killian, president of the
Massachusetts Institute of Technology. The panel was a subcommittee of
the President's Science Advisory Committee (PSAC).

> Unlike other commissions, which issued reports that were ignored,
> the TCP recommendations (at the personal insistence of President
> Eisenhower) accelerated the development of advanced weapons
> and intelligence collection systems that became vital to America
> during the Cold War. . . . One of the most significant recommen-
> dations came from the TCP's intelligence subcommittee, directed
> by Edwin Land, . . . which called for the Central Intelligence
> Agency to develop an advance reconnaissance aircraft proposed
> by the Lockheed Corporation, the U-2.[15]

In the pivotal meeting of 7 February 1958, Land and Killian discussed the program that became CORONA. In his memorandum summa-
rizing this meeting with Eisenhower, Goodpaster recorded his observations
as follows:

> Subsequently, because of my feeling that there might not have
> been full understanding between the President on the one hand
> and Dr. Killian and Mr. Land on the other, I met with the latter
> two and then talked further with the President. They [Land and
> Killian] clarified that what was really intended was that General
> [Bernard] Schriever and the Air Force would be in charge of the

program. I told them that I did not think the President had that understanding or intention. I then talked to the President who stated emphatically that the project should be centered in the new Defense "space" agency [Advanced Research Projects Agency (ARPA)] doing what the CIA wanted them to do. I then informed Dr. Killian.[16]

Eisenhower had thus made clear that CORONA should be run by civilian leadership rather than by the Air Force or other military agencies. This anecdote is an illustration that, throughout his career, Goodpaster was intimately involved in these kinds of covert, off-the-books operations.[17]

In fact, the work of Killian and Land, among others, gave the United States a significant boost in its research activities dealing with space flight, aerial intelligence-gathering, long-range missile development, weather observation, and so forth. Furthermore, given Goodpaster's already proven interest in, and knowledge about, the possibilities of technology in the cause of maintaining peace or prosecuting war successfully, his involvement in this aspect of presidential concern was naturally congenial to him. He was at the heart of these activities both as presidential liaison and as a knowledgeable observer.

Deterrence and Détente

Many books have been written about the meanings of the terms "deterrence" and "détente"—as was true also for "containment" as we have just seen. The central role of deterrence and détente was to rein in the nuclear arms race, while at the same time retaining a creditable threat posture in the event of a Soviet attempt to "blackmail" the United States. Calculations of "throw-weight" and other attempts to draw comparisons between dissimilar stockpiles became the stuff of agonized analysis and heated debate. Goodpaster would have been aware of these goings-on, of course, throughout his career, and especially while he was serving as NATO's supreme allied commander later on. Nevertheless, his assignments (and presumably interests) lay more in the implementation side of the debate, rather than in strategically conceptualizing.

Goodpaster had this to say about deterrence: "The proper question was not whether NATO could have defended successfully; it was whether the USSR could have attacked successfully. . . . A calculus of deterrence today—by almost any concept of rationality that can be imagined—must inevitably lead to a quick rejection of the vast bulk of conceivable conflicts between the super powers."[18] In a way, this was a reformulation of Eisenhower's use of the deterrent. As Goodpaster put it: "You knew that in due time, the Soviets were going to build the same kind of capability. But Eisenhower had a great sense of how these things would be viewed by the other side, in other words, of the deterrent as a strategy. He just comprehended that. He thought in those terms—how does this affect the other man—and he saw that as a very powerful deterrent."[19]

It is possible that this was intentional, for, as Kennan commented, in the context of Solarium: "The President . . . spoke about the whole range of these problems. He spoke, I must say, with a mastery of the subject matter and a thoughtfulness and a penetration that were quite remarkable. I came away from it with the conviction (which I have carried to this day) that President Eisenhower was a much more intelligent man than he was given credit for being."[20]

In contrast, a narrow definition of détente was used by one scholar: "Some have taken the word 'détente' to mean a state of near-bliss between Washington and Moscow. It simply means 'the easing of strained relations, especially in a political situation.'"[21] In fact, the term became a propaganda instrument directed not only at each other, but also by each with their respective domestic audiences. In other words, the term had both policy relevance and emotional relevance, depending on the circumstances and purposes for which it was employed. Analytically, as well, "deterrence" and "détente" are linked together.

Furthermore, Goodpaster mentioned in discussing Solarium: "In assessing the Soviet threat, there was a flat statement that there was very little chance of any deliberate Soviet attack or any desire of the Soviets for a general war, that the only way that was likely to happen was by mistake or miscalculation. It was assumed, however, that the Soviets would try all the other things which were possible to try to expand their area of influence."[22]

Another way of looking at it would be to consider détente in terms of its possessing an ideological component: "The President was arguing that, because the Soviet menace was basically ideological, or 'philosophical,' it was also indivisible and thus posed a threat everywhere in the world. . . . But Eisenhower's approach led to confusion, for it blurred over the fact that the ties between Communist ideology and other types of Communist power varied greatly in different parts of the world."[23]

The United States learned later on, to its regret, that pasting the same label of "Communist" on every form of anti-American or anti-Western self-government emerging throughout Asia and Africa (and also for that matter, Latin America) imposed simplicity on an extremely complex and diverse historical evolution.

It is safe to say that after the Suez crisis of 1956, in which the United States sided with a newly independent (and anticolonial) government in Egypt against its erstwhile NATO allies, Britain and France, the stage was set for America's entry into competition for the "hearts and minds" of the new nations of Asia and Africa, as well as the ongoing cultural rivalry in Europe.[24]

Goodpaster summarized Eisenhower's concept of how to adjust American policy in the face of rapid decolonization (some of which was unexpected): "His idea concerning Third World nations was to work with them on development, to show them the opportunities for self-government and tell the story of what the West had to offer and what has been achieved by Western civilization. He was always one who tended to put things in positive terms—that we should tell the story, that we should provide the assistance to them so that they could begin to better the life [sic] of their farmers and improve their industry and trade and so on. This would give a more reliable and more rewarding basis for development than the so-called shortcut of Communism."[25]

It is useful to recall here, however, that when it came to Southeast Asia, the picture was muddled. There was one military faction in Washington that advocated what has been termed the "all-or-nothing" approach—meaning to settle the ideological ambiguities through military means, at least initially by the use of airpower. The dilemma was put starkly when the French were facing defeat at Dien Bien Phu in 1954. Harkening back in disapproval as to how the Korean "police action" was settled, this group favored either intervening in order to achieve an unequivocal victory or remaining out. Eisenhower favored this approach, as did General Ridgway, the Army chief of staff at the time, even though he had succeeded General Douglas MacArthur in Korea precisely to bring about a negotiated settlement at the 38th parallel. In any event, "sobered by this hard-boiled cost-benefit analysis, Eisenhower rejected military intervention altogether and decided to try to deal with the consequences of the now certain French defeat through diplomacy."[26]

In contrast, in the 1958 crisis over the offshore islands of Quemoy and Matsu, Eisenhower recognized the danger of a local conflict escalating out of control, when he disagreed with his JCS by refusing to pre-delegate to them the decision to use tactical nuclear weapons if it seemed necessary to forestall a Communist Chinese invasion. But this did not imply that these weapons would absolutely not be used—only that the president reserved to himself that decision based on the circumstances at the time. Fortunately, the invasion never occurred.

In any event, even though Eisenhower had hinted broadly that if the Chinese did not accept a negotiated settlement in Korea, nuclear weapons might be used, by then it was clear that no president would delegate what would have been a fateful decision as to whether or not to introduce nuclear weapons of any kind in any crisis other than a direct Soviet attack in Europe. Simply stated: "It was the possession of atomic bombs by America and the possible intention to use them which brought about the Armistice, not the conventional military operations in which UN fire power was counterbalanced, to a large extent, by Communist manpower. This was possibly the only time that nuclear weapons could have been used without causing World War III. The Communists probably knew this but the West was not so sure."[27]

The danger of escalation was simply too great. The nuclear arms race would continue in the "what-if" mode. During the Eisenhower years, the nuclear stockpile grew both larger and more diversified, which implied that, in the opinion of some observers, automatic escalation was not necessarily a foregone conclusion. As it was put: "The smaller atomic weapons, the tactical weapons, in a sense now became the conventional weapons."[28]

Goodpaster elaborated on why, as a consequence of the dangers of an endless nuclear arms race, a policy of détente made sense. For the United States and USSR, it placed constraints on the size and capabilities of each nations' nuclear arsenal. In Goodpaster's opinion, the "détente process shap[ed] and constrain[ed] U.S. and USSR military capabilities," especially "the size and composition of strategic nuclear forces" of each nation. Additionally, multilateral organizations like NATO and the Warsaw Pact used the umbrella of détente to find common ground to reduce conventional forces. Beyond European, Russian, and U.S. soil, Goodpaster observed,

> Détente manifests itself in further ways in such areas as the Mid-East and the Far East and particularly on such issues which are of high interest in the United States and the Soviet Union but which do not, however, touch directly and vitally on the question of their national survival. . . . In these so-called "third areas" of the world, it is an important military implication of détente that, short of

issues involving the most vital interests of the United States and Soviet Union—on which each will feel constrained from challenging the other—threats to peace and order must be expected to continue to occur, and it must be expected that these will from time to time occasion intervention and conflicting measures of many kinds by both powers.

Ultimately, he concluded, with détente came the very real possibility that "peace and security may derive through 'linkage' to other détente-related agreements in which the Soviet Union has interests that are of value to it."[29]

If there was a time when the post–World War II world appeared to be permanently divided into two "camps," it was during these Eisenhower years. In an earlier but similar period, the nomenclature was different but the attitudes were alike: "From an individual struggle, a struggle of families, of communities, and nations, the struggle for existence has now advanced to a struggle of empires."[30] The biggest single diplomatic challenge for Goodpaster, and for the Eisenhower administration in its first term, was how to reconcile the policy of détente—seeking negotiable areas of mutual interest between the United States and the Soviet Union, and which would result in a lowering of tensions—with the concurrent maintenance of the highest stage of readiness.

By his second term, Eisenhower de facto adjusted his overall strategic concept to take account both of "means other than war" vis-à-vis the Soviet Union and of the relevance to America's national security of so-called peripheral wars. It was not understood generally that, as Goodpaster put it, Eisenhower was "slow to pick up the sword." "He repeatedly sought negotiations with the Soviets on the reduction of arms. Ike avoided involvement in 'brush fire wars' that could escalate into a nuclear confrontation. He ended the war in Korea in 1953, declined to intervene militarily in Indochina in 1954, and, above all, refused to support his World War II allies in their attack on Egypt in 1956. Eisenhower was the least interventionist of any modern president, although he approved activist covert operations in places like Iran and Guatemala."[31]

Part II
Goodpaster with Eisenhower

Chapter Six

Presidential Staff Secretary and Counselor

"The old soldier is accustomed to well-staffed work."
—ROBERT CUTLER

When "compared to the rest of government, the White House barely qualifies as an organization at all, if the term organization implies the existence of a fixed plan that is likely to look about the same tomorrow as it did yesterday. The very vibrations of the place differ markedly from president to president."[1] Nonetheless, first it must be said that the White House chiefs of staff, first Sherman Adams and then Wilton Persons, were definitely the men "in charge" of the Eisenhower White House. How could a former military commander have it otherwise?

Not far behind was Goodpaster: "Goodpaster was [Eisenhower's] Staff Secretary, a position akin to today's National Security Adviser, and took part in nearly every meeting the President had, in addition to serving as his chief liaison to the foreign policy bureaucracy. It was not without justification that Goodpaster was known as 'Ike's alter ego.'"[2]

Furthermore,

The dozen members of the top-echelon of the White House staff were men with whom Eisenhower had recently worked. Among them were his wartime associates, Walter Bedell Smith, Wilton "Jerry" Persons, and Andrew Goodpaster; others were Bryce Harlow, Gabriel Hague, and C. D. Jackson, men from government, academia, and business whom he had met during the postwar period. The responsibilities of these presidential assistants were grouped under four headings: domestic affairs (cabinet secretariat, departmental liaison, congressional liaison, state and local relations); foreign affairs (defense, national, and mutual security, intelligence); special projects established by order of the president or Congress; and routine scheduling and coordination.

Like everyone else, members of the White House staff had access to the president through a single person: Sherman Adams. . . . He gave and withheld permission to enter the Oval Office on the basis of whether the information was vital and the president receptive.[3]

Vice President Richard Nixon figured into this, of course, but more in a collateral way. Eisenhower had made his vice president more aware of what was going on than did any of his predecessors. Nixon's biographer Stephen Ambrose captured the situation: "He was by no means privy to all of Eisenhower's secrets, but he knew more than anyone else. This is not to say that he was the closest to Eisenhower, because he was not—Andrew Goodpaster, Foster Dulles, George Humphrey, Jim Hagerty, and some others were closer."[4]

As far as National Security Council affairs were concerned, "the NSC was also subjected to White House staff procedures by the appointment of Robert Cutler and later Gordon Gray as its secretariat. These men had been Eisenhower's associates in wartime and postwar defense policy assignments; he trusted them and knew they were capable and conscientious. Cutler and Gray were included in the NSC inner circle along with Generals Andrew Goodpaster and Walter Bedell Smith, two former military aides now in mufti as presidential assistants. Eisenhower relied on these four men when sudden foreign crises called for an immediate decision rather than a full-scale council discussion."[5]

Their style was to convene an inner group after the weekly NSC meeting to go over the more important and relevant matters that were on Eisenhower's mind. Press Secretary James Hagerty reported, for instance, on a 9 December 1954 meeting: "Comparatively quiet day. . . . After the NSC meeting broke up I attended a meeting at two o'clock in Jerry Person's office with Fred Seaton, Jerry Morgan, Jack Martin, Andy Goodpaster, and Murray Snyder on the military plans, which the NSC discussed this morning."[6]

Later in his administration, recognizing that the NSC meetings were becoming unwieldy, Eisenhower began the practice of assembling, a half hour before a regular meeting, a smaller planning group to identify the most significant matters needing decisions. As reported: "Staff Secretary Andrew Goodpaster worked closely with Gordon Gray in coordinating these meetings as an adjunct to formal Council meetings."[7]

Goodpaster as Staff Secretary

In his memoir, Eisenhower described the functions given to Goodpaster's immediate and only predecessor:

> To look after all communications of a top-secret character from or to the White House, I selected an outstanding young Army officer, Brigadier General Paul T. Carroll, who had served in World War II with distinction and had been with me both in the Pentagon and in SHAPE Headquarters in Paris. . . . His successor in 1954 was another Army officer of exceptional capability, Colonel (later Brigadier General) Andrew J. Goodpaster.[8]

In this position, Goodpaster served officially as an observer at all NSC meetings.[9] Besides carrying out what Eisenhower euphemistically called "communications," the main feature of the new position, that of "staff secretary," was maintaining total confidentiality. Eisenhower wanted "to have close substantive liaison on official matters of all kinds with the departments involved in international affairs. And that was a special duty of mine, with the State Department, the CIA, the Defense Department, the AEC [Atomic Energy Commission], and I think that was about the extent of it, but international activities of all of the departments."[10]

Goodpaster and his immediate colleagues were also on hand to record the substance of presidential communications—especially memoranda of conversations, or "memcons." These would "cover defense and space programs, strategic planning, nuclear testing and disarmament, intelligence matters, foreign policy, budgetary problems, government organization, and administrative subjects."[11]

Furthermore, "the staff secretary (and the chief of staff if need be) will subject papers for the president to a tough procedural scrutiny. Are memoranda verbose? Are they larded with extraneous details? Has the author slanted the options? . . . The staff secretary is the funnel for papers coming back out of the Oval Office. If a decision is marked or notes scribbled on briefing papers, he scoops up the inscribed documents, notifies those concerned of the chief executive's action, and builds the archival record."[12]

One important reason for Eisenhower's strong desire for confidentially was that, in his public diplomacy, "Ike employed hints rather than threats, and always succeeded in keeping his options open."[13] The British parallel, although not by any means exact, shared some significant characteristics:

The immediate circumstances, however, which gave rise to the formation of such a group of civil servants came from the war-making responsibilities of the British government. . . . A secretary who performed a coordinating role had always to maintain unobstructed channels to all the governmental bodies, groups, and leading individuals in the policy-making process. While he might be asked his opinions on some issue—and he often was [as was Goodpaster]—he should not, according to the tradition which was being built up, have taken stands on issues in such a way as to interfere with his access to and his credibility with those political persons and organs that he was serving.[14]

To interpret further this statement, self-effacement and discretion came to be hallmarks of the position, and Goodpaster's temperament fitted this requirement perfectly. "Improving on procedures he had learned from the British, Ike created a White House secretariat, headed first by General Paul Carroll and after 1954 by General Andrew Goodpaster. Other administrative changes were also made. The most important was to promote the National Security Council (NSC) to become the central forum for making cold war policy, though in practice the president and the secretary [of state] determined significant matters."[15]

Even more to the point is this observation about the role of Sir Maurice Hankey (later Lord Hankey), who was the key individual in adapting the British secretariat method to the machinery of the Paris Peace Conference, which settled World War I: "It would be inaccurate to infer from this that either the CID [British Committee of Imperial Defence] secretariat or its successor international secretariats had little power just because they were to behave in a politically neutral manner in policy-making."[16]

As far as Eisenhower's staff is concerned,

whereas the talents of the staffs under Roosevelt and Truman were to be found largely in their possession of highly sensitive political antennae, their overarching loyalty, or their creativity, the top echelon of Eisenhower's staff was noted for its functional professionalism. . . . A newly created staff secretariat . . . kept track of all pending presidential business and ensured the proper clearances on all papers that reached the Oval Office. A two-man operation within the secretariat prepared daily staff notes for the president, giving him advance notice of actions to be taken by the

departments and agencies. [Chief of Staff Sherman] Adams coor-
dinated White House work through early morning staff meetings,
generally three times a week. The sessions also were used for briefings by the CIA and preparation of suggested answers to questions
that might be asked at presidential press conferences.[17]

Also involved in these activities were the office of Executive Branch
Liaison and the legislative liaison team. All of these entities were designed
to avoid misstatements and departments working at cross-purposes, to
keep in touch with key congressional leaders, fact-check speeches, prepare
background briefs and summaries, and so forth.[18]

The Influence of Personality on Bureaucratic Relationships

As defense liaison officer, Goodpaster "would give the daily CIA briefing
to President Eisenhower, and also the exchange of messages, the overnight
exchange of messages from the State Department, and a report of activity in
the Defense Department as well. And out of that, he would very often ask
for additional information or ask for something to be looked into. And I
would communicate that back to the responsible departments. So that's the
way we began to work."[19] Goodpaster, in fact, was the person from whom
"Eisenhower had no secrets . . . something that could be said of no other
man, not even the Dulles brothers. . . . He gave Eisenhower a 30-minute
briefing every morning, because he . . . had the information and knew how
to present it the way the president wanted it."[20]

For example, Allen Dulles sent a classified report on a private dinner
meeting he had at the German embassy with Konrad Adenauer, chancellor of West Germany, when the latter was in Washington for the funeral of
Dulles' brother John Foster. His note read: "Dear Andy: I would appreciate
it if you would kindly show the attached to the President and then it can
either be destroyed or retained in your file."[21]

Nevertheless, there were limits to what Goodpaster could do. He
described an incident that occurred when he was fresh on his job. It
involved drafting a stiff letter from the president to his secretary of defense,
Charles Wilson, which was intended to assist Wilson in curbing the chiefs'
tendency toward parochialism rather than putting together an integrated
budget. Goodpaster inserted some language in the draft that softened what
Eisenhower had said orally in a meeting with the secretary and the chiefs.

"And that's when he looked up at me and said, 'Now Andy,' he said, 'ultimately this can either be done your way or my way and I guarantee you that ultimately it's going to be done my way.' And I said, 'Yes sir, Mr. President.'"[22]

Earlier in this chapter, Goodpaster has been described as fulfilling a communications function; then it was said he served as an "advisor"; now he is being described as virtually a third extension of the president in matters of national security policy formulation *and* implementation. Perhaps this ambiguity is a necessary adjunct of the kind of largely unobserved— and unobservable, except to a few—role that Goodpaster performed.

If anyone doubted the multiplicity of roles that Goodpaster played, note this assertion:

> Andrew J. Goodpaster played a significant role in the development and implementation of U.S. national security policy in the Cold War years from the late 1940s through the 1970s. His formative impact in such key areas as nuclear strategy, military modernization, and the maturing of NATO as a politically and militarily integrated alliance is largely obscure, however. He avoided the limelight and preferred the position of the loyal and expert assistant who gave substance to the leadership and direction of others. As President Dwight D. Eisenhower's principal White House aide on national defense issues, he enjoyed an especially close and influential working relationship with Eisenhower on virtually every foreign and military decision of that administration.[23]

In one respect, Goodpaster's role was not too complicated, because "Eisenhower's argument for the New Look was not sophisticated, but he believed it and insisted that others believe it. His feeling was that the economy was the pillar of U.S. strength and security, and unbalanced budgets threatened that pillar."[24]

It might at first glance appear useful to compare Goodpaster's role with that of Colonel House as he served President Woodrow Wilson at the Paris Peace Conference of World War I. This, however, does not seem apt because historians have concluded that House was more a de facto secretary of state.[25] However, a comparison with President Franklin Roosevelt's "man Friday," especially in Harry Hopkins' wartime role, might be a closer fit. In personality, Goodpaster and Hopkins could not have been more different. Roosevelt's ghostwriter Robert Sherwood "met this bright-eyed, intrepid, and deeply loathed and deeply loved man. . . . Plainly he was 'a master of the naked insult,' and no less plainly his fervor shone out in spite of his frailty."[26] What a contrast to Goodpaster! Where they were similar is in the trusted relationship that each had with his respective president.

Here is a description of Hopkins' role: "The fact is that by 1940 Roosevelt valued the peculiar kind of service rendered and the companionship provided by Hopkins to such an extent that he converted his friend to war purposes."[27] It is this uncanny ability of two persons to be drawn to each other in trust and even affection that stood both Roosevelt and Hopkins apart from most of their peers. Something similar was said of Goodpaster: "He played the role of envoy, and confidante and managed to do so without inflaming potential rivalries with other members of the [White House] team."[28]

Trust is a trait that military persons understand readily, since there is no place where trust between or among the participants is more decisive than on or near the battlefield. Literature is replete with narratives of the kind of male "bonding" that occurs under such circumstances. What often is not generally understood is that the same expression of human behavior can also occur between two persons who share over time great responsibility. The loneliness that accompanies high office—or high command—is one reason; another is simply that physical attraction stimulates trust, and conversely, mistrust almost naturally accompanies feelings of repellence between two persons.

Just as Roosevelt needed Hopkins' companionship so badly that Hopkins moved into the White House during the war, Eisenhower came to rely on Goodpaster's companionship almost as much as on his executive skills. As far as Goodpaster was concerned, Eisenhower possessed an "inner power," a sense of being "necessary."[29] These were the same traits that had attracted Goodpaster very early in his career to Abe Lincoln and to Marshall.

Goodpaster's obituary described him thus:

> Later, President Eisenhower asked General Goodpaster to serve as staff secretary in the White House. He became known as the president's alter ego for his ability to carry out orders in his wide-ranging national security portfolio with minimal need for instruction. His mandate included work on the so-called Solarium Conference to plan for the American role in a post-Stalin Soviet Union. Some called him "the man with the briefcase" for his silent but essential backstage role in practically all military matters. General Goodpaster, wrote one reporter for the *New York Herald Tribune*, "looks like a business executive and hides his

White House importance behind a quiet façade that lends itself neither to anecdotes nor stuffiness."[30]

One of the ways that Eisenhower employed Goodpaster in a national security/foreign policy dimension came up in February 1955, during the heated emotions of the crisis with Communist China over the islands of Quemoy and Matsu in the Formosa Strait, which had been occupied by the Chinese Nationalists. Eisenhower explained: "To get further information and a sensing of the problem, as it appeared to an observer firsthand, I should ordinarily have called in at such a moment the Commander-in-Chief of the Pacific Fleet. But in a time of such tension, with the enemy scrutinizing our every move, I could not possibly call Admiral [Felix] Stump back to Washington. I therefore sent Colonel Goodpaster, the brilliant and trusted White House Staff Secretary, to Pearl Harbor to confer with Admiral Stump. On March 15 Colonel Goodpaster's report was in my hands."[31]

Eisenhower also gave this profound reply to a reporter's question as to whether he would use atomic weapons if the islands were directly challenged by the Communist Chinese: "I said that I could not answer that question in advance. The only thing I knew about war was two things: the most unpredictable factor in war was human nature, but the only unchanging factor in war was human nature."[32]

Further examples, from *The White House Years*, of Goodpaster's usefulness are:[33]

1. On July [1957], I discussed with Under Secretary [Douglas] Dillon and General Goodpaster a message from Chris Herter at Geneva. In it the Secretary expressed the opinion that the conference seemed to have reached a stalemate. [p. 406]
2. I next landed at Okinawa [in 1960], the most important of the Ryukyu chain, seized at fearful cost by the Americans in World War II. . . . The chief representative of the Ryukyuan people was Mr. Seisaka Ota. . . . Mr. Ota earnestly protested a cut of about a million and a half dollars in the United States' appropriations for economic support of the Ryukyus. . . . So I asked General Goodpaster to make a transpacific call to General [Wilton] Persons in Washington with instructions to mobilize all possible effort for the restoration of the money. [pp. 565–566]

3. As Phoumi [Vongvichit] proceeded [in 1960] to retake Vientiane [Laos] General Goodpaster reported the events to me. "Two points are giving me concern: the fact that Phoumi has not yet taken the airport at Vientiane, which is of great importance to the Soviets' airlift; and the fact that the pro-Communists are probably advancing on Luang Prabang—the royal capital." He then posed several questions: "First, should we seek to have Thai aircraft transport supplies into the area. Second, if the Thais can't do the job, should we use United States aircraft? Third, should we suggest that Thai forces seize the airfield at Vientiane and hold the one at Luang Prabang? Finally, should we support reconnaissance of Laos by Thai aircraft and of North Vietnam by United States aircraft?" [p. 609]

4. My assistant, General Goodpaster, once showed me, in a state of complete exasperation, a press account on the subject of presidential functioning that ran about as follows. . . . Goodpaster was so perturbed at such a distortion of fact that I laughed aloud. "Andy," I said, "let's not worry about how decisions are made, let's just be sure they are right." [p. 632].

An unhappy example of misapprehensions that not even Goodpaster could have corrected was the Suez crisis of 1956, which occurred during the run-up to the presidential election. This "shooting" crisis appeared to take the White House by surprise, and yet, for months prior to the Anglo-French invasion, Eisenhower had been deeply involved in trying to settle differences—especially the concerns of the British—with the Egyptian government.[34] At the Bermuda Conference of France, Britain, and the United States in December 1953, Eisenhower had already made clear to Churchill that "any attempt by European powers to sustain by force their dominant positions in these territories would have long since resulted in furious resentment, unrest, and conflict."[35]

Notwithstanding, British prime minister Anthony Eden, in spite of an opinion by his own legal staff that Gamal Abdel Nasser's seizure was legal as long as he did not close the canal to traffic, planned to reoccupy the canal. As to the United States, "He was not really worried. . . . When it came to the crux, Eisenhower was in charge of the United States—and Eisenhower would not let him down. After all, he was an old friend and comrade, and he knew about war. As Macmillan kept on saying, once Great Britain took action Ike would 'lie doggo' and let them get on with it, and that was all they needed. It was the costliest miscalculation the British had ever made."[36]

Although Eisenhower's aides, as well as the State Department, claimed that the events of the Anglo-French-Israeli military action were unexpected, the United States had in fact received ample short-run notice. Goodpaster, in his official role as White House liaison with the CIA, must have been "witting"—in CIA terminology. He also would have learned from Department of Defense (DOD) sources that the U.S. Sixth Fleet in the Mediterranean was observing the Anglo-French invasion force as it assembled on Malta and then sailed toward Suez.

There is some room for attempting, in hindsight, to understand the situation. Not only was Robert Murphy, the American special envoy sent to London to calm Eden, unsuccessful, but even Secretary of State John Foster Dulles went to London to try to do it and did not succeed. There was, in fact, a sense of alarm among both the British and American senior diplomatic community in London. The following episode underscores why:

> The well-known military expert, Captain [Basil] Liddell-Hart, had come to see the prime minister at 10 Downing Street. Eden had asked him for an outline of how a military campaign should be fought in Egypt, and Liddell-Hart had written one for him— only to have it sent back, with curt demands for alterations, no less than four times. Finally, rather than do a fifth revision, he had sent in the original outline and decided to leave it at that. Eden summoned him and said: "Captain Liddell-Hart, here I am at a critical moment in Britain's history . . . and it takes you five attempts—plus my vigilance amid all my worries—before you get it right." "But sir," Liddell-Hart said, "it hasn't taken five attempts. That version, which you now say is just what you wanted, is the original version."
>
> There was a moment's silence. Eden's handsome face went first pale and then red. He looked across at the long, languid shape of Captain Liddell-Hart, clad in a smart off-white summer outfit, then he reached out a hand, grasped one of the heavy, old-fashioned Downing Street inkwells, and flung it at his visitor. Another silence. Liddell-Hart looked down at the sickly blue stains spreading across his immaculate linen suiting, uncoiled himself, picked up a government-issue wastepaper basket, and

jammed it over the prime minister's head before slowly walking out of the room.[37]

The United States could hardly support an intervention in the Suez against Egypt, and then point the finger at the Soviets for their actions. In any event, only propaganda support was given to the Eastern Europeans, while active opposition through the United Nations as well as bilaterally placed the United States in open disapproval of its two NATO allies.[38] In CIA circles, the fact that the United States offered only verbal support while Hungary was following Poland in rising up against their Soviet masters underscored the futility of any notion of "rollback."

Goodpaster's Formal and Informal Influence

It was observed: "Not all defense matters came to the president through the NSC. If a defense issue did not involve the formulation, revision, or clarification of an NSC policy, then it was not part of the NSC system. These matters were handled by the Staff Secretary (who was also the defense liaison officer) directly with the president. The procedures might involve informal briefings by Brigadier General Andrew J. Goodpaster on operational or intelligence matters or meetings with cabinet level officials and others, which Goodpaster normally attended."[39]

In recognition of this role, in July 1956 Gen. Maxwell D. Taylor, the Army chief of staff, recommended Goodpaster for promotion to brigadier general. Taylor reported: "He has demonstrated superior performance of duty in the very sensitive area in which he has operated, thereby reinforcing past indications that he is an exceptional officer, entitled to promotion ahead of his contemporaries. I request [the adjutant general] that this letter be transmitted personally to the president of the Brigadier General Selection Board to inform the board that I strongly recommend that Colonel Goodpaster be selected for promotion to brigadier general."[40]

There is no doubt that Goodpaster's influence went beyond the strict confines of his formal title. In fact, "I knew from my service with Eisenhower at SHAPE that he had confidence that I could analyze and provide advice and recommendations on serious issues of policy."[41] It is quite clear, in fact, that Goodpaster was involved in foreign affairs generally, and not just acting as the White House liaison with the Department of Defense and the CIA.

Here is how Goodpaster put it: "On many occasions the President and I talked about his views—the views he was developing regarding nuclear weapons and what to be done about them. . . . And we often talked about what could be done to head off and reduce the possibility that this would ever occur. . . . He asked me to follow closely the work of Harold Stassen whom he had appointed as his first disarmament advisor. . . . I talked to him many, many times about proposals for crash programs. . . . He wanted an orderly program rather than, as he said, stops and starts that just waste money."[42]

One of Eisenhower's biographers, in fact, described Goodpaster's role in the White House as that of "adviser."[43] An example was Eisenhower's decision to appoint Gen. J. Lawton Collins to assist in the 1954 crisis in Vietnam: "The president's staff secretary, Colonel Andrew J. Goodpaster, suggested Collins for the Vietnam assignment."[44] Then: "In view of [the] pessimistic outlook contained in National Intelligence Estimate 63-7-54, November 23, 1954, and pessimistic cables received from Collins, OCB [NSC Operations Coordinating Board] agreed on December 8 to request early review by NSC of the U.S. position in Indochina. Collins has been requested to submit an appraisal on the prospects of achieving U.S. objectives in Indochina on or prior to January 15. NSC will be requested in light of further report to review U.S. program and position in Indochina."[45]

Goodpaster also would have understood how Eisenhower manipulated the public media to serve his own purposes. A good instance is the famous "Open Skies" proposal made at the 1955 Geneva Summit, from which neither side expected much.

> But it was the president who, on 21 July, put forward what came to be known as his "open skies" plan. He had, in fact, discussed it with his advisers but, according to his later account, he "extemporized some of the proposal" and "just threw it right in [the Russians'] faces." . . .
>
> Declaring that he had been "searching my heart and mind for something that I could say here that could convince everyone of the great sincerity of the United States in approaching the problem of disarmament," . . . he proposed that they should "give each other a complete blueprint of our military establishment" and provide "facilities for aerial photography to the other country." Then, "as Ike finished his earnest and impressive peroration, in which he pleaded for peace with security, there was a great clap of thunder like some cosmic round of applause and all the lights went out."[46]

The drama of the occasion could not, however, conceal the fact that the Soviet leaders who were present—and especially Khrushchev—looked upon this more as a propaganda stunt than as a serious proposal. The reason was obvious:

> As Ike recorded in his memoirs, the American "plan was to keep the Soviets on the defensive" by proposing measures of general appeal. This was certainly true of the "open skies" plan, which had the additional advantage that the open United States would gain by it more new information about the closed Soviet Union than vice versa. On the other hand, one of Ike's closest confidants, his staff secretary Colonel (later General) Andrew J. Goodpaster, asserted that the proposal was not disingenuous or made for propaganda purposes. . . . On balance, it seems, Ike was hoping to have it both ways. He wanted a propaganda advantage that would also reduce the risk of nuclear war and might just lead to some form of agreement that would clearly benefit the United States.[47]

In fairness to Eisenhower, it could also be argued that he perceived, in order to avoid what seemed during those times a catastrophic nuclear war, that "a form of behavior becomes out of date only when something else takes its place, and in order to invent forms of behavior that will make war obsolete, it is a first requirement to believe that an invention is possible."[48] Was arms control leading to disarmament achievable? Disregarding the overwhelming body of skeptics surrounding them, to their credit Eisenhower and Goodpaster—along with Stassen—considered disarmament worth a try.

One of Goodpaster's notable traits was that he combined the sometimes abstract nature of diplomacy as practiced by the professional diplomat with the practicality of the professional soldier. Few general officers of his generation could manage to achieve this blend. In describing the problem, he inadvertently described himself in both his national and multinational roles, which is one important reason why his career took the form that it did:

> The national security environment is also a complex one, in which relationships are intricate, often unstable. Below the President, participation is widely diversified into strongholds vested with particular interests, values, and responsibilities. Viewing security problems from the White House, one has the ineluctable

impression that only on the President's desk does everything come together. The big issues affecting national security arise, in particular, between the departments of Defense and State. Not only in dealing with security problems but also in framing them, the military and the diplomatic approaches are inherently different.

Still, it remains necessary to draw them into some coherent combination. There is nothing diplomatic about a machine gun, nor can an aide memoire of itself stop subversive infiltration and terror; yet, in the modern world it is clear that both must be employed in some higher security context if security and safety are to be served. . . . The interest of the State Department is to limit the scale and extent of violence, while that of the professional military man, once higher authority has decided to resort to force, is to seize and hold the initiative and to gain quick preponderance over the adversary, employing force decisively and aggressively to accomplish the mission with minimum loss of life and minimum risk to the United States.[49]

For example, on 18 July 1958, Allen Dulles wrote to Goodpaster: "Dear Andy: I enclose for your files, a copy of the Briefing Notes which I used at the meeting which the President had with Congressional Leaders, July 14, 1958, 2:30 p.m., in connection with the Middle East crisis. These notes were closely followed in my presentation, but with some additions and there was, of course, a question-answer period not included in these notes."[50]

Another example is this memorandum from Goodpaster to the State Department:

Memorandum for: Mr. John A. Calhoun, Director, Executive Secretariat, Department of State, 26 May 1959. The President today indicated general acceptance of the recommendations in Secretary [Douglas] Dillon's memorandum to him of May 22nd concerning the Baghdad Pact Council session this fall. In so doing, he indicated that the State Department should prepare for him a short speech of welcome rather than anything amounting to a major address. He also said that before any move is made in this matter, the State Department should consult very carefully with appropriate Congressional leaders concerning the proposals. A. J. Goodpaster, Brigadier General, USA, Staff Secretary.[51]

All of the foregoing suggests that one scholar's appraisal of Eisenhower as a "figurehead president" is not accurate—in fact, it is a complete distortion of the reality. As reported: "[Richard] Neustadt presents an account of a leadership style that, by relying extensively on delegation, renders the president ill-equipped to advance his policies." A contrasting view was put forth by another scholar, who titled his study of the Eisenhower period, *The Hidden-Hand Presidency: Eisenhower as Leader.*[52] Where to strike the balance between "hands-on" and detached is impossible to determine because administration comes down to matters of human temperament and bureaucratic culture.

The amount of detail that Eisenhower could consume is reflected in this note to an assistant secretary of state: "A man named Henry A. Kissinger has just written a very provocative book entitled 'Nuclear Weapons and Foreign Policy.' The book was brought to my attention by Cabot Lodge. . . . I have not read the complete book, but I am sending you herewith a copy of a fairly extensive brief made by General Goodpaster of my office."[53]

Furthermore, drawing on this as a parallel, Eisenhower's public discourse and private commentary projected sharply different images: "His remarks in press conferences were colloquial and folksy. His speech rhetoric was dignified, but simple and direct enough 'to sound good to the fellow digging the ditch in Kansas.' In private, particularly when he conveyed his thoughts to his aides on paper, his prose was crisp and detached, revealing a cognitive style in which deductive clarity played a central part."[54]

Eisenhower, like all presidents before and after him, could not possibly achieve what they initially expected was possible. "It is never long enough to do any real planning, to think about where the country ought to be, even in the next decade, and to design programs to get from here to there. . . . He never really ran the government as he had expected. Rather, he found that the job was to try to keep the social fabric intact; to keep the peace if possible; to defend the nation from aggressors; to maintain the nation's place in the world, even by force; to attempt to balance economic growth and stability; and at best to make some new initiatives that the history books would record as his."[55] In doing all of this, Goodpaster was, quite literally, at his side.

Eisenhower confirmed this in his 1956 efficiency report on Goodpaster: "Colonel Goodpaster is Staff Secretary at the White House and serves also as Department of Defense Liaison Officer. He has the full responsibility for the operations of the 'Secretariat' in the White House Office, a department that during the past year has taken over increasingly important duties.

Colonel Goodpaster sees me frequently during the day; all military, diplomatic and intelligence matters are brought to me by him, as well as many additional important problems. He participates in Cabinet, National Security Council, and other high-level meetings, and sits in on intimate meetings in my office with top-level military, intelligence and State Department personnel. His post is one of highest importance."[56]

Even when not at his side, Goodpaster was in the picture. This excerpt of 11 February 1955 from Press Secretary Hagerty's diary illustrates the point: "At the press conference Wednesday, Joe Harsch of the *Christian Science Monitor* . . . [asked]: 'Mr. President, is that invitation to General [Georgy] Zhukov still open?' . . . Goodpaster told me Thursday morning Harsch had received a call from the third secretary of the Russian Embassy. The third secretary said he would very much like to talk to Harsch and they made a luncheon engagement at the Metropolitan Club. . . . The sounding out of Harsch by the third secretary was a very interesting development and, of course, Harsch confidentially reported it to the CIA. Goodpaster was sure that the President would want to hear of this."[57]

Thus, during the Eisenhower years, both in theory and in practice, the staff secretary's role grew because "of its position at the intersection between politicians and the military."[58] As Goodpaster described: "Here was a senior executive working with his immediate subordinates but supported by a staff system which took care of the flow of paperwork and information. And we the staff people were charged with the follow-up on meetings in the president's office, where decisions were made, to check to see that they were indeed carried out and to keep an eye on operations and activities within the department, and if there was a discrepancy between them and the policy guidance that had been given, to bring that back in to the president."[59]

Eisenhower firmly believed that the NSC machinery should operate as intended, which meant that it was advisory rather than a decision-making body, and he regularly attended the Thursday meetings. As reported: "Eisenhower hoped that the NSC would become a 'corporate body' of top officials, who would act as personal advisers to the president. Moreover, he wanted the NSC planning board to serve as the council's 'planning arm' by providing 'sound security policy recommendations.'"[60] He was actively interested in attempts to rein in the three services' attempts to "go around" him to lobby Congress for their needs, especially if they ran against the official set of priorities, meaning in particular the Army.[61]

The same could be said of the JCS's Joint Staff, on which Goodpaster also served. Later, in the Johnson presidency, then-JCS chairman Gen. Maxwell Taylor hoped that he could consolidate the authority of the JCS into the single office of the chairman, thus bringing under control the constant interservice rivalries that hampered the military establishment from insisting on a larger policy-making role in national security affairs. Although he was unsuccessful, this is what he envisioned (viz. Goodpaster's role):

> Taylor thought Congress should "dissolve the JCS" and replace it with a single "Defense Chief of Staff" and a "Supreme Military Council." The defense chief of staff would have "great authority" and report directly to the secretary of defense and the president. Now that he was chairman, Taylor thought that he could become a de facto "defense chief of staff." In an effort to centralize authority, he gave his special assistant for policy, Maj. Gen. Andrew Goodpaster, formerly President Eisenhower's national security assistant, unprecedented responsibilities and latitude. Goodpaster became, in effect, a deputy. Previously, in the absence of the chairman, the senior service chief presided over important sessions as acting chairman. When Taylor was out of town, Goodpaster as his "deputy" attended White House and other high-level policy and planning sessions in place of another [Service] Chief. . . . Taylor tried to formalize Goodpaster's position and make it permanent. He wanted him promoted to lieutenant general and his title changed to Assistant Chairman, Joint Chiefs of Staff, a maneuver that required considerable political support.[62]

Certainly, the efficiency report that Eisenhower wrote on Goodpaster in 1958 could apply as well to this later period of Goodpaster's service: "He handles the most delicate and sensitive material that ultimately comes to my attention. He is an invaluable assistant. It follows that I have in him the utmost confidence. In character, ability, performance, and dedication he is of the very highest classification."[63]

Chapter Seven

A Functional National Security System

"The military policy to be adopted by the nation would have a significant bearing on the courses of action open to it in the area of foreign policy."
—DONALD F. BLETZ, *The Role of the Military Professional in U.S. Foreign Policy*

Goodpaster's upward career trajectory rested in large part on both the conceptual and the accompanying bureaucratic evolution of the "national security" dimension of presidential leadership. Both dimensions suited Goodpaster's temperament as his career unfolded along a parallel trajectory.

To begin at the beginning: it seems difficult to comprehend in hindsight, but during most of the first half of the twentieth century, when the United States had become a world power, there was no systematic scheme in place to coordinate within the government what later came to be known as national security policy. General Marshall recognized this deficiency early in World War II when he asked the War Department General Staff to create a unit "solely responsible for thinking and planning improved methods of warfare."[1] He thus used a "think-tank" approach to develop a global vision and strategy for the army.

Marshall said at one point: "You should organize in your division a small planning and exploring branch, composed of visionary officers, with nothing else to do but think out improvements in methods of warfare, study developments abroad and tackle such unsolved problems as measures against armored force, night bombardment, march protection, and the like."[2] This certainly was a step in the right direction, and was one that, undoubtedly, both Abe Lincoln and Goodpaster would have welcomed.

When the United States entered World War II, it "did not have a politico-military body such as the British War Cabinet or our present National Security Council. . . . It was not until December 1944 that a politico-military body was created. It was the State-War-Navy Coordinating Committee (SWNCC), composed of assistant secretaries of the represented departments. . . . It was the direct ancestor of the National Security Council."[3]

The SWNCC advised President Roosevelt "regarding military strategy, military relations with our allies, the allocation of munitions and shipping, requirements of all kinds—including the manpower needs of the armed forces—and matters of joint army-navy policy."[4] Goodpaster served on the staff of SWNCC in the early postwar period. As he said: "I . . . saw [Eisenhower as Army chief of staff] during that spring of 1947 when I was working with the State-War-Navy Coordinating Committee in preparation for what became the Marshall plan, reporting to him on the work that our group was doing."[5]

An example early in his career of how close to the seat of power Goodpaster was: in 1945, he helped resolve a disagreement between Secretary of War Henry Stimson and then–Army Chief of Staff George Marshall. It had to do with the visit to Washington of President Sergio Osmana of the Philippines, who was very interested in knowing if the United States was going to honor its wartime commitment to grant full independence. Goodpaster was working at that time for Lincoln in the Strategy Section. Secretary Stimson wanted a general statement, whereas General Marshall wanted a more detailed statement. As Goodpaster recounted:

> At that point, Mr. Stimson came through the door between their two offices, the door that was never closed, and here these two men stood side by side, two men who revered each other, greatly respected [each other]. . . . At about that time, General Marshall turned to the three of us with a kind of frosty twinkle in his eye and said, "Well, I think we've given you all the help we can, it's time for you to go to work." And so we did. . . . We prepared a third solution. . . . And at ten o'clock, as President Truman had required, Mr. Stimson brought it over and the document was signed by the two presidents. . . . [Marshall] would say, don't bring me a problem, bring me a problem with your best solution. And, of course, that was why he was as successful and able as he was.[6]

It flows from this anecdote that one of Marshall's traits that appealed to Goodpaster (and to Eisenhower) was his insisting "that his principal assistants should think and act on their own conclusions in their own spheres of responsibility."[7] It was observed: "The former army general was a man who believed in both an orderly process and planning."[8]

It was in this assignment that Goodpaster came to admire Marshall firsthand. Goodpaster would have agreed with this statement: "On leaving Washington for the last time, that craggy veteran of seven administrations, Secretary of War Henry L. Stimson, said to Marshall, 'I have seen a great many soldiers in my lifetime and you, sir, are the finest soldier I have ever known.'"[9]

Marshall was working at that time, along with George Kennan, on developing the Truman Doctrine of aid to Greece and Turkey. In June 1947 Marshall delivered his famous speech at Harvard about the United States taking responsibility, in tandem with counterpart war-shattered nations of Western Europe, to rebuild their economies, thus removing them from the threat of Soviet Communism. The idea was soon dubbed the Marshall Plan.

The National Security Council

In tracing the evolution of what has come to be known as "national security," it is useful to recall that the creation of the NSC is usually considered the starting point. This is important for this biography because the NSC played an important role in Goodpaster's responsibilities as the president's defense liaison officer in the White House, and then later when he was involved in the NSC's activities. Its formation in 1947 was contained in the same legislation that unified the armed services. The enabling statute "provides a council 'to advise the President with respect to the integration of domestic, foreign, and military policies relating to the national security.' To do this, the council is to 'assess and appraise the objectives, commitments, and risks of the United States in relation to our actual and potential military power.' The council has no statutory function and operates with a staff appointed at the discretion of the president."[10]

One of the problems—both bureaucratic and political—in creating a new function, and especially if it involves the president, is that there is always maneuvering either to enhance its role or to sublimate its role. In the case of the NSC, Truman tried to have it both ways. He wanted to keep it in check, but at the same time, the legislative provisions meant that it could not be ignored entirely. So he appointed a fellow Missourian, Adm. Sydney Souers, to the post of executive secretary to the NSC.

To minimize intra-administration politicizing, "Truman, in one of his first assignments for his new assistant, had Harriman draft a presidential order limiting attendance at NSC meetings to members, plus others explicitly invited by the President himself. Nevertheless, a new power center in Washington would over the years evolve from Harriman's circumspect beginning as the first presidential assistant for national security affairs."[11]

Eisenhower also did not want to vest too much authority in the NSC, and in particular any policy-making role. The small staff could coordinate, facilitate, monitor, and so forth. Eisenhower did, however, create a position in the White House of special assistant to the president for national security affairs. Some years later, in response to a request for his opinion as to whether the special assistant should be confirmed by Congress, Goodpaster responded:

> I recognize that [today] when the functions of the office go beyond a purely "staff" character a problem of assuring appropriate accountability to the Congress arises. During the Eisenhower administration with which I was associated as a staff assistant in this area to the President, this difficulty did not exist. By specific instruction of the president, positions such as mine and that of the Special Assistant for National Security Affairs were limited to "staff" responsibilities, and were denied executive authority, the line for which ran directly from the president to the secretaries of the departments concerned, and the heads of the agencies concerned. In addition, our functions did not involve direct contact with the press and other media, those being reserved to the President himself and his press secretary. Moreover, it was not his practice to have members of his staff like myself engage in negotiations, or official discussions, with foreign authorities: this function was reserved to the State Department or, within their respective areas, to other departments and agencies of the government.[12]

No one would argue against the fact that the actual policy-making took place in the Oval Office: under crisis conditions, Eisenhower would meet with his principal advisers, using NSC staff for coordination purposes. In this respect, Goodpaster could play a useful role, moving both inside and outside the formal chain of command.[13] The so-called NSC process, like Solarium, became Eisenhower's method of engaging or creating a sense of participation and commitment with the various foreign and national security–related constituencies. He also "had a penchant for careful staff work, and believed that effective planning involved a creative process of discussion and debate among advisers compelled to work toward agreed recommendations."[14]

> The Special Assistant was made responsible for determination, subject to the President's desires, of the Council agenda, for briefing the President in advance of Council meetings, and for presenting matters for discussion at the Council meetings. As Chairman of the Planning Board he was responsible for scheduling Planning Board work and for the manner of presentation and quality of such work. He was to appoint (subject when necessary to the President's approval) such ad hoc committees, such consultants from outside the Government and such mixed governmental-nongovernmental committees as might be required. He supervised the work of the NSC Staff through the Executive Secretary.[15]

The Operations Coordinating Board (OCB), which monitored the implementation of NSC decisions, derived its authority from Executive Order 10483, which provided:

> Section 2. The National Security Council having recommended a national security policy and the President having approved it, the Board shall (1) whenever the President shall hereafter so direct, advise with the agencies concerned as to (a) their detailed operational planning responsibilities respecting such policy, (b) the coordination of the inter-departmental aspects of the detailed operational plans developed by the agencies to carry out such policy, (c) the timely and coordinated execution of such policy and plans, and (d) the execution of each security action or project so that it shall make its full contribution to the attainment of national security objectives and to the particular climate of opinion the United States is seeking to achieve in the world, and (2) initiate new proposals for action within the framework of national security policies in response to opportunities and changes in the situation. The Board shall perform such other advisory functions as the President may assign to it and shall from time to time make reports to the National Security Council with respect to the carrying out of this order.[16]

Overall, NSC 162/2, which was the official statement of the NSC authority, only partially filled Eisenhower's wishes, but it did enough so that he could be pleased publicly with the result. There were, for instance, reservations about when and under what conditions troops could be withdrawn, and it failed to state clearly how and when nuclear weapons would be used. Furthermore, "the armed services did not yet have unencumbered access to nuclear weapons. . . . The lack of weapons in sufficient quantity and appropriate design was a constant impediment that the services said hindered them from carrying out the President's desired changes in policy and strategy."[17]

In 1953 President Eisenhower adopted a reorganization plan for the Department of Defense and the JCS that enhanced the powers of the secretary of defense and the chairman of the JCS at the expense of the separate services. The chairman of the JCS, Adm. Arthur W. Radford, became the principal military adviser to the secretary of defense and to the president (he replaced Eisenhower's wartime colleague, Gen. Omar N. Bradley).[18]

A few years later, in a further consolidation of power, the Defense Reorganization Act of 1958 removed the service secretaries from the chain of command leading from the president to the operational forces, and authorized the president, with the advice of the Joint Chiefs, to create unified and specified commands that took their orders directly from the secretary of defense. In addition, the chairman of the JCS gained increased influence in JCS deliberations and greater control over the Joint Staff.[19]

Goodpaster described the law's intended and unintended consequences:

The Act of 1958, in clarifying the authority of the Secretary of Defense, has had a result not anticipated or consciously intended by those who participated in its formulation. With regard to operational planning and the military and tactical advice that is offered to decision makers, the intent of the legislation was to concentrate responsibility in the Joint Chiefs of Staff, thus ending the situation in which the individual services, acting separately, extended operational influence over field commands. The Secretary of Defense and his immediate office would exert policy direction and control. But in the application of the Act, a further shift has occurred, resulting in a detailed treatment of a wider range of matters at the civilian level of the Office of the Secretary of Defense than was then foreseen. . . . Where the act visualized fixing the responsibility for military operational matters in the Joint Chiefs of Staff and assigning the conduct of combat operations to the unified commands, there has evolved in practice a sharing of the Joint Chiefs of Staff role and a retention of operational decisions on a more centralized basis at the Secretary of Defense level of control than was anticipated in 1958.[20]

Eisenhower's first national security assistant, Bobby Cutler, described Eisenhower's approach: "President Eisenhower used the National Security Council as a vital mechanism to assure that all sides of an issue could be known by him before coming to his decision. He wanted a skilled planning arm to gather from informed sources the material relevant to each issue, to winnow and to test that material in the crucible of argument, and to bring the integrated, exactly phrased result before the Council for debate in his presence."[21] Cutler further enthused: "The National Security Council has emerged as a mechanism of the executive branch . . . equal in importance to the Cabinet. . . . Out of the grinding of these minds comes a refinement of the raw material into valuable metal, out of the frank assertion of differing views, backed up by preparation that searches every nook and cranny, emerges a resolution that reasonable men can support."[22]

Goodpaster's National Security Role

All told, Goodpaster, living up to Eisenhower's expectations, described his role

> while Bobby Cutler was there, then Dillon Anderson, then Bobby again, and then Gordon Gray. They would deal with the policy papers that would come via the NSC route, broad plans, major programs, things of that kind. I would get the day-to-day flow of things that involved the president. If these matters came to the White House for coordination but did not require the president's attention, they would oftentimes go to the Operations Coordinating Board, which was part of the structure that was under Cutler's and then Gray's supervision.[23]

One feature that distinguished the Eisenhower administration's approach to "national security" from that of the Truman administration was precisely the role that Goodpaster played:

Beyond State and the NSC, Ike also had a third resource for foreign policy management: his staff secretary Andrew Goodpaster. The formal job was created in 1954 when Eisenhower lost his temper over mismanagement of White House paperwork—"Andy's" initial task was to be sure it flowed smoothly to the right people. But once Goodpaster solved that problem, he was available to do much more. Quietly and efficiently, he handled much of Eisenhower's most critical national security and intelligence business. He sat in the West Wing, down the hall from the Oval Office. He organized and took notes for the president's many informal meetings with senior advisers on international matters.

He smoothed communications between Eisenhower and Dulles, and perhaps even more between the president and Dulles's successor, Christian Herter. . . . He did not provide independent substantive advice, nor was his stature equal to that of Eisenhower's formal national security assistants, Bobby Cutler and later Gordon Gray. But he played a key operational coordination role. And Eisenhower trusted him totally—he would remark that every man would want his son to be like Andy Goodpaster.[24]

Furthermore, acting just barely within the formal operational structure of the NSC—if formalities were to be employed—Eisenhower would regularly meet alone with Goodpaster. "These informal meetings accomplished precisely what contemporary critics of Eisenhower's foreign policy-making took the NSC to task for not accomplishing— rapid, flexible decision-making by the president himself. . . . Goodpaster was not just the note-taker in the informal policy-making meetings in Eisenhower's office: his role was like a combined Planning Board and OCB. He saw that critical participants were not frozen out of discussion and that Eisenhower's decisions were carried out. In this sense, his duties paralleled those of Cutler. Indeed, their two positions came to be combined in later presidencies."[25]

After leaving the White House, Eisenhower deplored the dismantling by the Kennedy administration of the elaborate NSC committee structure, and the de facto downgrading of the NSC in highest-level decision-making. "I explained to [Kennedy] in detail the purpose and work habits of the Security Council, together with its two principal supporting agencies—the Planning Board and the Operations Coordinating Board. I said that the National Security Council had become the most important weekly meeting of the government."[26] Nonetheless, one observer recalled: "The elaborate organizational staff reforms of the Eisenhower White House were stripped away with an almost evangelical glee; in particular the downgrading of Eisenhower's cherished National Security Council (NSC)."[27]

Later, witnessing the Bay of Pigs debacle, Eisenhower would observe that Kennedy and his principal advisers might have avoided their mistakes if they had had Eisenhower's less impulsive national security decision-making apparatus. Goodpaster agreed wholeheartedly with Eisenhower, having himself been a product of the more hierarchical system of policy formation and decision.

John Eisenhower's Role

Whether Goodpaster welcomed the presence of the president's son at his elbow can only be an object of conjecture. A hint, however, shows in a handwritten note that Goodpaster wrote to himself:

> President asked, on my first day back from leave, how long I had been here, indicating he was wondering whether I wouldn't be thinking I should leave in another year or so (he thought I had been here about 2 years—was surprised when I told him 3). I told him I had no definite period in mind—that when I was ordered in I accepted idea of serving here if my service were thought to be needed, and as long as they were thought to be needed [sic], recognizing but disregarding the possibility of adverse effect on my future in the military service.
>
> He then said he had thought about this in relation to the possibility of bringing John in as my replacement as Staff Secretary and Defense Liaison Officer (in which post he had been serving during my leave).
>
> I told him my only thought was to serve here if, in such capacity, and so long as needed. He said John should be available in early 1959 (after he finishes Armed Forces Staff College), and that, if he comes here shortly after that, I would be available for other duty. He said he had in mind that I might continue to serve here as a special assistant, or military adviser, unless for some reason I should be returned to Army duty.
>
> I told him any of these actions would be all right with me— that I was hoping, on leaving here, to get an assignment such as

Asst Div Comdr or CG of one of the missile commands, such as the one in Italy.[28]

Goodpaster recalled: "In 1958 John Eisenhower came aboard as an assistant to me and he worked on the international side of the house. And this was a great help to me because he and I could substitute for each other in taking these meetings and writing up the results of the meetings and then following them up in the government." John Eisenhower described his duties: "I spent about a month, a little more than a month, between stations and the White House in '57 filling in for General Goodpaster while he was gone on leave. Then, in October of '58, I came on a permanent basis for the rest of the administration. I was General Goodpaster's assistant and our functions were paper flow: to make sure that every action that came to the president's attention had everybody's contribution to it. We were a device for insuring that the last one in the office was not the one who got his way. That when something was brought to the president's attention, everybody had a chance to comment on it first."[29]

Other assistants would monitor follow-up to the various presidential meetings. "It was an informational channel and it was really quite helpful in keeping a flow of specific information of particulars of what was going on in the government, getting down below the kind of broad generalities and major programs which could be reflected in, say, budget and the money provided, to knowing some of the quite specific things that were going on which did or did not conform to and support the line of policy that the President had in mind. . . . This helped to discipline the system and keep it aligned with the policy directions that the President gave."[30]

Furthermore, John Eisenhower recollected:

My particular functions were daily intelligence briefings. I sat in on them and made records of quite a few of the meetings that Dad had in his office. We tried to arrange it so that there would be no meeting of any importance that was not recorded. The great exception to this, which is too bad historically but I guess it was certainly the way they wanted it, was John Foster Dulles. Nobody was in the room with Dad and Dulles so that what they've said has just been lost except for what Dad recorded from his own memory.

When [Christian] Herter took over, General Goodpaster and I would sneak in one at a time. We would go in and see if we were thrown out! And we weren't! So, from that time on we were able to record the private conversations between the president and the secretary of state.[31]

Thus, "it was necessary for us to work very closely together and to pass tasks or topics back and forth, to check with each other to see that each was informed of any significant thing that the other was concerned in."[32] What this implies—almost asserts—is that Goodpaster and then later also John Eisenhower, were intimately involved at the presidential level, in virtually all matters of a "national security" nature, even though not technically charged with the responsibility to do so.

Chapter Eight

National Defense Writ Large

"War is the most controversial strategy that great powers can employ to increase their share of world power."
— JOHN J. MEARSHEIMER, *The Tragedy of Great Power Politics*

It is useful here to recall, in capsule form, Eisenhower's notion of national defense, made in 1954. Both houses of Congress had shifted to the Democratic Party, and therefore more challenges would be forthcoming to Eisenhower from various military-related interests.

> [Eisenhower] said that the controlling thought that the leaders must keep in mind was that the United States was really never frightened about enemy attack until the advent of atomic bombs and the long-range bomber. . . . But the invention of the A-bomb and nuclear weapons and the long-range bomber to carry them has caused us all to take a different look at the world. "It seems to me that the great emphasis that we now should put on national defense should be centered on two main objectives: (1) massive retaliation, which simply means the ability to blow hell out of them in a hurry if they start anything and (2) a system of advance warnings developed through our radar system to minimize any such attack. . . . Now, everything points to the fact that Russia is not seeking a general war and will not for a long, long time, if ever. Everything is shifting to economic warfare, to propaganda, and to a sort of peaceful infiltration. . . . What we want to do is to lessen the priority we have been keeping on Army ground troops and those parts of the Navy that do not deal with air and with submarines. I want you to know that this judgment is my own."[1]

Goodpaster explained, although a bit eloquently, why the national security process is important: "The first and overriding characteristic of national security affairs is that . . . the stakes are high. They concern the continued existence of the United States as a free nation, with free institutions. What is really involved is self-preservation, the first law of life. In this sense—and to this degree—military and security needs take priority over almost all other considerations. While these are not of themselves primary goals of a national society—as are the freedom and self-government, and the education, health, economic well-being, and the cultural and moral advancement of its people—without the protective shield of the power and readiness to defend itself, it is not likely that these others could be attained."[2]

The Overall Political Framework

More important is the observation that "the final characteristic of the national security environment is the fundamental fact that the conduct of policy and action occurs within an over-all political framework. The framework is political both internationally and domestically. Internationally, it is evident that considerations of security guide both the foreign policy activities of peace and the warfare that continues foreign policy by other means."[3]

> This leads to the question of what is meant by having the best men assigned to the Joint Staff. Obviously, the best way to insure that the Joint Chiefs of Staff provide thorough, well-reasoned, professional military advice, particularly in times of crisis and war, is to make sure that only the best officers are selected to head their Services. . . . What is meant by the term "best-qualified"? Of course, there are all sorts of ways one could measure qualifications. However, when it comes to the Joint Chiefs of Staff providing military advice in times of crisis or war, the best-qualified individuals are those highly professionally adept, combat-experienced (if possible), tough-minded, and willing to state the bald-faced truth as they see it. Such officers must be bright (and few rise to that level unless they are), but need not be intellectuals. And while at least a modicum of diplomacy and tact is essential, it is neither necessary nor desirable—in such times—for such men to be military diplomats (politicians).[4]

This definition fit Goodpaster, although perhaps the term "scholar" could also be appended to him, given his lengthy list of correspondence, articles, and speeches after his retirement. It is a credit to both Eisenhower and his close colleague Gen. Alfred Gruenther that they saw in Goodpaster the qualities that Brig. Gen. George Lincoln recognized, and which led to

Lincoln first drawing Goodpaster into the planning world of the Pentagon, then bringing him to Paris to participate in the creation of SHAPE, and then bringing him to the White House itself.

Overall, Goodpaster, in furtherance of his responsibilities, was a model of the officer corps of his day. "A study of the alumni of the National War College in 1969 revealed a surprising acceptance of political-military emphasis on the part of the graduates. 'The study of our national strategy, to include the integration of military and foreign policies . . . is clearly seen as the most important base of study for the course, regardless of year of graduation, service, branch of government or rank of the respondent.'"⁵ What is also most interesting here is that Goodpaster was commandant of the National War College in 1967–1968.

To summarize: "Eisenhower introduced a variety of staff entities and roles that hitherto had been absent from the presidency, among them a White House chief of staff, Cabinet and National Security Council (NSC) staffs, and a special assistant for national security affairs. . . . [There also was] his informal national security policy-making operations, which involved such fluid procedures as daily consultations between Eisenhower and Secretary of State John Foster Dulles, informal meetings in the Oval Office between Eisenhower and core aides, and one-to-one meetings of the president and an extensive network of public and private advisors."⁶

There were strong pressures from both Congress and the administration for reducing the Pentagon's budget, and this in turn introduced into the situation the continual bickering among the services over their respective budgetary justifications. Thus the confusion was twofold: (1) a president confronting the most basic concept of how to fight and win the most likely (at least it seemed then) kind of warfare (i.e., nuclear); (2) a JCS that bickered and competed among themselves over how to equip themselves and for what war-making purpose. Overall, the "ultimate absurdity"—as Herbert York termed it—was that with increasing expenditures on armaments, American security was in fact declining.⁷ Thus, any hope of an orderly system of war planning fell by the wayside because of this situation, which had taken on a dimension that was more than just a "roles and missions" dispute.

To make matters even more confusing, the chiefs would air their complaints before Congress, to Eisenhower's intense displeasure. However,

One Chief who, over the course of several years managed to attain a closer than normal relationship with President Eisenhower, was Admiral Arleigh Burke. Years later Burke recalled: "'He'd call me up on the white phone . . . maybe four-thirty, five o'clock and say, 'Could you come over for a discussion or a cocktail or something?' 'Yes, sir. Of course.' And I went over. And he might ask me a question . . . on the Army. I said, 'Mr. President, I don't know a damn thing about that.' He was an impatient man. 'I know you don't know anything about it, damn it. I want to get your views.'"[8]

It is a safe bet that Goodpaster was on hand during these occasions.

Concepts of "National Security"

There have been criticisms, from time to time, that the chairman of the JCS had either too much authority to speak out or too little. "Critics of the system seem to have forgotten that one of the complaints about the Joint Chiefs in the mid-1950s . . . was that Admiral Arthur Radford had too much influence with President Eisenhower, not too little." In fact, the Army's chiefs of staff at the time, Gen. Matthew Ridgway and then Gen. Maxwell Taylor, claimed that Eisenhower's massive retaliation strategy and his reduction in the Army's size represented an excessive dependency on the military advice of Chairman Radford.[9]

Moreover, "Part of the problem of the service Secretaries has been the Joint Chiefs of Staff channel to the Office of the Secretary of Defense [OSD], the National Security Council, and the President; part of it is OSD; part also is the nature of centralized military planning in an armed service department. . . . [The service secretaries] . . . were not permitted to participate in the discussions . . . of the top management—i.e., the National Security Council and the Secretary and Deputy Secretary of Defense—by whom policies affecting [their] enterprise were considered and determined."[10]

Goodpaster recalled that "some of the changes introduced by the Act of 1958 clearly reflected dissatisfaction at the higher levels of the government with the form and degree of service rivalry then manifest. The act took steps to eliminate such sterile rivalry. It created a chairman with statutory powers, and emphasized corporate responsibility. It strengthened the role of the Vice Chief in each service, to enable him to shoulder a larger part of the burden of service operations, thus clearing the agenda of the Chief and allowing him to spend more time on his corporate responsibility."[11]

Eisenhower delegated downward, letting the various issues clinging to a large issue of policy either fall away or become more clearly defined.

Given his leadership style, Eisenhower preferred not to deal directly with the military—that was [Secretary of Defense Charles] Wilson's job. Recognizing Wilson's lack of a military background, Eisenhower tried to buttress the secretary's position when he reorganized the Pentagon on July 1, 1953. Wilson's authority was strengthened, as the number of assistant secretaries increased from three to nine. In a bow to the military, the president also gave the chairman of the Joint Chiefs the authority to manage the joint staff and approve the selection of those who were to serve on it. Eisenhower wanted the chairman to recruit officers who would focus not just on the interests of their own service, but on "national planning for the overall common defense."[12]

He was only partially successful in this endeavor, however, undoubtedly placing a burden on both his own chief of staff and on Goodpaster to monitor happenings at the higher echelons in the Pentagon. Goodpaster, inevitably, was always in danger of being caught in the middle of a contretemps. He had worked for Army Chief of Staff Ridgway at SHAPE when Ridgway was SACEUR, and now Ridgway was the "bad boy" in Eisenhower's eyes for vigorously advocating an increase in conventional forces.[13]

Furthermore, to the skeptic, massive retaliation was nothing more than a slogan to use as a budgetary axe rather than signaling a sharp change in grand strategy. So-called peripheral actions were still taking place with no open consideration of using the "nuclear option"—at least since the Korean truce.

The enunciation by John Foster Dulles in January 1954—before Goodpaster had arrived—that "local defenses in many areas . . . were inadequate against aggressors who could strike without warning, and therefore these defenses 'must be reinforced by the further deterrent of massive retaliatory power.' America's shield would be its 'capacity to retaliate instantly, by means and at places of our choosing.'" However, in Berlin, in Korea, in Indochina (including Vietnam), and in regard to a so-called Sino-Soviet bloc, Eisenhower and Dulles could not move American public opinion beyond what the *Economist* termed "a spectacle of vociferous inaction" to favor more fighting, even if they had wanted to.[14] Even the Communist Chinese claims and threats regarding the offshore islands of Quemoy and Matsu did not trigger any military response. In fact, instead of "unleashing" Chiang Kai-shek, he was in effect "leashed."[15]

This debate over the efficacy of deterrence over offense—or vice versa—raged especially vigorously during the Eisenhower period of the Cold War.

"Massive retaliation" was partly a declaratory policy and partly a justification for sharply increased expenditures on both nuclear warheads and the means of delivering them. Furthermore, "many have argued against reliance on deterrence alone, since the adversary could punish the United States in return for any strike we might deliver."[16]

This brings to mind some contradictory elements to any notion of a nuclear "grand strategy." First, it is easier to articulate a strategy than it is to identify the circumstances under which it can assist the tactician. Thus, "new technology, even when properly integrated into weapons and systems with well trained and highly motivated people, cannot erase the difficulties that impede strategic excellence. A new device, even innovative ways to conduct war, is always offered as a poisoned chalice. . . . Every new device and mode of war carries the virus of its own technical, tactical, operational, strategic, or political negation."[17] That, in essence, is massive retaliation, if it is to be considered an operational guide rather than merely a political slogan.

Goodpaster, having studied the nature and impact of technology on both military strategy (trying to reduce the unknowable to educated guesswork) and weapons innovation (the unforeseeable setting), would have taken this for granted. Many of his civilian and military colleagues, however, even if they had known better, would have sidestepped this reality in the interests of furthering budgetary or career ambitions.

The "Arms Race" That Wasn't

One area of national security that virtually paralyzed Eisenhower was the persistent assertions, by both some of his more right-wing Republican colleagues and virtually all of the Democratic political opposition, that he had neglected to keep abreast of the Soviet Union missile for missile. After all, in the minds of the public, that was what the arms race was about. Nevertheless, because of *how* he obtained his information, he felt he could not reveal *what* that information contained as to any notion of a superpower "balance." Not only was there no balance, there was a lopsided advantage in the Americans' favor.

A particular thorn in Eisenhower's side was his former Army chief of staff, Gen. Maxwell Taylor, and his notion of "flexible response."[18] Taylor, when chief of staff, had lobbied aggressively for an increase in the Army's conventional war-making capability, arguing that the "nuclear option" had cancelled itself when both the Soviet Union and the United States had achieved a kind of parity. Goodpaster appeared to have supported the

Taylor argument, observing: "In the latter part of his administration, probably under the impetus of Foster Dulles, Eisenhower was almost driven to recognize that there was more to it than just the nuclear weapons, that problems were arising in the so-called 'third world' that [required] conventional military strength and a conventional military position. . . . The President was reluctant to acknowledge that. I think part of that reluctance came from a concern that he would lose the ability to keep a limit on the buildup of military forces."[19]

For example, "Dulles's reconsideration of Massive Retaliation symbolizes the turmoil within the Eisenhower administration as different actors attempted to challenge with new ideas and new bureaucratic alliances the prevailing commitment to the strategic nuclear deterrent."[20] The intra-administration debate had even spilled over into congressional politics. As it was reported:

> Eisenhower also contemplated ways to control the testimony of the active-duty chiefs. In a White House meeting on 25 January 1960 with Joint Chiefs of Staff chair [Nathan] Twining, and his staff secretary Army Col. Andrew Goodpaster . . . General Twining admitted that he too had become tangled up on the "argument over intelligence based on intentions v. capabilities." . . . Twining was troubled by [the] Preparedness Committee's practice of requiring the members of the Joint Chiefs of Staff to testify under oath. . . . The president had a simple solution for such situations: "Any military man who appears before the group and is required to take an oath," he said "should refuse to give opinion and judgment and limit his testimony strictly to facts."[21]

Eisenhower had to endure many more partisan attacks during the forthcoming presidential election, and since the electoral outcome between Nixon and Kennedy was so close, this lingering, apparently irresolvable issue may have tipped the scales in Kennedy's favor. It is easier, for example, to cry wolf than to make an appeal based only on the assertion "believe me because of who I am." The embarrassment and moral confusion of the U-2 incident further weakened the argument.

Note should be taken here that Eisenhower took very seriously the third "leg" of his concept of national security—arms control and disarmament. It was easy for the skeptics (or the disillusioned) to dismiss this aspect, but according to Goodpaster, this was not, in fact, the case.

Goodpaster ordered Eisenhower's security-related priorities as follows: (1) defense capability; (2) deterrence; (3) arms control. He explained that "[Eisenhower] had, of course, just been over in NATO. And in NATO, they formulated the security policy as being a dual policy of defense and deterrence, deterrence being linked primarily to superpower nuclear parity. . . . But he was one of the first to see that control of armaments was really a third main line of policy. . . . Eisenhower, interestingly, had a very great interest in this and he felt—and I speak of this because I spoke to him many times, we had long talks about this—and I shared with him, I think, a view that action in the field of disarmament was really a third major link or line of our policy at the time. I discussed this with him and, over the years, it has seemed to me that he was one of the first to see it in those terms."[22]

Nonetheless, "since an acceptable treaty for controlled disarmament was not realized, we continued to build an overpowering military establishment as the only feasible defense against the menace and probing of international Communism and as the indispensable platform from which to continue negotiations for a peaceful world."[23] Eisenhower commented: "It seems a wry and sad commentary on human intelligence that the development of a unique weapons system [the Polaris submarine-launched missile] did more to restore a feeling of Western confidence in a stable future than had all the disarmament talks conducted over a period of years."[24]

As to any contradiction between the New Look and disarmament, Goodpaster felt that, to the contrary, Eisenhower recognized that embracing the New Look almost demanded a careful examination of the possibilities of disarmament. The destructive potential of nuclear weapons had changed the character of war to such an extent that, without linking an evolving nuclear arms race to an equally evolving nuclear arms reduction effort, the world would be left as a hostage to the superpower rivalry. The overarching danger was that this rivalry could spin out of control at any time. For this reason, Eisenhower felt that the superpowers would recognize the need to engage in arms reduction negotiations, difficult as they might be.

Even so, Eisenhower left a noteworthy legacy, especially because—as the Cold War persisted and eventually collapsed—negotiations did in fact produce results that would have pleased him. To quote: "The Arms Control and Disarmament Act (P. L. 87–297, 75 Stat. 631) was landmark legislation designed to entrench arms control as a key component of United States national security policy during and after the Cold War. Congress achieved three main tasks: it set ambitious goals and purposes for coordinating disarmament with other defense strategies; it created the U.S. Arms Control and Disarmament Agency (ACDA), a body that would make the country's commitment to arms control a part of its governing institutions; and it established standards and procedures for integrating all aspects of security policy."[25]

The new agency was to have four principal tasks:

1. To conduct, support, and coordinate federal research on arms control issues
2. To prepare for and manage U.S. participation in international arms control negotiations
3. To inform the American public about arms control
4. To prepare for and operate or direct "control systems" that might be useful in monitoring and enforcing compliance with international arms control agreements

The agency's director became "the principal adviser to the secretary of state and the president on arms control and disarmament matters." This double responsibility—reporting to both the president and the secretary—was often referred to as a "dual-hat" mechanism. The director was an "independent voice" in the most senior-level national security debates, while not straying too far from the secretary of state's leadership in international diplomacy. Obviously, the more closely the director was tied to the top national leadership, the greater the agency's influence.

The act made arms control a legitimate tool of U.S. policy. The concept of seeking enhanced security through negotiation, rather than solely through arms procurement, became an accepted feature of the political landscape, and even national leaders who were not inclined to value diplomatic approaches were frequently nudged in that direction by the arguments and information provided by ACDA.[26] Although it was only after the demise of the Soviet Union that credible and binding international disarmament treaties were negotiated, the administrative framework was set in place shortly after Eisenhower left office.

Incoming president John F. Kennedy recognized Goodpaster's value by requesting from President Eisenhower that Goodpaster be held over in the White House beyond the transition period, even though he already had his orders for the command assignment that he coveted.

Eisenhower reported:

Senator Kennedy was very much concerned with the activities of General Goodpaster, and said he would like to hold Goodpaster

for two months into the new Administration. I told him that I
thought a better solution would be for him to appoint a man
right now who could take Goodpaster's post (the duties of which
I detailed at some length) and allow Goodpaster to leave with
the rest of us on January 20th. He said he would be handicapped
unless he had Goodpaster for a month or two, really favoring
the second. Of course I had to say that he would soon be the
Commander-in-Chief and he could *order* [Eisenhower's empha-
sis] General Goodpaster to do anything, and those duties would
be efficiently performed; but told him also of Goodpaster's great
desire to go to active line duty and that a particular spot was being
held for him. I asked the Senator if he would assure me that that
spot would be held. (That evening I called [Army Chief of Staff
George] Decker and told him the details of this conversation and
asked him, as a personal favor to me, to make it his business to
protect Goodpaster's future to this extent. He said there would be
no trouble about this.)"[27]

Subsequently Eisenhower wrote: "Dear Senator Kennedy: I have now
heard from both Secretary [Thomas] Gates and General Decker regarding
your desire to retain General Goodpaster temporarily after your inauguration. They have arranged, as you asked, for him to stay on in your office
for a period ending sometime in February or March, the exact date to be
determined later. At the same time, they have taken steps to see that, as we
agreed, when he ends his service here he will be sent to the same assignment
that is now planned for him."[28]

When Kennedy immersed himself in plans to oust Cuba's Castro,
"though the President's initial orders seemed restrained, Kennedy proceeded to rob himself of the machinery that Eisenhower had created
to exercise close control. . . . More than ever before business was trans-
acted directly with the new NSC staff, yet Kennedy showed little interest in consulting Ike's White House staff secretary Andrew Goodpaster,
who had most of the relevant information at his fingertips."[29] Significantly,
Goodpaster was not privy to Richard Bissell's tightly held plans, nor were
the agency's Cuba experts.[30]

This was unfortunate because, although the Kennedy administration suffered the opprobrium of failure in its anti-Castro Cuba policy,
the seeds had been planted earlier during the Eisenhower administration,
and Goodpaster was at the center. "On November 9, Andrew Goodpaster
informed [Secretary of State Christian] Herter of the approval [to disrupt

Castro's regime]. At the White House, knowledge of the action was to be restricted to Goodpaster himself, Ike's son John S. D. Eisenhower, and one confidential secretary."[31]

No greater compliment could be paid to Goodpaster than this: "Transition aide Richard Neustadt stressed repeatedly . . . the need for 'a Personal Assistant to the Commander in Chief-Elect' to handle duties that 'roughly corresponded to (and expanded upon) the work now done for Eisenhower by General Goodpaster. . . . When Kennedy saw the President on December 6 he extracted Eisenhower's reluctant assent to Goodpaster's staying on for a month after inauguration day, deferring his transfer to the active-duty post that Eisenhower was instrumental in holding for him."[32]

During this "interregnum," Goodpaster received many notes from well-wishers; one in particular stands out because it captures Goodpaster's personal as well as professional traits. It read: "Dear Andy: This word of appreciation to our Staff Secretary, one of the most able, most influential, and most anonymous men in the United States Government. And one of the most congenial and considerate. The value, to the President and to the country, of your knowledge, judgment, and loyalty is great— beyond estimation."[33]

In April 1961 Goodpaster became, as promised, commander of the Eighth Infantry Division in Germany. But just a year later, in April 1962, he was recalled to Washington to serve as assistant to the chairman of the Joint Chiefs of Staff, and in 1967 as director of the Joint Staff. These assignments are mentioned to show how much Goodpaster was valued in and around the uppermost echelons of the Pentagon after his service in the White House.

Somehow, Goodpaster had, over the six years that he worked in the White House as staff secretary and defense liaison officer, moved among the "movers and shakers" of the Eisenhower administration without attracting unwanted attention or controversy. He was trusted, even admired for qualities that appeared contradictory to persons in and around the seat of power. By not seeking to enhance his personal influence in an intensely competitive bureaucratic environment, Goodpaster made himself an essential part of the policy process.

As Eisenhower's staff secretary, he occupied an all-important position that had relevance to this observation: "In government, as in every institution, information is blood. Clamp it off from any part and the member cannot function. At the White House, the national security assistant [and staff secretary] is a carotid artery to the president."[34]

Chapter Nine

Eisenhower's Health Crises

"The effect—of the fearless leader, the happy warrior, the father figure on whom the nation relied—was as central to his own equilibrium as it was to the country's."
—H. W. Brands, *Traitor to His Class*

As his presidency unfolded, an unanticipated—but understandable—situation arose concerning the state of Eisenhower's health. The persons around him and in the White House writ large found themselves distracted during significant periods of time while Eisenhower was recuperating from several serious maladies. There also was the brooding possibility that, if Eisenhower had been fully healthy, or even able to give concentrated attention during a specific incident, the outcome might have been for the better. This did not mean that during his two terms of office he ceased to function effectively, but these events had an inevitable unsettling mood on those in his immediate circle as well as in the larger world.

The Heart Attack

The first crisis came in September 1955, while Eisenhower was vacationing in Denver prior to engaging in pre-election activities. He recounted: "I went to bed at about 10 p.m. and slept. Sometime later—roughly 1:30 a.m., I think—I awakened with a severe chest pain. . . . [Mamie] urged me to lie down and promptly called the White House physician, General [Howard] Snyder. She thought I was quite sick. . . . I was helped into a car and taken to a hospital . . . but never after that night did I feel any pain or any other symptoms connected with the attack."[1]

Following custom, Eisenhower wrote a "Dear Dick" note to Vice President Nixon, saying: "I hope you will continue to have meetings of the National Security Council and of the Cabinet over which you will preside in accordance with the procedure which you have followed at my request in the past during my absence from Washington."[2] Thus, Eisenhower made a situation appear routine when it was anything but! Although other efforts were made to show that, with Nixon acting for the president in Washington, matters were going forward "as usual," in fact, there was considerable maneuvering taking place among the administration's chief players. John Foster Dulles took the helm, shutting out Nixon; instead he relied on Sherman Adams to be in Denver to coordinate matters. The truth was: "Eisenhower simply did not like Nixon."[3]

As an example of Dulles' control at this stage, note the following: "During the subsequent Geneva conference of the four foreign ministers between 27 October and 16 November 1955 . . . in a letter to the president, who was recuperating in Fitzsimons army hospital in Denver after his September heart attack, Dulles wrote that Molotov had delivered 'one of the most cynical and uncompromising speeches which I have ever heard,' when the Soviet foreign minister completely rejected any discussion of the reunification of Germany except on Soviet terms."[4]

Goodpaster had to have been privy to all of this as he continued to perform his functions from the Denver "White House."[5] He also, along with the president's personal secretary Ann Whitman, was constantly monitoring his moods. As she put it, "The doctors do not think (and perhaps this is partial guess work on my part) that any serious decision would upset him, but the little minor crises do upset him and worry me so terribly."[6]

In a memorandum to Sherman Adams in December, Goodpaster wrote: "When the President returns, it would be of great value, I suggest, to have a generally understood pattern for appointments, etc. While not rigid, such a pattern would make for a better organized, more orderly use of the President's time and energy. . . . As the above indicates, it would appear that there would be, at most, an opportunity for eight appointments with the President, on official matters . . . in a week—and this number might be as low as three."[7] The cabinet, the National Security Council, and such were expected to step in.

When Eisenhower went to his Gettysburg farm for further recuperation, Goodpaster was readily at hand there also. "We would fly up to Gettysburg after he went up there for his recuperation, either every day or every other day. Adams would fly up once a week. We would transact all of our business. We, by that time, had the secure telephone put in there and I could work with him in that way. So that's the way we worked it out."[8]

However,

> access to the president became more of a problem than it had been previously. . . . Dulles had access to the President. . . . But

there was no Dulles in the Pentagon, and in the period after the heart attack, access was not easy for either Secretary Wilson or Chairman Radford. . . . There was, however, one individual of lesser military rank who did have access—Brigadier General Andrew J. Goodpaster. Goodpaster was both staff secretary under Adams (subsequently under Persons) and defense liaison officer. In this latter role, he was pretty much on his own. Eisenhower considered Goodpaster's work in national security affairs as more important than his other functions and viewed it as overlapping the role of the special assistant for national security affairs.[9]

Also, to provide a private place near the Oval Office where Eisenhower could rest during the day, "he ought to have a little room where he could just relax, read, even do any painting that he wanted to do. . . . I [Goodpaster] designed a way to cut off part of the room that was used by his scheduling secretary, and make use of that space and a space just across the walkway so that he could use that as a place to go and spend a little time just relaxing and taking off the pressure."[10]

During the reelection campaign, Eisenhower recalled, "First I reiterated the decision to accept the Republican nomination (should it be tendered to me). Then, because five months earlier I suffered a heart attack, I explained the latest findings of the doctors—optimistic findings, by and large. There was no denying that in view of my illness I was more of a risk than a normal person of my age, but not great."[11]

Ileitis

Not too long after the heart attack, Eisenhower suffered another illness that also came during the reelection campaign. John Eisenhower reported: "The blockage had been in the ileum, a small tube which connects the small and large intestines." His ileitis required surgery, which was successful; nonetheless, it "had wide repercussions. First of all, it intensified the health issue for the 1956 political campaign. . . . And with a temporary loss of stomach muscles, he walked slowly and hunched over."[12]

As Sherman Adams recounted,

Shortly after midnight, Andy Goodpaster called me from his home and told me that the President was about to undergo surgery. "I am leaving right now to go to Walter Reed," Goodpaster said to me. "For what purpose?" I asked. "To observe his competency should any military decisions become urgent," he said. . . ." Goodpaster was already at the hospital when I reached there a half-hour later. Hagerty joined us and the three of us stood in the corridor at the door of the operating room and watched the surgeons as they worked on the body of the President of the United States. . . . Goodpaster said something about how we would have to change the office routine again.[13]

Eisenhower commented: "Strangely enough, although I was truly miserable for several days I was never disturbed in this instance by the doubts that beset so many others. My current ailment was something acute which was corrected by immediate surgery; and once I was conscious again and in possession of my faculties, I did not bother with the question of full recovery."[14]

This was not the first time that Eisenhower had been afflicted with ileitis. While president of Columbia University, he had suffered an attack. "His doctor, Howard Snyder . . . told Eisenhower to stop smoking. He did so immediately. . . . When asked how he did it, he said he had simply given himself an order to quit."[15]

As to the latter medical emergency, "it was also not noted that the unexpected illness had required a postponement of a meeting with the heads of the Latin American states: 'The original dates had been set for June 25–26, 1956, but it was rescheduled after my ileitis operation.'"[16]

Eisenhower insisted that more, rather than less, information should be given to the press and general public as his recuperation advanced. Goodpaster would have been consulted about what to say and what not to say when it came to matters of state. Otherwise, health details were left to others. For example, this is an exchange in a press conference dealing with his heart attack, arranged at Walter Reed Hospital for the president's personal physician, Dr. Howard Snyder. After reporting that the president had walked around his room, the question was asked whether he had some support: "Would you describe it as less support than yesterday or about the same?" Dr. Snyder: "About the same." The next question was: "Just one elbow?" and so forth. The idea was that with this kind of detail, the people at large could grasp the general state of affairs while Eisenhower was hospitalized.[17]

This leads to a consideration of the overall effect of illness on presidential leadership. With the memory of Woodrow Wilson's disabling illness having been covered up by his wife and others around him—including Colonel House—as a negative example, Eisenhower was determined that the general public should not be left in the dark about his own health maladies. Wilson had been experiencing "cerebral episodes" as early as 1896, and in April 1919 he suffered what a neurologist termed a "a stroke so destructive as that it made of him a changeling with a very different personality and a markedly lessened ability."[18] To claim that illness did not alter the running of the presidency would be an obvious misstatement. Nevertheless, to say that the effective running of the presidential office was disabled would also be inaccurate and misleading, because the "office," as distinct from the incumbent, was an ongoing agency of government.

This is where persons such as Goodpaster enter the scene, for their tasks become more complicated, decisions become more tentative, coordination more imperative, and overall (including the morale of the spouse and family) a different situation obtains. Goodpaster understood this and adapted himself accordingly. He possessed the gift of being able to subordinate himself to his chief executive's wishes, while at the same time making sure that the running of the office—and for lengthy periods of time this would mean from, literally, a hospital bed—did not suffer more than was necessary. Put another way, what would have been seen as an inconvenience to Eisenhower—albeit a serious one—would have been in fact a major alteration of procedures and scheduling to those persons immediately around him.

Added to this was the fact that Adams was determined that Nixon not be considered primus inter pares among those with direct access to Eisenhower. One of the fears of presidential bureaucratic loyalists is that their chief, in times of crises, would be cast in the shadows by overweening aides, and that would include the vice president. For example, the instruction was that "3. For most items, departments will bring problems to attention of White House Staff before contacting the Vice President. 4. Staff members should take particular care to assure that matters they send for President's attention or signature really require it. 5. Material intended for President's attention or signature should be submitted through Staff Secretary to Governor Adams. 6. Staff members should let Staff Secretary know when they expect to be absent from the city."[19] Furthermore, during the Denver period, Goodpaster penned a note: "On basis guidance from Gov. Adams . . . I will select from State Daily Summary and material sent by CIA (which will be sanitized) material for Denver, and I will send it out over WH [White House] facilities."[20] Clearly, Goodpaster had almost a "choke hold" on communications for the president.

Understandably, it would come as no surprise that those persons closest to Eisenhower would have been thinking what Goodpaster expressed:

"Still, in the back of our minds, there was always the unmentionable dread of a next attack."[21] However, something even more unexpected and less amenable to purely medicinal control occurred.

The Stroke

Goodpaster had to perform a different, and perhaps more delicate, form of diplomacy when Eisenhower had what was termed a mild stroke in November 1957. Eisenhower recalled that after experiencing some dizziness,

> I sat down quickly and rang for my secretary. As Mrs. Whitman came to my desk I tried to . . . I could not express what I wanted to say. . . . Actually my performance must have been worse than I suspected, for Mrs. Whitman . . . became thoroughly alarmed and called for General Goodpaster.
>
> Andy Goodpaster wasted no time asking questions or making any attempt to diagnose the difficulty. He knew something was wrong and concentrated on getting me to my room in the Mansion. . . . I responded without protest to Goodpaster's grasp of my arm and his urgent, "Mr. President, I think we should get you to bed." . . . Goodpaster helped me to undress and lie down.[22]

John Eisenhower recalled that "on that Monday afternoon, Ann Whitman came into my office on the verge of tears. 'The President has gone back to the house,' she said. 'He tried to tell me something but he couldn't express himself. Something seemed to have happened to him all of a sudden.' When she had called Dr. Snyder the President refused to leave his desk. 'Go away from me,' he tried to say. But Goodpaster had been able to persuade him to leave the office and had walked back to the living quarters with him. . . . 'And just now [Eisenhower] gave up and went home,' she said. 'I can't imagine what's wrong with him.'"[23]

Looking toward the future, Adams

> called Nixon on the telephone and explained the situation to him. . . . Then I asked Goodpaster to accompany me while I had a talk with Mrs. Eisenhower. . . . While we were talking the President walked casually into the room. He was wearing a long robe over his pajamas and his feet were in bedroom slippers. He smiled at us, as if to let us know that nothing was wrong with him. He

started to say something. "I suppose you are dis-" but he stammered, hesitated and then struggled on with the rest of the sentence: " . . . talking about the dinner tonight." We saw that he was trying to talk about the plans for the evening but he was frustrated and getting angry at his inability to form words. "There's nothing the matter with me!" he said finally with effort. "I am perfectly all right!" . . . Flushed and upset, he shook his head abruptly and said, "If I cannot attend to my duties, I am simply going to give up this job. Now that is all there is to it." Then he turned away from us and walked out of the room.[24]

Eisenhower probably came to rely even more on Goodpaster, because "even today, occasionally I reverse syllables in a long word and at times am compelled to speak slowly and cautiously if I am to enunciate correctly. This is not, I am told, particularly noticeable to anyone else, but it certainly is to me."[25]

Goodpaster informed Gen. Lauris Norstad, then NATO supreme allied commander, that "by now you will have seen the reports on the President's condition. To preclude undue concern on your part, let me say that the doctors indicate he is in no danger whatsoever, his general condition is excellent, and he is resting easily and has already improved tremendously. We are much heartened. It is clear, however, that one must assume that he would not attend a NATO meeting in December. Accordingly, the arrangements about which I wrote you must be put in abeyance at least temporarily. I would like to stress that, except for the impairment of speech—which is rapidly decreasing—there is no other impediment whatsoever that is perceptible."[26] Eisenhower's entourage, including Goodpaster, respectfully disagreed. The problem with the aftereffects of a stroke is precisely that they can be imperceptible yet consequential.

Another kind of aftereffect would be Eisenhower's desire to calm down the public (and political) uproar when *Sputniks I* and *II* were suddenly launched, thus appearing to give the Soviet Union an edge in the space race. He asked Goodpaster and his speechwriters to craft a series of three addresses to the nation on the general subject of space science, but the third speech had to be cancelled because of his stroke.

Even up to the very conclusion of his presidency, Eisenhower's health remained on everyone's mind, and this included emotional considerations. Immediately after hearing the disappointing results of the 1960 election, Eisenhower recalled: "As I wrote to a friend several weeks later, when I heard the outcome, I felt as though 'I had been hit in the solar plexus with a ball bat,' as though eight years of work had been for naught. It was a low moment, and about all I remember of November 9 is that when I began debating whether to cancel my previously planned trip to Augusta, my staff—and my son in particular—objected violently, almost shoving me aboard the plane. At the moment, I had little spirit to argue. (The doctors, I later learned, had been concerned in the last days that I had temporarily used up all my available earlier reserves in the closing weeks of the campaign.)"[27]

Personality, temperament, opportunity, and competence all play a role in the "mix" of relationships in the hotly competitive and pressure-cooker environment of the White House. Eisenhower, with insight, once remarked, "After a bit of cool reflection, I realized that the cause of the difficulty lay more in my own failure to make myself unmistakably clear than in the failures of others to understand me."[28]

It may be too much to say that as a consequence of these serious illnesses, the relationship between Goodpaster and Eisenhower was gradually evolving into one of at least partial dependency, but it probably isn't too much off the mark.

As for international politics, if the cause for the misalignment of international conferences at the highest level can be attributed to the health of the participants, then perhaps even vital interests might be compromised for reasons having little or nothing to do with the actual negotiating postures.

To put it rhetorically: "In a summit conference the health of the negotiator becomes a significant factor. Could someone suffering from a heart condition withstand the labors of a prolonged summit conference or one hastily called in a dangerous crisis? An upset stomach could leave a president in a poor state to negotiate. If an illness should suddenly strike, will it be considered a diplomatic affliction by others? Dare the statesmen risk postponement after there has been so much preconference publicity?"[29] Goodpaster would recognize immediately the relevance of this line of consideration to his responsibilities coping with Eisenhower's illnesses.

Post-Presidency Health Issues

In the nine years after his presidency, before his death in early 1969, there were several "ups and downs" to Eisenhower's health. In almost every case, Goodpaster was on hand in one way or another, whatever and wherever his assignment.

In Eisenhower's final illness, this story is recounted by Eisenhower's grandson David: "Eisenhower . . . had long ago resolved never to reveal weakness to his wife. With her now, he refused to concede that he was failing. He tried, futilely, to persuade the doctors to withhold news from her about his situation and strictly forbade his wife to speak morbidly. Finally, he conceded. Prone, under the 'bulldozer' life support machine and flanked by [the Surgeon General, Dr. Leonard] Heaton, . . . and several nurses, Eisenhower scolded her for any remorse about their life together. 'Now Mamie,' he growled, 'don't forget that I have always loved you.'"[30]

He asked that the tubes and machines be removed and shortly thereafter, on 28 March 1969, Eisenhower died with his family gathered around or near him. He wanted to end the suffering, which by then appeared to be for no appreciable purpose. Thus concluded Goodpaster's nine years of formal and informal liaison with three of Eisenhower's successor presidents. But Goodpaster's advisory role to future presidents continued well beyond his retirement from active duty.

Finally, it is important to note that Goodpaster's relationship with the president's personal secretary, Ann Whitman, was warm and trustful. They probably bore the burden of most of Eisenhower's lesser day-to-day indispositions as well as his major health setbacks. Behind that ruddy, famous, and endearing grin lay a temperament that was prone to outbursts of irritable frustration and anger. In closing this chapter, offered here is an example of how the three of them shared a concern for each other:

Andy,

This is a perfectly miserable thing to have happen on Christmas day. I am so sorry. [She is referring to the death of Goodpaster's father.]

I'm sure you aren't in the mood to be thanked for everything just now, but I do—mostly for your understanding, for your broad shoulder, and—for the gay and handsome scarf that lifts me out of the two hundred letters that lie ahead of me.

If you don't know, our leader decided to drive to Gettysburg, and for the first time in their history, the secret service had to beg for additional time. He gave them, reluctantly, ten minutes more to produce a driver. He is charged up within an inch of his life and off in a cloud.

Ann[31]

Chapter Ten

The U-2 and Overflights

"For the first time since Independence, the United States government had publicly admitted that it had committed espionage in peace-time and deceived the world about it."
—MICHAEL R. BESCHLOSS, *Mayday: Eisenhower, Khrushchev, and the U-2 Affair*

Without a doubt, the technological innovation of the U-2 spy plane, which promised to help break the American impasse with the Soviet Union over the problem of inspection and verification of its nuclear arsenal, ended in a diplomatic disaster. To put it mildly, it ruined Eisenhower's hoped-for triumphal conclusion to his presidency. In many books recounting this episode, the word "incident" is used—a euphemism if ever there was one.

The Justification

Eisenhower's reason for initiating research on both aerial reconnaissance and photography was to "give us information about what the Soviets had, and to some extent, what they did not have. And also it would be very useful to see if there was any massing of troops that could be used for surprise attack."[1] Then, the president continued: "When the Soviets rejected my Open Skies proposal in 1955 I decided that more intelligence about their war-making capabilities was a necessity. So I directed that we would begin aerial reconnaissance, making use of the then relatively invulnerable, high-flying U-2 aircraft. . . . From 1956 onward its basic mission was to provide us with current information on the status of the Soviet missile and armaments programs."[2]

As usual, Goodpaster was at the center of things. In 1954 he had penned: "Authorization was sought from the President to go ahead on a program to produce thirty special high performance aircraft at a cost of about $35 million. . . . The President directed those present to go ahead and get the equipment, but before initiating operations to come in for one last look at the plane."[3] It was his job to coordinate this highly secret spying activity with the CIA, which had the operational responsibility. Goodpaster explained, "I served as Eisenhower's liaison with the CIA with regard to the whole U-2 program, and assisted him in considering the proposals for each of the flights. When the final flight went down, I just have to say that we handled the situation in a very miserable and unsatisfactory way. We had not thought through the use of a cover story, looking at all the what-ifs that we should have considered."[4] This was odd, considering the stakes involved.

Eisenhower gave full support to the work of the CIA, which also meant, of course, that Goodpaster as the White House liaison with the CIA was fully in the picture as well.[5] "In fact, because the administration focused heavily on covert operations, countless conversations took place behind permanently closed doors."[6] To recall: "To the extent that their busy schedules permitted, [Eisenhower and John Foster Dulles] ended the day by meeting in the Oval Office, mostly alone but sometimes joined by Central Intelligence Agency (CIA) director Allen Dulles, or one or two others."[7] It can safely be inferred that Goodpaster was one of those "other" persons who were present, although he was excluded from the sessions of just the two of them because Dulles preferred that no notes be taken. When Christian Herter succeeded Dulles as secretary of state, Goodpaster became a regular attendee.

To illustrate how central Goodpaster was: "In a meeting Eisenhower held with Secretary of Defense Neil McElroy, Richard Bissell of the CIA, and Goodpaster on 7 April 1959, covering various reconnaissance flights and related matters, Goodpaster recorded: 'Earlier the President had discussed this matter [reconnaissance flights to gather information on the Soviet missile program] at length with me. In response to his request for my advice, I analyzed the proposal as to the importance of possible costs and possible gains.'"[8] How more central to presidential decision-making could he have been?

Eisenhower always kept in mind the budgetary outlays and the consequences. One of his motives was to use the information obtained from the U-2 to verify the various alarmist claims being put forth by the armed services to justify ever-larger budgets and weapons acquisitions. For each flight that was approved, Eisenhower insisted on knowing what were the reasons for doing it and how useful was the information, both in terms of knowing what the Soviets were doing, and how it would affect the many pressures that were being exerted by the military establishment.[9]

Goodpaster as a West Point Cadet

In a brace

With NATO's first supreme allied commander

SACEUR with the family

Secretary of State
George C. Marshall
in his office

With "The Boss"

With Eisenhower at London dinner for Churchill (Goodpaster at top right)

Maj. Gen. Goodpaster
receiving parachutist's
badge

As NATO SACEUR, reviewing the troops

Official photo as SACEUR

With Mrs. Goodpaster (second from right) in the Marshall Foundation Library

Goodpaster later pointed out that when an overflight was brought in for approval, "we kept necessary informal notes, but my recollection is that we did not write up an official permanent record on those. Those were regarded as too sensitive and the knowledge of those was very, very closely restricted."[10] In addition, Eisenhower assembled a small consultative group, which had as its members the secretaries of state and defense, the JCS chairman, the CIA director, and Richard Bissell.[11]

Bureaucratic Momentum

Secretary of State Dulles considered that "Richard Bissell Jr. was one of the rising stars of the CIA. A tall, amiable, cultivated man, with an interest in ornithology, sailing, and ecology—all pursuits that the top echelons of the Agency strongly approved—he had previously worked for the Marshall Plan in Germany and the Ford Foundation in Washington. He had known Allen Dulles since 1948, was a friend of Frank Wisner, and had first met Foster when Eleanor threw a party at McLean for her brothers, Vice President Nixon, Bob Bowie, and other members of the administration."[12]

Bissell, who believed that covert operations should be the prime function of the CIA, was appointed deputy director for plans (DDP) in 1958, replacing Wisner (who had suffered a mental breakdown).[13] Bissell's deputy was Richard Helms.[14] In other words, the person who had been placed in charge of developing and operating the most technologically superior instrument of aerial espionage—the U-2—was virtually a novice in the business. Furthermore, by that time, DDP reportedly controlled over half the CIA's budget and was responsible for what was known as the CIA's black operations.

Even more puzzling, if not alarming, "part of Bissell's job description was to develop new espionage technologies, including the authority to give a bureaucratic jolt to promising projects through funding and management support. His office became a hothouse for ideas and was responsible for the U-2 spy plane and, later, spy satellites."[15] Even with all of this bureaucratic energy devoted to the technology of spying, Eisenhower believed that "only spies, not gadgets, could tell him about Soviet intent to attack."[16]

After the plane—little more than a jet-propelled glider—had proven airworthy, arrangements were made to base it in Wiesbaden.

They were now ready to go. Bissell alerted Allen, who in turn informed his brother. A meeting was held in the White House in

the spring of 1956 at which Bissell laid out his plans for a number of flights over Russia. He was told to wait outside while the
President discussed them with Allen, Foster, and his military secretary, General Andrew Goodpaster. Presently, Goodpaster came
out and said to Bissell, "Well, you've been authorized to conduct overflights for two weeks." "I hope that means fourteen days
of good weather," Bissell said. "In other words, bad days don't
count." "It doesn't mean anything of the kind," Goodpaster said.
"It means two weeks. You're free to go for two weeks."[17]

Eisenhower also could draw upon his military background and experience in war to shape his attitude toward these very expensive as well as dip-
lomatically dangerous overflights. Bissell, for example, noted that "Andy
Goodpaster sees Eisenhower's military background—his experience as a
field commander and the importance of intelligence when he was supreme
allied commander—as influencing his interest in and active management
of the U-2 project. His understanding of the various intelligence disciplines
made him acutely sensitive to the critical role U-2 intelligence could play in
maintaining national security. . . . Almost every morning, Goodpaster used
the CIA's overnight intelligence report to brief him. . . . He would then take
this information and fit it into a worldview that had been shaped by years
of 'reviewing and studying and pondering.'"[18]

The Ill-Fated Flight of 1 May

The rationale was: "Eisenhower approved another U-2 flight even though
the summit conference could be endangered. There was fear lest a détente be
reached at the Paris [four-power summit] meeting which might lead to a permanent grounding of the U-2 planes. Because this might be the last flight,
one more mission ought to be attempted. The Central Intelligence Agency
had information that a new Soviet rocket rested on its launching pad near
Sverdlovsk. [Francis Gary] Powers's mission would be to photograph this
rocket."[19] As the world came to learn, Powers' plane was shot down; he para-
chuted to the ground and was captured. No amount of dissimulation could
hide the fact that the United States had been caught publicly engaging in aerial espionage over the Soviet Union (and China) for several years.

It should be no surprise that in 1960 "the president and Dick Bissell
were locked in an increasingly intense struggle over the control of one of the
biggest secrets of all—the U-2 spy plane. Eisenhower had not allowed any

flights over Soviet terrain since his talks with Khrushchev at Camp David six months earlier. Khrushchev had returned from Washington praising the president's courage in seeking peaceful coexistence. Eisenhower wants the 'Spirit of Camp David' to be his legacy."[20] That legacy was soon to be destroyed.

Along the way, this entire matter of testing and verification was causing deep discomfort at the highest levels within the administration—and particularly between the State Department and the Atomic Energy Commission. This was especially so in regard to the notion of ceasing testing altogether, including underground. As the journalist Arthur Krock recounted, Eisenhower held a meeting on Thursday, March 24, 1960. "Secretary of the Air Force James H. Douglas, and Gordon Gray, Eisenhower's special assistant on national security matters, and other insiders [presumably including Goodpaster]" along with Christian Herter, the secretary of state, were all in attendance. In an already tense atmosphere, John A. McCone, the chairman of the Atomic Energy Commission, "strongly argued" for continuing the U.S. "show me" policy when it came to inspections and the dangers associated with an extended moratorium on underground nuclear testing. The president, however,

pounded the table and said he intended to follow Herter's counsel in favor of taking these ventures. Later he calmed down, but his rebuke to McCone scared the Pentagon also into silence.

At the same meeting, the President directed that any speeches on the subject be approved by Herter's department. McCone, who was flying that afternoon to make such a speech in Los Angeles, left his transcript behind for Herter's inspection. When he got to Los Angeles an AEC aide informed him Herter had flatly vetoed the whole speech. McCone got Herter on the telephone, but the Secretary would say only that he had sent the speech to the White House and would have no more to do with it.

McCone then got in touch with Col. Goodpaster of the White House staff who told him the speech was "out." Then, inquired McCone, does this mean we have changed our test policy entirely? McCone's reaction must have induced second thoughts at the White House, because soon afterward Goodpaster phoned McCone to say that if he would put in one sentence estimating the Soviet proposal as "hopeful," the remainder would be acceptable. McCone put in the sentence and delivered the speech as written.[21]

This was hardly the first time that dissension had arisen over the risks and benefits of overflights over the Soviet Union. For example, after the U-2 flights had been suspended, the Air Force pushed for using the RB-57D in its stead. After receiving assurances that the Russians would not detect such flights, Eisenhower agreed. When this assurance proved misplaced, "Eisenhower, according to Allen Dulles, was furious . . . he said he was going to 'order a complete stoppage of the entire business.' He instructed Colonel Goodpaster to call Secretary of Defense Wilson, JCS chair Radford, and DCI [Director of Central Intelligence] Dulles and inform them that, effective immediately, there were to be no flights of U.S. reconnaissance aircraft over Iron Curtain countries. Each man confirmed that he understood."[22]

As later events confirmed, the pressure to overfly did not diminish. After the downing of Powers and its attendant embarrassments, the overflight procedures were changed but the flights themselves had not been discontinued:

> One of the most important changes in the overflight program after the loss of Francis Gary Powers's U-2 was the institution of more formal procedures for the approval of U-2 missions. During the first four years of U-2 activity, very few members of the Eisenhower administration had been involved in making decisions concerning the overflight program. The President personally authorized all flights over the Soviet Union and was consulted by Richard Bissell and either the DCI or the DDCI [deputy director of central intelligence] about each proposed mission. In addition to CIA officials, the President's discussions of individual U-2 missions or of the program as a whole generally included the Secretary of State or his Under Secretary, the Chairman of the Joint Chiefs of Staff, the Secretary of Defense or his deputy, and the President's secretary, Colonel (later General) Goodpaster.
>
> The approval process under President Eisenhower was thus very unstructured. There was no formal approval body charged with reviewing overflight proposals; the President kept this authority in his hands and simply consulted with selected cabinet officials and advisers before reaching a decision.[23]

Eisenhower had anticipated this situation as early as 1956:

After the election he authorized additional flights. The Soviets protested privately but strongly. On November 15, Eisenhower met with Herbert Hoover [II], [Admiral] Radford, and Allen Dulles to discuss the flights. Eisenhower thought that they were beginning to "cost more than we gain in the form of solid information." Hoover pointed out that "if we lost a plane at this stage, it would be almost catastrophic." Eisenhower agreed, and added "Everyone in the world says that in the last six weeks, [because of its reaction to the Suez crisis] the [United States] has gained a place it hasn't held since World War II." The country had to "preserve a place that is correct and moral."[24]

The Overall Setting

Building on "the Spirit of Camp David," Eisenhower agreed to attend a four-power summit in Paris in May 1960. It was to be the crowning achievement of his foreign policy, even if there were no dramatic breakthroughs over such a thorny question as Berlin. Consequently, "never was there a worse time for the President to be forced to take responsibility for an espionage affair, no matter how many may have been informed of the mission. . . . [Allen] Dulles considered that one more flight was so important that it should take precedence over foreign policy. . . . In Washington, the U-2 no longer served American foreign policy. Instead, national policy was endangered for the sake of the U-2. Intelligence gathering had become important for its own sake."[25] In contrast: "In a revealing moment, [Eisenhower] remarked that nothing would make him 'request authority to declare war more quickly than violation of our air space by Soviet aircraft.'"[26]

By this time John Foster Dulles had died and was replaced by Christian Herter. Bissell commented later that "I would have thought that, if they wanted, they could have got the maximum propaganda advantage out of shooting down the plane. . . . It was a misreading of the situation which, one suspects, Foster Dulles would never have made. . . . A more percipient man than Eisenhower would have guessed that they would try to get out of the summit. A more experienced Secretary of State would have warned him that there were crises coming. A more alert Director of Central Intelligence would have warned his deputies to stay away from all anti-Soviet provocations until the summit was over."[27]

Before Eisenhower left Washington for Paris, word had come in that Powers was shot down on the Communists' celebrated May Day.

Eisenhower was at his Gettysburg farm when the unfortunate event took place, so it was left to Goodpaster to pass the bad news to him.

Bissell's hindsight was better than his foresight. Both symbolically and propagandistically, the timing could not have been worse. It seems obvious that sending Powers aloft posed an excessive risk, unless the summit itself was considered expendable, which from all appearances appeared unlikely. As mentioned, summits in general are surrounded with skepticism, even cynicism. Yet for Eisenhower, this one—if for no other reason—would be an occasion to celebrate the culmination of his extraordinary career of wartime and subsequent public service. To be caught up in such a major embarrassment had to be devastating for him as well as for those persons closest to him, Goodpaster in particular.

History had not yet given its initial assessment of Eisenhower's handling of the Cold War as president. But his ability to use his personality, or public persona, to engage adversaries as well as allies in mutually rewarding endeavors was already well-recognized. There is a photograph of Eisenhower taking leave of his official French hosts after the failure of the summit. Goodpaster, famous briefcase in hand, is exiting along with him, illustrating why Goodpaster's near-constant presence had come to be taken for granted, and thus rendering him even more effective as the end of their official time together drew closer.

John Eisenhower recalled: "Monday morning, May second, General Goodpaster told me about the plane going down. He and I both were cleared for the U-2 project. Our only reaction was just feeling sorry for the pilot, and that was about all there was to it because we were assured that nobody would ever be taken alive."[28] Later, President Eisenhower commented: "My acknowledgment of responsibility for espionage activities was practically unprecedented in history, but so were the circumstances."[29] On 5 May, during a meeting of the Security Council, "General Goodpaster, with the missing U-2 very much on his mind, got up and left the meeting to arrange for the complete text [of Khrushchev's statement to the Supreme Soviet] to be sent to us by secret teletype."[30]

The consequence was that "[Eisenhower] knew that at such a summit there would be no sign, even on the surface, of geniality. . . . By no means did I intend, at the forthcoming conference, I told them [President Charles de Gaulle and Harold Macmillan, the British prime minister], to raise my hand and swear that we would never again do anything in the field of espionage. I would not permanently tie the hands of the United States government for the single purpose of saving a conference."[31]

This sounds a bit self-serving, as the United States had just been caught dissimulating over an intelligence activity, so why could not Eisenhower have made the promise, which would not have tied the hands of his successor, who would be in place in a matter of months? Goodpaster would not, in his oral interviews, claim that "plausible denial" dictated that covert operations carried on during the Eisenhower years were not specifically authorized by the president. The flights of the U-2 were an exception, where Eisenhower, after tentatively trying to employ plausible denial, took personal responsibility (as did President Kennedy over the Bay of Pigs covert disaster). As Richard Helms commented, in testifying before Congress: "I just think we all had the feeling that we're hired out to keep those things out of the Oval Office."[32]

The timing of the U-2 crash could not have been worse, for virtually all the senior members of the administration, including Eisenhower, were going through an emergency exercise in case of a direct attack on Washington. They were gathered at a "secret command center dug deep into Mount Weather in the Blue Ridge Mountains and built on a series of giant nuclear shock-absorbing steel springs. Its code name was High Point, but members of the president's inner circle also called it simply 'the hideout.'"[33]

This inner circle gathered at the bunker to decide how to handle Chairman Khrushchev's claims. After five days of silence from Moscow, "the Soviets were not only taking credit for blasting the spy plane out of the sky with a missile, they were pointing the finger of responsibility directly at the president." Assuming that all Khrushchev had was a dead pilot and 'a stack of scrap metal,' the men in the bunker decided to stick with the NASA weather plane story, especially given that Allen Dulles had given the White House 'absolutely categorical' assurances that a U-2 pilot would never survive a crash." Later, "top Eisenhower aide Andrew Goodpaster [commented] that 'we had an understanding . . . that the plane would be destroyed and that it was impossible for the pilot to survive.'"[34]

A "wall of lies" now began to be constructed to shield Eisenhower from confessing to direct responsibility, and this must have been agonizing to Goodpaster. He had had to pass the word that "the president wants no specific ties to him of this particular event." After all, career officers had been taught from their earliest days to "stick to the facts" and leave the interpretation to others. Unfortunately, it was the facts that were being reinterpreted, until finally the façade could no longer be sustained when Powers was produced and parts of the downed plane were placed on display in Red Square.[35]

Khrushchev observed: "It was as though the Americans had deliberately tried to place a time bomb under the meeting." Before he left for Paris, Eisenhower met with Herter and Goodpaster in his office and "told them in no uncertain terms that all further U-2 overflights of the USSR would cease. 'Inform Allen Dulles,' he said abruptly. The next day Eisenhower was to depart for Paris and a long-awaited summit conference with Khrushchev. He wanted no more surprises."[36]

It also turned out that, ironically, Eisenhower's method of dealing with problems—through indirection rather than otherwise—worked to his disadvantage in this, possibly the greatest embarrassment for the United States in the Cold War period. His style was described thus:

> Visible leadership on the outside, persistent and continuing presidential pressure on the inside. . . . But this was not the way Eisenhower operated. His approach was successful in maintaining his public popularity and in retaining the loyalty and respect of senior officials within the government. It prevented, presumably, any number of unwise actions. It contributed, however, to his administration's disappointing conclusion. Eisenhower relied upon an organizational approach to addressing issues of a national security nature, and on the whole it served his purposes well. But he also understood that flexibility was needed to address both complexity and unexpected events.[37]

Allen Dulles defended the use of the U-2 as an espionage tool:

> It is extremely difficult for me to sum up in words the significance of the effort to our national security. I do not wish to exaggerate, nor do I wish to belittle other vital intelligence programs. The photographic coverage and the data derived from it are an inseparable part of the whole national intelligence effort. But in terms of reliability, of precision, of access to otherwise inaccessible installations, its contribution has been unique. And in the opinion of the military, of the scientists, and of the other senior officials responsible for our national security it has been, to put it simply, invaluable.[38]

Just as the Eisenhower administration was winding up its affairs, another spy scandal involving the Soviet Union broke out. The Strategic

Air Command had been flying reconnaissance flights using the RB-47H. On 1 July 1960 an electronic intelligence-communications intelligence (ELINT-COMINT) flight was shot down near the Soviet Union, although the United States claimed it was over international waters. The crew of six, from the 55th Strategic Reconnaissance Wing, were captured. Only two crew members survived. "The Soviets' immediate protest of an incursion infuriated President Eisenhower. He ordered an investigation to see if the plane had actually crossed into the Soviet Union as the protest note indicated. The initial investigation revealed that the flight was over international waters about seventy miles north of the Soviet border when it was shot down. . . . Khrushchev refused to return [the two survivors] as a protest of the U-2 and other overflights."[39]

John Eisenhower, as assistant staff secretary, forwarded to the president a joint memorandum from the secretaries of state and defense that delineated the American response to this further embarrassment: "Following State-Defense study of the problem, we have concluded that the unilateral military measures listed in the enclosure might be effective in obtaining the release of the RB-47 officers if diplomatic measures continue to be unavailing. We have rejected as unpromising at this time economic and cultural measures and measures involving cooperation of our allies. . . . We think that our efforts to date have had some success in impressing upon the Soviets the connection between the release of the officers and the prospects for improving relations with the U.S. or indeed of entering into negotiations with us."[40]

Partly as a consequence, "on August 9 the president summoned Allen Dulles, [Ambassador] Livingston Merchant, General [Nathan] Twining, Gen. John Persons, Gen. Robert Breitweiser, General Goodpaster, and Col. John Eisenhower to discuss the resumption of COMINT-ELINT flights. . . . Before he left office, he decided to pull all the Air Force, Navy, and special reconnaissance activity together under the Joint Chiefs of Staff to provide effective and unified operational control and coordination of all flights. . . . The Joint Reconnaissance Center became operational before Eisenhower left office on January 16."[41]

It is worth noting here, however, that the American and Soviet conceptions of "negotiations" had become very divergent. Whereas Eisenhower and his foreign policy advisers conceived of heads-of-state conferences as a useful diplomatic tool to help narrow the differences between the superpowers during the Cold War, the Soviet Union under Khrushchev had a different motive.

These conferences all too often were purposely used by Khrushchev as occasions to discredit the "warmongering" Americans and to propagandize the Soviets as "peace advocates." Generally speaking, "in the postwar summit meetings too little attention has been paid to purpose and content; the conferences tended to become charades that would save the world. . . . At the Paris Summit Conference of 1960, four statesmen could not negotiate because of one U-2 plane that had been shot out of the sky."[42]

Above all else, it was indeed wretched for Eisenhower that he had to defend the clumsy U-2 espionage failure as his presidency drew to a conclusion. As his science adviser, Dr. George Kistiakowsky, remarked: "Eisenhower began to talk with much feeling about how he had concentrated his efforts the last few years on ending the cold war, how he felt that he was making big progress, and how the stupid U-2 mess had spoiled all his efforts. He ended very sadly that he saw nothing worthwhile left for him to do."[43]

Part III
Arrival at the Top

Chapter Eleven

Deputy Commander and Commander-Designate in Vietnam

"Having fought the fight, lost 50,000 of our young people . . .
having in hand a situation that could be sustained in much the
same way as Korea . . . all of that was cast away. . . . And that's
the ultimate tragedy of Vietnam in my view."
—GEN. ANDREW J. GOODPASTER

Like most of his contemporaries, Goodpaster viewed experience as a combat commander as the true measure of his capabilities as a career Army officer. The fact that early in his career he jumped from the usual assignments as a junior officer to occupying the ultimate staff position of his generation in the Eisenhower White House did not sway him from that belief.

Although his tour was brief in terms of his overall career assignments, Goodpaster regarded being promoted to four-star rank and assigned as deputy commander in Vietnam in 1968, with the clear prospect of becoming commander, as the true consummation of his career. Before this, having served as director of the Joint Staff under the aegis of the Joint Chiefs of Staff, along with other JCS-related assignments, had made him very much professionally engaged in the planning aspects of that unfortunate war.

For example: "At this point, the Joint Chiefs of Staff were tasked by [Robert] McNamara to come up with a comprehensive strategic review of the Vietnam situation to determine what assurance the United States could have of winning the war 'if we do everything we can.' Lt. Gen. Andrew J. Goodpaster was put in charge of an ad hoc staff group to conduct the study. The resulting 'concept and appraisal,' completed in less than two weeks, indicated that victory was possible given the establishment of a military force capable of seizing and retaining the initiative."[1] Goodpaster then inserted this significant caveat: "Within the boundaries of reasonable assumptions . . . there appears to be no reason we cannot win if such is our will . . . and if that will is manifested in strategy and tactical operations."[2] Goodpaster in particular must have been reminded about Eisenhower's advice to him: "The United States was 'not going to be run out of a country we helped to establish.' Since the President [Lyndon Johnson] had 'appealed to force,' the United States 'must win.'"[3]

Eisenhower, from Gettysburg, was not reluctant in expressing his thoughts concerning the ebb and flow of a conflict that defied an easy definition or a simple solution. For example: "Through General Andrew Goodpaster, now secretary of the Joint Chiefs of Staff, Johnson kept Eisenhower informed in advance of bombing halts and troop level increases and his efforts to enlist allied support and to open conversations with the communists."[4] Eisenhower urged Johnson not to give away gratuitously the option of negotiating an end to a war that seemed to be becoming crippled more by domestic than purely military conditions.

Goodpaster and his JCS colleagues had defined the Vietnam problem as a military problem, requiring a military solution, thus favoring escalation as a means toward a negotiated victory. They promised that escalation could bring victory nearer. There was also the opinion that the JCS should have been more aggressive in advocating its views as to how to conduct the war, rather than leaving the policy initiative to the McNamara "Whiz Kids." In their defense, the JCS claimed with some justification that they were shut out of the policy debate. It was reported that "the president's deep distrust of his senior military officers manifested itself in exclusive advisory forums that limited JCS access to the president."[5]

In any event, Goodpaster's JCS role placed him squarely among the often bitter clashes of policy, whether among the military leadership or between the military and the civilian leadership. He ultimately came down on the side that drew the conclusion that "the Vietnam War had been lost at home by incremental policy decisions and mismanagement."[6] Goodpaster shared the previously unthinkable realization that "few would deny that the United States was a vastly more powerful state than North Vietnam, yet the weaker state was able to defeat the stronger in the Vietnam War (1965–72) because non-material factors trumped the balance of power."[7]

The seemingly endless escalation on the battlefield had brought with it, in the American public's eyes, an escalation in the perception of what constituted an acceptable (or even "honorable") victory. Complicating matters was that by the time Goodpaster took up his command in 1968, to accept a stalemate would have been tantamount to humiliating failure; to the enemy it would have represented a stepping-stone to complete success.

A Battlefield Commander

Goodpaster succeeded Gen. Creighton Abrams as deputy commander, U.S. Military Assistance Command, Vietnam. Abrams, in turn, had replaced Gen. William Westmoreland as commander, U.S. Military Assistance Command, Vietnam (COMUSMACV), when Westmoreland became Army chief of staff. As deputy, Goodpaster would serve as acting COMUSMACV in Abrams' absence. Goodpaster's most noteworthy action was to implement the order from Washington to halt the bombing campaign. "By that time," Goodpaster said, "we'd come to the judgment . . . that we could accommodate this, that the situation of our military operations had gone far enough so that this would not have any damage to us that we couldn't manage quite well."[8]

Goodpaster might have felt that way, but Washington was by no means completely convinced. Clark Clifford, who had succeeded a self-doubting Robert McNamara as secretary of defense, had by then turned against the war. In a private meeting of senior officials in March 1967, Clifford "had called for a 'reduced strategy' of a bombing halt or a reduction in bombing of the north, abandonment of isolated military positions, and a new ground strategy that used U.S. troops as a shield around populated areas in order to give the South Vietnamese time to assume the burden of the war."[9] "When asked by Clifford if a military victory could be won, [Ambassador Philip] Habib answered, 'Not under the present circumstances.' 'What would you do?' Clifford asked. 'Stop bombing and negotiate,' Habib replied."[10]

Furthermore, Johnson's self-imposed war-making limitations had skewed a central strategic aspect of war. Goodpaster recognized this as the enemy's center of gravity. "We had adopted a strategy that focused on none of the possible North Vietnamese centers of gravity—their army, their capital, the army of their protector, the community of interest with their allies, or public opinion. . . . Instead, by seeing the Viet Cong as a separate entity rather than as an instrument of North Vietnam, we chose a center of gravity which in fact did not exist. The proof that the Viet Cong guerrillas were not a center of gravity was demonstrated during Tet-68, when, even though the enemy had incurred huge losses, the war continued unabated."[11]

At the operational level, Goodpaster described where the friction lay: "In Vietnam, the relationship between the civilian leadership there under Ambassador Ellsworth Bunker and a couple of really very able assistants that he had and our military leadership was very close and very positive.

The division was between those who were out there on the ground and the high leadership back in Washington."[12]

Goodpaster had experienced firsthand the taste of this division when, before taking up his Vietnam assignment, he was a member of the American delegation to the ill-fated Vietnam peace talks in Paris. The incident is worth reporting in full:

> Harriman did indeed get the Paris assignment, being posted there in May 1968 with Cyrus Vance as his deputy, Phillip Habib as political advisor, and Lieutenant General Andrew J. Goodpaster as JCS representative. Potential problems surfaced as early as the plane ride to Europe—indeed, even before the mission began—recalled Goodpaster. "From the outset, Governor Harriman tried to get approval for offering a 'scaling back' of our military operations in Vietnam as a negotiating gambit with the North Vietnamese, hoping they would reciprocate. I opposed this at all times, beginning with our delegation's meeting with President Johnson, who disapproved Governor Harriman's proposal, and approved my position."
>
> But Harriman apparently had no intention of being constrained by anything as mundane as instructions from the President. Soon after the delegation's aircraft departed Washington, he offered the view that "now it's our job to end this war—to get the best terms we can, but to end the war." Goodpaster immediately objected. "That's not my understanding," he retorted, recalling LBJ's statement that the delegation was to negotiate, but not in any way compromise, the "maximum pressure" he wanted put on the enemy. "That's not right, General," Harriman countered. "I think it's clear what our position is—what the president ordered."

In this instance, true to form, Goodpaster insisted that the president's instructions be closely adhered to: "Goodpaster would not be intimidated. 'No, sir,' he shot back. 'The president would not want us to endanger American lives. We have not been instructed to end the war on the "best terms we can."' By this time the autocratic Harriman, not accustomed to being contradicted, was angry. 'We're going to end this war,' he insisted. 'That's what the president said we should do.' Goodpaster had the last word. 'Sir,' he said in acid tones, 'that is not what the president said. Those are *not* [Goodpaster's emphasis] our instructions.'"[13]

What Is "Victory"?

In sharp contrast, Goodpaster and Abrams were in complete harmony as to the strategic concept. As Goodpaster said—reflecting the Army view: "We did not have clear guidance from the national level but we worked up our own overall strategic plan. . . . My ideas coincided completely with those of General Abrams. . . . I found that the situation was extremely well assessed."[14]

This is not surprising, because in 1965 their strategic concept had been developed in the Pentagon by Goodpaster and his colleagues. Their study influenced the thinking of senior Army leaders. A variation, known as PROVN (Program for the Pacification and Long-Term Development of Vietnam), was then being implemented. Also noteworthy was that Goodpaster's approach was at variance with General Westmoreland's notion of "search and destroy." PROVN became an inspiration for village-level pacification efforts intended to ensure that the South Vietnamese could resist the constant pressure from the Vietcong.[15]

The concept essentially argued that the "Vietnamization" of the war was a realistic objective, given enough consistent American support. South Vietnam was divided into four zones, with each zone adapted to the local conditions. Overall, this meant attacking the supply routes both within and outside of the country. Within the four zones, air support, including in particular logistics for both the South Vietnamese as well as the American forces, depended upon CIA air drops and secure landing areas.[16] Thus, the CIA was playing an important role in attempts to gain control over the supply routes of the North Vietnamese, and in particular the Ho Chi Minh Trail that led through Laos.

This was a matter of great concern to Goodpaster, given that his specific duties were twofold. One was to travel to the units to observe through briefings how the situations in both the American and Vietnamese areas of responsibility (i.e., combat areas) were going; he would report on what he saw and heard in his weekly meetings with Abrams. Goodpaster's other major responsibility was the training of the South Vietnamese local and regional forces, upon which hinged the success of Vietnamization.

Overall, Goodpaster felt that the "conduct of the war was going well"—referring to Vietnam, however, and not Washington. It was estimated that "the successful pacification program, one repeatedly cited in enemy communications as a threat that had to be countered, was extending not only security but also elected government, trained hamlet and village officials, and economic gains to most of the population."[17]

A related argument could be made that just when the Abrams-Goodpaster strategy was being implemented to bring about a favorable resolution of the conflict—which meant putting in place a pro-Western democratically elected government—the domestic political situation in the United States further hampered such efforts. The split between the civilian and military leadership cadres was getting deeper, with a growing doubt that the war, even assuming it could be won, would result in a victory worth the expenditure, not only in troops and matériel, but also in national honor. For example, Dean Acheson, responding to a statement from JCS chairman Gen. Earle Wheeler that "the Pentagon was not bent on a 'classic military victory,' . . . but only helping the Vietnamese to avoid a Communist victory," declared that Wheeler was simply using semantics to justify the presence of a half million American soldiers.

In other words, the term "victory" had itself lost much of its currency as a justification for continuing the war, and this situation was increasingly compatible with general domestic public opinion. "The American public's attitude seemed to be, 'Either get in or get out,' and there was little taste for negotiations, which appeared to be either useless or a betrayal of how the war had been displayed during the earlier years of escalation."

The level of frustration both politically domestically (win or get out) and militarily in Vietnam (give us the means and the time) had never been higher than while Goodpaster was deputy commander. Even though the "clear and hold" concept had replaced Westmoreland's "search and destroy" concept as to how to conduct the war in the countryside, it could not be a war-winning strategy; it could serve by then only as a basis for a negotiated "honorable" withdrawal. Although the transition in strategy from Westmoreland to Abrams was symbolized by these two terms, to the American public it simply appeared that one dubious slogan had been substituted for another. Regrettably for the historical record, Goodpaster's approach appeared to be catching hold under Abrams, but by then it was too late, politically speaking.

How Goodpaster could still draw a conclusion that his mission was achievable, after having demonstrated in his previous assignments that he could "think strategically" as well as tactically, is puzzling. Surely, analytically, he could recognize that

> the difficulties of fighting the war on terms disadvantageous
> to the United States' real military strengths reflected a larger

political problem—the discrepancy between the means and ends (as Clausewitz might have put it). The North Vietnamese and the Vietcong were fighting for what they believed in very strongly; those who were not were undoubtedly subject to the discipline of a total-itarian, passionately nationalistic regime. The South Vietnamese governing system, by contrast, appeared corrupt, unpopular, and in a distinct minority, opposed by the Buddhist monks, unsup-ported by a frightened, exploited, and war-weary peasantry; those native units loyal to the regime and who often fought well were not sufficient to compensate for this inner corrosion.[18]

Fortunately, Goodpaster was not directly involved in Vietnam long enough to have his career tarred by the Vietnam brush of perceived failure. "In Vietnam, General Fred Weyand reported for duty as deputy to Abrams. 'What's the mission?' he asked. 'Who the hell knows?' Abrams retorted. 'You know what has to be done. I know what has to be done. Let's get on with it.'"[19]

Battlefield conditions did not rattle him any more than did service in staff assignments. It is worth recalling an interesting episode reported by the military historian Lewis Sorley: "At a Harvard lecture series given in 1967 by McGeorge Bundy, Bundy asked Dr. Edwin Deagle [who later was to write about Abe Lincoln] what he thought should have been General Westmoreland's assignment after Vietnam. Deagle responded: 'You should not make General Westmoreland Chief of Staff of the Army, as he will have to go to great lengths to justify his record. Make him the new NATO com-mander, where he will have no responsibility for Vietnam policy. The chief of staff should be General Andrew Goodpaster, who is brilliant and wise in the ways of Washington.'"[20] Instead, of course, Westmoreland went to Washington, where his professional integrity was in doubt, and Goodpaster went to NATO, with his integrity intact.

Clearly, Goodpaster was caught up in the almost total national fixa-tion on the use or misuse, or the unilaterally conditional employment, of American political-military power in Southeast Asia, which was at that time serving as the cockpit for the Cold War superpower rivalry. In American eyes, this meant a rivalry with a Sino-Soviet "bloc," which in fact had been rapidly deteriorating into its own form of Great Power competition. In contrast, the European "front" of the Cold War had been largely stabilized by the late 1960s, and the Afro-Asian "third world" was still evolving out of its recent decolonization.

Chapter Twelve

As NATO Supreme Allied Commander

"For human activity is complex, human motives exceedingly mixed."
—ALDOUS HUXLEY, *Ends and Means*

The two most coveted assignments before retirement for the most senior Army officers were chief of staff and NATO supreme allied commander. How and why Goodpaster came to the NATO position rather than the other post was linked to the fact that in the years since his time as a lower-ranking officer in the Eisenhower White House, he had become, willy-nilly, a widely respected "wise man" and adviser to presidents.

Goodpaster Arrives at SHAPE

Goodpaster became SACEUR on 1 July 1969. As was customary, he first became U.S. commander-in-chief, European command, in his national role, and thereafter he assumed his multinational command as SACEUR. There was also a third "hat" called Live Oak that was not talked about openly.[1]

As SACEUR, he worked within the framework of multinational institutions to the extent considered compatible with American foreign policy and national security interests. Certainly Eisenhower believed in this approach. His own experience commanding a multinational army in World War II and in initiating similar principles of political cooperation in the formation of NATO's military arm had inescapably defined the position.

Likewise, Goodpaster also had had extensive exposure to the multilateral approach to framing American military policy, having served at different times at the United Nations as well as at NATO in its formative years. In summary, Goodpaster had already played a role that was compatible with both his beliefs (peace is preferable to war under defined circumstances) and his career interests.

He seemed to embody the best aspects of leadership, as expressed in their different ways by his two immediate predecessors, Gen. Lauris Norstad and Gen. Lyman Lemnitzer. Norstad was handsome, innovative,

124

and sensitive to public relations. Lemnitzer was solid, reliable, cautious. Goodpaster was tall, trim, gray-haired, and spectacled, and in addition, he appeared to have a more reflective temperament than most generals. He had a quietly persuasive manner; bellicosity was not his style.

Goodpaster also understood very well this observation by Gen. Alfred Gruenther, an even earlier SACEUR: "I am not really worried about governments. They believe in NATO, and have no thought of scuttling the organization. However, no government does much about keeping the subject alive with the people. That takes effort and imagination, and a lot of time."[2] Further, Goodpaster was quick to recognize that the SACEUR's effectiveness depended on political factors as much as military expertise. He was already aware, of course, having served so many years in and around the political leadership in Washington, that to realize fully the role of SACEUR would require from him adroit political talents. He certainly understood that "consultations with Europe are neither simple in execution nor a panacea for our deeper differences: the process is fraught with as many complexities as are the issues."[3]

The general setting would have been obvious to Goodpaster—especially given his close ties with Nixon and Kissinger: "It was geopolitical decline that preoccupied the architects of U.S. foreign policy especially in the early 1970s."[4]

The Tasks Ahead

Goodpaster's greatest immediate challenge as SACEUR was dealing with the strong antiwar sentiment fueled by the frustrations of the war in Vietnam, not only among the European allies, but also in North America with the Canadians. Put succinctly: "There was uncertainty about the future of Europe. The attitude to the common defense was a curious mixture of unwillingness to augment European efforts and fear of American withdrawal."[5] Ever since taking office, the Nixon administration had been searching for ways to balance increasing domestic discontent over war expenditures, brought on partly by a conflict situation in Vietnam that seemed to be endless, with the need to convince the European allies that the real battlefront of the Cold War remained the division between East and West in Europe.

This was indeed a challenge given that opposition to the war in Vietnam had forced Lyndon Johnson to step aside in the 1968 presidential election, enabling Nixon to win by promising an "honorable" conclusion to the war. Goodpaster no doubt understood, having just come from Vietnam, that the weaker party in the military confrontation could not dictate the terms of the conflict. The facts on the ground defined the outcome, and the Europeans, no strangers to inconclusive wars, understood this.

The state of affairs that Goodpaster faced can only be described as alarming, "because of both the demands of the war in Vietnam and the turbulent social conditions at home. . . . This resulted in units that were grossly understrength, wracked by continual massive turnover in those who were assigned, plagued by widespread problems of drug abuse, racial disharmony, dissent, and indiscipline, and thus not only much reduced in operational capability but also poor examples for the NATO Allies that the U.S. was trying to contribute more and better forces to the Alliance."[6] The United States had reduced its forces in Europe from 408,000 to 300,000 between 1963 and 1969.[7]

Goodpaster later recounted that "the crumbling of support from the United States couldn't be stopped but it could be controlled, and I think that the focus then shifted to Kissinger's negotiations, most of which were extremely secret. I helped him on occasion keep them secret."[8] This is another example in which Goodpaster's proximity to Nixon (and later to President Gerald Ford) showed itself.

It was Goodpaster's responsibility to urge the Europeans to do more while America was doing less. This was a challenge indeed! Nonetheless, he had some support among the allies, especially in the Federal Republic of Germany, which was on the front line of the East-West standoff. "There is nothing surprising in a professional soldier asking for the forces to which he belongs to be taken seriously. But when at a semi-official meeting in Bonn, General Goodpaster, the highest officer in the Atlantic Alliance, does not shrink from making a drastic comparison of the military forces in Europe that is clearly unfavourable to NATO, the whole public must take notice, because normally the outspokenness of a military leader diminishes with the importance of his post. . . . What Goodpaster indicated without saying it in so many words is that a military balance does not at present exist and will only come back if the Soviet Union reduces its forces."[9]

One of the most frustrating aspects of the situation in which Goodpaster found himself was that, to make a policy of détente credible, the forces of the two opposing sides must be roughly equal. This equality—or "equivalence"—can be calculated in some combination of ground troops and tactical nuclear retaliatory forces, but essentially this translates into some sort of stalemate between East and West. Paradoxically, it was just such a battlefield stalemate that the United States was unable by then to achieve in Vietnam, and this was weakening Goodpaster's hand in his attempt at a diplomacy of détente in Europe.

Another of Goodpaster's immediate responsibilities was to attempt to counter the strong sentiment both in the United States and in Europe favoring withdrawal, rather than a further buildup, of forces. This included congressional attempts to reduce the American forces in Europe in the face of pressures from Vietnam. Goodpaster did not need to be reminded that "as a minimum, allies represented wartime capabilities, denied to an adversary. Moreover, allies not only contributed in a psycho-political sense to a state's ability to deter conflict, but also to its military potential for immediate combat."[10]

An example that further contributed to Goodpaster's frustration was when President Nixon was faced with how to counter the Mansfield Amendment, offered by Senator Mike Mansfield of Montana in 1971. The amendment called for the number of U.S. troops stationed in Europe to be halved. Goodpaster recalled, "President Nixon had his people call me one night and asked if I could immediately come back and work with him in trying to block that. And I came back and my helicopter landed on the White House lawn. The meeting had just begun and I came in and partic-ipated."[11] Fortunately for Goodpaster, on 19 May 1971, the Senate defeated the amendment by a vote of 61–36.

One innovation that Goodpaster introduced "was [to] set up a pro-gram called Alliance Defense in the 1970s. The idea was to use every means we could to improve the effectiveness and efficiency of the military funds and budgets that were being provided. And we shifted the accent to look-ing for those improvements and putting them into effect to get better use of our funds and our efforts. . . . We shifted the accent from fending off cuts to making the forces that we had more effective, using the funds in a better way."[12]

Even at that, no commander would have been satisfied with this state of affairs, but fortunately, for Goodpaster, as he exhorted the allies to do better than the Americans themselves could, his personal standing was not affected.[13] One reason was that he did not lecture his NATO part-ners; rather, in his speeches he adopted a "conversational" mode of address, which tended to disarm any personal resentment for the American general.

For example, in a speech to the Royal United Service Institution in London, he opened his remarks thus: "We live at a time when a valid understanding, broadly shared, of security problems is of tremendous importance. These problems are complex, difficult, burdensome—even irksome—and they are in important areas, obscure and hard to define and to grasp. . . . Yet public understanding and interest in security issues are truly indispensable if there is to be the support and confidence, widely based throughout our countries, on which the future strength and effectiveness of our military forces depend."[14]

This enabled Goodpaster to play a more effective role in stemming this combination of antiwar and anti-American sentiment and, in general, widespread opposition to increasing military expenditures for a conflict that they all hoped would never occur. For example, a Munich paper editorialized: "We cannot expect a general to bother about who will pay for his army. This is a matter which the political leaders must take up. But General Goodpaster did not hesitate to reiterate the call for a 'considerable' intensification of Europe's defense efforts, a call which is becoming louder and louder in the United States. . . . Nor should General Goodpaster overlook the fact that Europe merely is the front line of the United States. . . . And last but not least, playing a leadership role costs money."[15] What this implies is that the war in Vietnam was a constant drag on Goodpaster's efforts to increase the European members' contributions.

One way to achieve this goal was to engage in negotiations with the Soviet Union to bring about mutual and balanced force reductions (MBFR). The MBFR negotiations were extremely complicated because it was not easy to arrive at an agreed-upon definition of what was "mutual" and what was "balanced." Goodpaster, quoting Nixon, held: "Our objective should be to create a more stable military balance at lower levels and at lower cost." Goodpaster went on to observe that "I have long felt—as did my predecessor, General Norstad, more than fifteen years ago—that such a pattern of reduction is a valid theoretical and logical possibility—that in principle, it should be possible to provide the same level of security as now exists for both sides at lower levels of forces. But to get from the theory to the realization is, we already know, a difficult and time consuming business of great complexity, just as it is of great importance and consequence."[16]

Goodpaster explained his approach to shaping NATO's grand strategy: "There are three intricately interlinked components of military power that give reality to our strategy. They are conventional forces, tactical nuclear weapons, and strategic nuclear forces. The conventional military forces provide much more than what some have called a 'symbolic presence.' Rather, when properly manned, equipped, and trained, they afford an essential means to meet any aggression at the level it occurs. The second element is tactical nuclear weapons; these provide the flexibility in firepower required by the strategic concept. And the third element is strategic nuclear forces; these constitute the ultimate deterrent and, should it ever be necessary, the ultimate defense."[17]

The dilemma was that "no militarily acceptable and apparently negotiable MBFR scheme has been discovered which successfully compensates for the Warsaw Pact advantages in existing forces, geography, and initiative."[18] Goodpaster observed, trenchantly, that "equal reductions in unequal forces could result in forces that are even more unequal."[19] Goodpaster also commented: "The Mutual and Balanced Force Reductions (MBFR) negotiations . . . are testing whether the process of mutual forces limitations developed in SALT [Strategic Arms Limitation Talks] can be in some way applied to military forces below the strategic nuclear level."[20]

Another of Goodpaster's responsibilities as SACEUR was to keep a careful eye on SALT as the negotiations unfolded. Put succinctly: "The most demanding game that the Americans played during the last weeks of 1969 was the game of arms control."[21] Goodpaster pointed out: "In the SALT negotiations on the size and composition of strategic nuclear forces, the détente process shapes and constrains U.S. and USSR military capabilities that, by any standard, are in a class by themselves. . . . The effect will undoubtedly be to narrow the strategic options for their employment, as well as the kinds of missions and objectives that may be assigned to them."[22]

Perhaps even more important, and by implication referring to the notion of "linkage," Goodpaster observed that "I have long felt that one of the collateral effects of strategic nuclear parity has been to narrow the range of issues over which the strategic nuclear forces can be relied upon to provide an effective deterrent. . . . Reliance must not be placed on expectations that détente consultations and negotiations will have enough motivation behind them on the part of the Soviets to keep them from challenging U.S. objectives and interests."[23]

The End Approaches

Career-wise, Goodpaster's reputation is often linked to his service in the Eisenhower White House as the president's staff secretary and defense liaison officer. However, in terms of influence and prestige at the highest international level during the Cold War, there could be no assignment more coveted than that of NATO's SACEUR. Quite naturally, therefore, when the news surfaced in October 1974 that Goodpaster was about to be replaced as SACEUR by Gen. Alexander M. Haig Jr., it created some interest and even consternation internationally as well as in Washington. As is generally true for four-star generals, this event was not without its underlying political narrative. Yet the politics at this time was well beyond what might be called normal.

The political environment in post-Watergate Washington was in extreme flux, with a disgraced Richard Nixon having resigned in August before his second term had ended and a largely unknown Gerald Ford having ascended to the presidency under circumstances without precedent in American politics. The immediate problem at hand was what to do about Haig, who had served as Nixon's chief of staff and had ably helped engineer Nixon's resignation. Haig was a senior general and yet still too young to be retired without implying dissatisfaction with his performance. This had created a dilemma in that there were few appropriate assignments for Haig. Complicating matters was the fact that the Army hierarchy did not want such a controversial "politicized" officer returned to its highest ranks.

Conversely, Goodpaster had had some reason to think that his position as SACEUR was still secure in spite of the major political earthquake that had occurred in Washington. Earlier that year he had written to one of his career mentors, General Gruenther: "Whether we look at Washington, which is swamping itself in Watergate and related activities, or at NATO, which is having a rough passage on the fundamental issue of Alliance solidarity, things are far from good. . . . While I was on a brief visit to the States two weeks ago, I had the opportunity to meet with President [Nixon] and discuss a good deal of this. Interestingly, he remains strong for NATO, while insisting that the Allies not gang up in opposition to the U.S."[24]

This presidential relationship was well established, not only because both had been involved in the Eisenhower White House, but also because immediately after Nixon had won the 1968 election, Goodpaster was drawn into the post-election transition. As he said, "I spent a number of weeks, I think probably four weeks or more, at the Hotel Pierre as he was getting his administration organized. I worked closely with Henry Kissinger during that time."[25]

According to one observer, "Although Goodpaster is a close friend of President Richard Nixon he was not appointed as [Army] Chief of Staff during Nixon's tenure because the President felt he was irreplaceable at NATO."[26] Goodpaster had another explanation: "One reason Nixon wanted me to go [to NATO] was to keep closer to Washington and come back and meet with him from time to time and discuss the European situation but more broadly, the whole—his whole approach worldwide . . . issues of security. And I did that. Initially perhaps in his first year, several times and then I would come back to the United States probably twice a year while I was serving as SACEUR and always have conversations with Nixon."[27]

Nonetheless, to his dismay, Goodpaster discovered (or perhaps rediscovered) that at the highest level in the nation's foremost political-military alliance—NATO—virtually nothing is "nonpolitical." Hence, nothing and nobody is irreplaceable. In a White House meeting that included Secretary of State Kissinger and National Security Advisor Brent Scowcroft with the new President Ford to discuss what to do about Haig, they examined various alternatives and then decided to move Haig to NATO as SACEUR. The dilemma was that this would require cutting short Goodpaster's tenure. Ford suggested that Kissinger should inform him, and Kissinger in turn looked squarely at Scowcroft, who then picked up the telephone and called his good friend Goodpaster, who, of course, was not at all pleased with the news. Goodpaster explained:

> I had talked with Abrams, who was chief of staff of the Army by that time, about my own tenure and he said they would like to think of a retirement in the spring of 1975. And I said that would be fine with me. . . . And then suddenly . . . I got a call saying that the Americans would like to terminate my assignment and assign General Haig—who had, of course, served with President Nixon—to the post. This clarified something that had occurred.
>
> I had had a call from a couple of my senior European commanders, military heads of their forces, saying that they had just heard that I had requested retirement. And I said well I haven't requested retirement and then I got this call. And what had happened was that the White House had sent out a message saying that I had requested retirement and that General Haig would take over. So it was a little embarrassing and awkward and it was a clumsy affair.[28]

The Change of Command

So now, here he was, suddenly devalued by a new and unexpected presidency, within months of ending a truly remarkable career. He was justifiably annoyed and perhaps also somewhat embarrassed after being asked, even ordered, to step aside for what obviously was an arrangement for political convenience.[29] To illustrate why, this statement describing how Haig rose nearly to the top could never be said *under any circumstances* about Goodpaster:

> From the start, he used his position as NSC military aide to become Kissinger's indispensable, across-the-board assistant. . . . Less than three weeks into the administration, Haig wrote a memo to Kissinger urging that he appoint a deputy. "I am not volunteering," wrote the not-so-subtle officer, but "would be honored" to serve. It was 1970 before Haig was given this formal designation, but in the meantime, he employed his assiduous service to Kissinger and his perceived political loyalty to Nixon to build up his role. The fact that other [NSC] Council members did not respect Haig intellectually actually helped in his rise, for it meant they did not perceive him as a threat.[30]

All of this goes a long way in explaining Goodpaster's unusual behavior at the change of command ceremony. It was reported: "The ceremony at which General Haig assumed command was one of the rare occasions where the private General Goodpaster became involved in a public dispute. In a break with custom, he was not present at the ceremonies. Some said he was resentful at being retired; others said he had stayed away because of recent minor surgery. The general did not say."[31] Nevertheless, he did appear alongside Haig at a subsequent news conference on 15 December 1974.[32]

The sensitivity of the episode was such that on 16 December the Associated Press reported: "General Goodpaster explained that he was not at the previous ceremony because he needed to convalesce from a minor operation. . . . 'It is a point of principle and a point of honor with me—I have never turned down an assignment and I have never asked to be relieved of any task.'"[33]

Even earlier, he had sent a message to his NATO commanders: "Apparently some of the messages and letters that were sent out by U.S. authorities stated that I had requested (repeat requested) retirement. This is untrue, and I am deeply troubled at the implication, which is erroneous of willingness on my part of continuing to serve the Alliance as SACEUR. I have not now or previously requested retirement or relief from my duties. I wanted you to know this from me personally."[34] But he was not alone in being disgruntled; some months after Goodpaster had relinquished the command, there was grumbling in NATO circles about the United States sending a "political general."[35]

It is interesting, if not significant, to note that, notwithstanding a particular SACEUR's background and career inclinations, at least through the time of Haig the officers so designated appeared to be appropriate to their respective times and circumstances. For such disparate personalities as Norstad, Lemnitzer, Goodpaster, and Haig, every one of them were experienced in the international political as well as the purely military arenas.[36] Persuasiveness, combined with almost endless patience, were among the hallmarks of their success.

Eisenhower put it well during World War II. In a letter to General Marshall, Eisenhower commented with obvious frustration: "The sooner I can get rid of all these questions that are outside the military scope, the happier I will be. Sometimes I think I live ten years each week, of which at least nine are absorbed in political and economic matters." Ten years later, of course, Goodpaster found himself back in the same situation that Eisenhower was deploring earlier, and, as the record shows, no SACEUR can avoid the political and economic aspects of NATO defense.

Furthermore, as CINCEUR (most of whose day-to-day duties were delegated to the deputy), these generals actually had some troops under their direct national command. This provided a psychological as well as a material backup to their efforts as international commanders. Without a doubt, Goodpaster, with his long experience at or near the top of the national political-military policy-making and execution apparatus, could rightfully be considered almost an ideal choice for Nixon—notwithstanding his proximity to the president as counselor.

Chapter Thirteen

Returning to West Point as Superintendent

"This art [of war], like all others, is founded on certain and fixed principles, which are by their nature invariable; the application of them can only be varied: but they are themselves constant."
——HENRY HUMPHREY EVANS LLOYD, in *The Theory and Practice of War*

Upon retiring in 1974, and after a year and a half in Washington at the Woodrow Wilson International Center for Scholars and then membership on the faculty of The Citadel in South Carolina, Goodpaster found himself contemplating an unexpected assignment. It was one that would enable him to leave a lasting mark on the next generation of young officers to graduate from West Point.[1]

As he put it:

They had had this really large-scale cheating scandal. . . . They asked me, in general terms, what would I think of calling a retired officer back to active duty to do that. And I told them I thought that might be a good idea. And they said, "Well if we ask you to come back at the grade of three-star general, would you consider it?" I said, "Of course I would." . . . I said, "Well, I'd like to talk to the secretary of the Army to see that we have a full understanding, before I come back." I said, "I'd be happy to come and do the things I believe in to restore the academy to what it should be."[2]

Goodpaster's Welcome

At the time of his appointment as superintendent, a military man who had served with him said: "'This guy's just a brilliant guy without being domineering.' He said that the general gave the impression of being 'just a quiet guy' at first until it became clear that he had 'a few brain cells to rub together.'"[3]

134

This demeanor of modesty yet firmness of purpose showed itself in regard to one of the most sensitive aspects of a career officer's self-image—recognition of his rank. It is worth recalling here again that when Goodpaster returned to active duty in 1977 to be superintendent, he was reminded that the position was for a three-star lieutenant general and Goodpaster had by then achieved four-star rank. The administration offered to go to Congress for a special legislative act authorizing an exception to this rule, but Goodpaster demurred. He did not want to embark on an especially difficult leadership challenge, in which ethical behavior played such a prominent part, carrying the baggage of his own preferential treatment.

Goodpaster could still recall the last major cheating scandal at West Point, in 1951, involving the football team. He had this to say at that time:

> What I have seen to date has made it clear to me that the action and intent of the cadets involved was such as to constitute full culpability on their part warranting action of the kind taken. It strikes me, however, that some rather intensive soul searching is indicated on the part of those who bear responsibility for creating and maintaining the pattern and system within which the violation occurred. I am not thinking of the business of giving the same writ on successive days. I think that a sound honor situation could take a relatively minor test like this in its stride. . . . Those who gave the tremendous emphasis to football did not, I am sure, foresee this as one of the consequences turned up by the wheel of time. . . . I hope . . . that this athletic binge and its unsavory morning after will be enough to return West Point football teams to the Ivy League where they belong.[4]

Goodpaster also perceived in 1951 that the honor system was being applied indiscriminately to offenses, large and small, and that the offenders thought of themselves apart from the corps of cadets and its standards. The same proved to exist in the current scandal.

In the engineering episode, mirroring the football scandal, Goodpaster quickly discovered that he needed to not only determine how to deal with the scandal but also demonstrate that there was a scandal to be dealt with. As he said: "Initially I found people really saying that a cheating scandal of the kind that had occurred couldn't occur. I said let's agree it did occur and it wasn't two hundred [cadets]. It was probably four hundred and there may have been eight hundred. And that's the challenge we have and that's what we're going to set out to correct. And we did."[5]

The scale of the cheating could never be exactly determined, but it seems that "eventually 152 members of the class of 1977 were dismissed for violation of the school's Honor Code by cheating, or toleration of cheating, on a take-home electrical engineering (EE-304) examination."[6]

He went even further when he observed: "You know, there is a lot of nostalgia for the old days, but that's not this decade, that's not when we are living. Now, we've got to live in terms of the kind of country and the kind of Army that we have."[7] This remark would not have gone down well with what Goodpaster termed "the elite."

This "elite," however, could not be taken lightly. This was especially true concerning the Honor Code and System. It was intended to give life to the phrase "Duty, Honor, Country," by allowing the Corps of Cadets to discipline themselves. In the football cheating scandal, for instance, much consideration was given to explaining to the alumni exactly what had occurred (and what had not occurred). For example, in the football scandal, a carefully crafted letter addressed to the "Brothers" was sent to all alumni, pointing out that "the publicity on this affair cannot be said to have been foresighted and well planned."[8] Goodpaster would have been well aware of this earlier example.

In fact, cheating was a source of concern as early as 1970, when the Army War College produced a report on the general state of the officer corps that said: "The findings of this study surprised and, in some cases, shocked many of the Army's senior leaders. . . . In general, it discovered that the majority of the Officer Corps perceived a stark dichotomy between the appearance and reality of the adherence of senior officers to the traditional standards of professionalism, which the words duty, honor, and country sum up. Instead, these officers saw a system that rewarded selfishness, incompetence, and dishonesty."[9]

Knowing the ways of Washington, Goodpaster asked for a letter giving him complete authority to make changes. In addition, he wanted "an understanding that I'm here for an extended but indefinite period, so that the elite guard cannot wait me out. And that was part of the agreement that I had with the Secretary [Martin R. Hoffmann of the Army]. The other part was that I'd said to him and to Army chief of staff General [Bernard] Rogers, any time you want to do something different from what I believe in, you let me know . . . who my successor is, because if this is to be done, it has to be done systematically. And that's what I really intend to do."[10]

"Soon after he became Superintendent in 1977, General Andrew Goodpaster provided what might well serve as the best capsule explanation of the Honor Code's origins and evolution. 'The code, derived from the "code of honor" of the officer corps of the late 1700s,' he told a congressional committee, 'after many changes in statement, application, and interpretation evolved into the present code.'"[11] Further, and noteworthy, given changing public attitudes toward the use and abuse of authority: "The honor system has evolved to include greater respect for due process and the defendants' rights."[12]

To grasp a sense of how far the notion of appropriate behavior had advanced, note this comment by Gen. Fox Connor, of the class of 1898, who considered Eisenhower his most accomplished protégé and who also mentored Gen. George Patton and Gen. George Marshall—thus in direct line to Goodpaster: "In theory, cadets were governed solely by the regulations of the Commandant and his Tacs [tactical officers]. In practice, the upper-class cadets developed their own norms and values and enforced them physically. Cadet discipline took the form of bare fist boxing. Fourth-class cadets, or freshmen, are known as plebes. A plebe suspected of an infraction against the upper-class was required to square off against an upperclassman of similar weight. The fight continued until one of the parties couldn't stand."[13]

Implementing a Leadership Concept

Goodpaster was able to build on the steps already taken by his immediate predecessor, Lt. Gen. Sidney Berry, and by General Rogers, who had convened a study board to assess "what the situation was in terms of academics, the military side of cadet life, and the whole complex of activities there."[14] Goodpaster regarded the report as helpful in what he termed "an orientation of objectives."

Thus, when he arrived at the academy, he made a statement in which he recalled that "West Point exists to provide to the cadets of the corps academic, military, physical, athletic and [a] moral ethical experience of such high quality that it can serve as bedrock on which they as future military leaders can build their capabilities over time to make their contribution to the safety and well-being of our country."[15]

Being a pragmatist as well as an idealist, after assessing the situation, he decided that a radical reformation was unnecessary but that a clarification of the purpose of the academy was badly needed. He doubtless bore in mind that by the 1970s the cadets were coping emotionally with the social and ethical turmoil brought on in part by the war in Vietnam, which was also being reflected in the behavior of the troops themselves.

One of the objectives that Goodpaster highlighted was to rekindle a sense of duty. "For the last year, efforts have been under way to foster cadet development of a military sense of duty. Discussions with cadets and members of the staff and faculty have helped to produce the attached paper, which seeks to give focus and direction to this essential aspect of becoming an officer."[16] As superintendent, he obviously was talking about taking the entire military academy, and not just the cadet corps, back to "first principles."

This reveals how Goodpaster realized the importance of forming or changing attitudes, both institutional and personal. Here is an example:

> What is "duty" in this sense? Though an understanding of its full meaning can only be approached through a lifetime of study and experience, its basic principle is well and simply conveyed in "doing what ought to be done." An unremitting internal urge to act in all things in this way is the first requirement and serves as a distinguishing mark of the exemplary officer and officer-to-be. But given even this strong desire, the individual quickly confronts a second essential: to know where duty lies; that is, to know how to assess and decide what it is that "ought to be done."[17]

An example of how Goodpaster altered the outlook, rather than discrediting outright an undesirable practice, is the matter of competition. "As I put it, rather than emphasizing the competition with each other, think about it like a game of golf where you are going up against the course, competing against the course, not against each other. The whole idea is to do as well as you can with the tasks at hand and not to elbow your way ahead of this fellow officer or that fellow officer. . . . The role of senior leadership is to decide where that dividing line—dividing area—begins to occur, where the thing begins to get corrupted as we know it had been corrupted."[18]

Goodpaster explained how he approached his task of restoring integrity to where the nation's core Army leadership is nurtured as well as educated:

> First, [the program] centers on cadets. Cadets are the product of West Point and they measure the value of the contribution of the institution. Second, it is purpose-oriented, because there has to be

a clear concept of purpose, which everyone at West Point can recognize and work toward. It emphasizes a combined experience, one that is a combination of intellectual, military, physical, and moral-ethical experience. It is need-oriented because West Point must look at what the Army requires and to what our nation needs in the way of security and defense activities, which these officers-to-be will be responsible for directing and leading.[19]

In his remarks when he assumed command at West Point, Goodpaster concluded by saying: "We will face our problems with confidence and resolution, with integrity, justice, and human understanding and, not the least, with good humor and good will. Our common standard will be excellence. Our common inspiration will be duty, honor and country."[20]

One especially delicate task with which Goodpaster had to deal was the introduction of women into the cadet corps. He addressed and rejected the idea of putting the women in a separate barracks. Instead: "The real point is that if we are going to have an Army with women in it—and we have and we are going to continue to have—then officers in their pre-officer training should learn how to work in an Army which integrates the services of men and women. It becomes very important to do that during this preparatory period."[21]

It is not necessary to recount every change in procedures or in emphasis that took place during Goodpaster's four-year tenure, except to point out that he simplified the chain of command so that the senior officers in the administration became responsive to cadet self-governance to the extent that this was possible. Another area that he emphasized was that academics were as important as athletics—it seemed that the offending cadets would not have cheated on the playing field, yet they did in the classroom. Goodpaster viewed this as an erosion of values.

Even though the institution of the "military academy" was preserved, the glamour of West Point had lost some of its burnish. Tradition without substance—in other words, an empty shell—was worse than nothing. Goodpaster would have been painfully aware that the cheating scandal had drained the substance out of the tradition—at least temporarily.

In a way, this was mirrored in the perennial debate over football at West Point: is achieving fame and athletic respect by winning on the football field a useful symbol of military leadership—the true payoff of which would be winning in war? Conversely, would losing continually convey another kind of symbol, one that would not be congenial to Goodpaster and his contemporaries, who had graduated just at the eve of the greatest war ever fought?

To every superintendent, honorable conduct in the classroom was a vital aspect of leadership; dishonor, inversely, would discredit this effort to teach personal responsibility by example and deed. As it was affirmed, "The strength of the system . . . is that it belongs to the Corps of Cadets; it is theirs to manage; it is as good as they collectively and individually wish to make it."[22] Put another way, it doesn't take much to turn a positive symbol into a most undesirable symbol.

This was at the core of Goodpaster's tenure as the academy's chief executive and chief symbol of leadership and command behavior. He recognized this responsibility when he declared that "no one will take the Honor Code away from the cadets and this should be known to them. The Honor Code and its well-being is a shared responsibility. One of my prime responsibilities is to look after the well-being of the Honor Code. But this responsibility cannot be accomplished without the wholehearted support of the code by the cadets."[23]

Finally, on a more personal note, returning to West Point held special meaning for both Andy and his wife, Dossy Anderson Goodpaster—they had met there when she was living on the post with her father while he was a member of the staff and Goodpaster was a cadet. They married soon after he graduated, and the marriage truly unfolded in the best traditions of an Army family.

Conclusions

The Soldier-Scholar in the National Security Policy Process

"The increasing role of the American professional military officer in the foreign policy process has presented unique problems for the foreign policy planner and for the professional military officer as well."

—DONALD F. BLETZ, *The Role of the Military Professional in U.S. Foreign Policy*

The mix of presidential politics, wartime exigencies, and personal ambition can possibly trip up promising young officers serving either in or near the White House. They become more engrossed in their personal ambitions than the circumstances warrant. Yet there are other talented young officers, among whom was Andrew Goodpaster, who can enter into this particular career situation and emerge not only unscathed, but also even for the better, both career-wise and personally.

An Unambiguously Professional Officer

Goodpaster had received assignments at the international level from the very beginning of his career. He assisted in the formation of NATO, the most formidable military alliance in history, even crafting the general order creating its military component. From there, he moved in and out of national, international, and multinational assignments, developing an outlook that served him well both as staff secretary and defense liaison officer to President Eisenhower in the 1950s, and as NATO's supreme allied commander, Europe, in the 1970s.

Although Goodpaster had worked closely with Republican presidents, he steadfastly maintained his political neutrality concerning his own personal ambitions. He saw himself as, first and foremost, a serving officer in the U.S. Army. In this respect, he was reflecting the professional values of George Marshall. An example of Marshall's careful integrity was when

141

he went out of his way to protest, when accepting the appointment as President Truman's secretary of state, that "I am assuming that the office of Secretary of State, at least under present conditions, is non-political and I am going to govern myself accordingly."[1]

Goodpaster could look back on his years with Eisenhower—and his career in general—with sincere satisfaction. He had played a substantial role in enabling Eisenhower to declare in his last formal report to Congress:

> On January 20, 1953, when I took office, the United States was at war. Since the signing of the Korean Armistice in 1953, Americans have lived in peace in highly troubled times. . . . The nation can ill afford to abandon a national policy which provides for a fully adequate and steady level of effort, designed for the long pull; a fast adjustment to new scientific and technological advances; a balanced force of such strength as to deter general war, to effectively meet local situations and to retaliate to attack and destroy the attacker; and a strengthened system of free world collective security.[2]

Because Goodpaster entered the White House as a junior colonel and left it as a brigadier general, he could not cope at times on a completely equal footing with the various three- and four-star officers who had dealings with the White House, and especially those flag officers who were engaged in the sometimes fierce debates over the New Look and its budgetary implications. It could have been especially awkward for him in regard to those senior Army generals disaffected by Eisenhower's definition of "roles and missions." Even though he was close to Eisenhower on a day-to-day basis, Goodpaster appraised the nature of the dissent not as acts of disloyalty to the commander-in-chief, but rather as part of ongoing and ever-changing interservice deliberations. Eisenhower, in contrast, was openly more than annoyed with his former Army colleagues.[3]

Perhaps more significantly, Goodpaster was, in his unfolding relationship with Eisenhower, engaged de facto in the formation of what is today an extensive White House–based national security policy-making apparatus. In contrast to many of his successors, who achieved their White House status in part because of their political ties, Goodpaster regarded political considerations to be largely irrelevant to the successful execution of his duties. This does not mean, however, that he was insensitive to the kind of politics that of necessity must be ever present at this highest level of government.[4] Eisenhower commented on this point in his final report to the secretary of the Army regarding Goodpaster: "In his post of White House Staff Secretary he handles, quite naturally, exceedingly important, delicate and sensitive material, most of which ultimately comes to my attention."[5]

A Practitioner of Strategy and Policy

Goodpaster's success in maintaining his professional and service-oriented integrity while in the White House is exemplified by the fact that thereafter both Republican and Democratic presidents sought his advice. As it was put: "No longer adviser to the commander in chief, Goodpaster contributed to national security policy during these years as a troop commander, planner, and negotiator."[6] In fact, he was "on call" ever after.

For example, when McGeorge Bundy, first Kennedy's and then Johnson's national security advisor, organized an important mission to Saigon in February 1965, he included Goodpaster in the party. He was at that time assistant to the chairman of the JCS. This trip coincided with the Vietcong attack on the airfield at Pleiku, which meant that these important participants in the formulation of Vietnam war policy witnessed a huge propaganda victory for their enemy. "A barrage of mortar rounds caused explosions that killed eight American servicemen, wounded more than one hundred others, and set fire to twenty aircraft on the airstrip. Goodpaster and Bundy accompanied General Westmoreland to the site of the attack. The airfield was in shambles."[7]

How Goodpaster felt about this is not clear, but he was always inclined to measure battlefield events from the twin assessments of whether success was possible, and what price would be exacted to achieve that success. He understood the complexity and the tentativeness of decision-making at the highest level of government. In this sense, his innate modesty served him well.[8]

Although President Johnson had already decided to bomb North Vietnam, Pleiku brought home the destructive reality of the war—it was no longer just a matter of quantitative assessments from within the orderly confines of the White House or the Pentagon. Not only were strategic decisions being made within the tight political circle around Johnson, without input from the JCS, the JCS were being given only token acknowledgement of their responsibilities. This is one reason why Goodpaster believed that the military did not "lose" Vietnam—his view was that, under Johnson, there was no real opportunity to pursue the war as the military planners would have wished. He tended to agree with the school of military thought that argued for an all-out effort to achieve victory, rather than adopting a posture of "graduated response."

In contrast to Eisenhower (and Goodpaster), "[Kennedy] would refuse to consider or even to acknowledge the consequences of his decisions, and thus still imagined that he could pursue a policy of gradual escalation without involving the United States in a major war."[9]

Goodpaster's honesty took precedence over pandering to the prevailing public sentiment, such as when Gen. Earle Wheeler, then chairman of the JCS, asked Goodpaster "to establish what the United States would have to do to win the war in South Vietnam 'if we do everything we can.' Goodpaster's lengthy report envisioned the possible need for seven to thirty-five American battalions above and beyond the thirty-four American battalions called for in the forty-four battalion request."[10] The additional troops were not, of course provided, and this lay behind Goodpaster's feeling that the United States lost its "will" rather than its means, to achieve its war aims in Southeast Asia.

Goodpaster's unassuming manner, quiet courteousness, and serious yet not heavy demeanor fitted in well with whatever professional situation in which he found himself. This is why he was so highly regarded in all quarters. Perhaps not coincidentally, at every stage in Goodpaster's military career, he attracted the support of persons influential in furthering his interests. These associations also enabled Goodpaster to continue to participate in foreign and military policy discussions during his many post-Army years of unofficial and semiofficial activity.

While on active duty, he was able to inspire the confidence and even admiration of his troops at whatever level of command, and as a civilian, he was able to articulate policy issues persuasively at the highest political level. There were four areas of the security environment, according to Goodpaster, that were especially important. First was the "*paramount importance of national security.* Self-preservation is the first law of life," he argued. As a result, "government," he believed, "should be organized and run so as to place national security in the highest order of priority." The second key element was "*the dynamism of the security environment,* the constant change that is encountered with new technology, the rise of new nations, new factions, new leaders, the changing of old alliances and power arrangements, the rise of new interests, the secular shifts which take place as new generations mature which have not been marked by the problems of their predecessors." These forces naturally contributed to the third aspect, "*the factor of complexity.*" Nothing was simple when it came to matters of national security, which only are achieved through an intricate and inherently unstable process. "The fourth point to remember," declared Goodpaster was that, "in the security environment is that *it takes place within a political framework on both the domestic and international sides.* This [domestic] arena is rarely one in which the military officer will feel comfortable. . . . These are the issues in which the military is most likely to run afoul of the so-called 'politicization' of their advice and support. . . . The military man is an *advisor* [Goodpaster's emphasis here; author's emphasis in other instances above]."[11]

Goodpaster successfully carved out for himself a notable niche in America's Cold War history, and even beyond. Geoffrey Blainey observed, referring to Britain's Lord Palmerston and Germany's chancellor Otto von Bismarck in an earlier Great Power period: "It is vital to enquire how much of their influence came from their personalities and policies, how much from the contemporary international situation, and how much from their superior military backing."[12] In Goodpaster's case, his personality dovetailed with the manner in which he performed both as a trusted aide to and as a collaborator with Eisenhower.

A Final Comment

The purpose in writing this biography is to place Goodpaster where he belongs among the annals of the soldier-scholars of his historical period. Goodpaster excelled at (1) command at the highest military level; (2) command in combat; (3) leadership at the highest political levels; (4) cogent analysis of men and events. There are military figures who have excelled in one or another of these accomplishments, but few who excelled in all four.[13]

The histories of the Cold War that have been written—and those yet to be written—may not necessarily have Goodpaster listed in their indexes, yet he was one of the key figures during that ongoing crisis—one who remained behind the dominant personalities of those times, whether military or political (or both). Then later, he stood at the forefront himself, not only in regard to Vietnam and NATO, but also in restoring the integrity of West Point during a major ethical crisis. His presence on the Washington scene was always welcome, even in those instances in which he was be a dissenting voice in some policy debate.

Given the strains to the national fabric that warfare can impose on a society, and given that in his time the Cold War appeared to be endless,

Goodpaster and his contemporaries in the governing process were fortunate to conduct their affairs "[largely] under a set of conditions in which an able civilian government maintained national interests by effective diplomacy [and] closely supported by a capable military who were willing to remain in their proper place."[14] Goodpaster witnessed this process almost daily before, during, and after his years in and around the White House and the Pentagon.

In conclusion, the military historian Donald Kagan observed that "Thucydides . . . understood war as the armed competition for power . . . 'by a necessity of their nature [human beings] rule as far as their power permits.' . . . In the struggle for power, whether for a rational sufficiency or in the insatiable drive for all the power there is, Thucydides found that people go to war out of 'honor, fear, and interest.'"[15] Gen. Andrew Jackson Goodpaster was a modern-day soldier who understood the human motivations that underlie the persistence of armed warfare in human affairs, even while engaging in a career that embraced the technological complexities of contemporary war.

This biography intends not to celebrate an era; rather, its purpose is to celebrate a noteworthy figure of that era. Even so, as the historian Robert Conquest, put it: "I am well aware that there is much more to be said on the themes I have covered; and that there are important issues which I have passed by, or barely touched on."[16]

Afterword

Gen. Andrew J. "Andy" Goodpaster, USA, was a person who defied the cliché "soldier statesman" by actually being one; he was also a consummate organizer, diplomat, humanist, and friend to so many.

I met him late in his career and regretted all those lost years and experiences, but I had known of him for decades, as the quiet, unassuming man who was "present at the creation" so many times, and who was both adviser to and steadying influence for many of modern American history's more famous leaders. For so long, if one of these leaders, with a sense of the nation's destiny and of the need to get the job done and done right, was in need of the best possible counsel, he would call upon Andy Goodpaster to do what had to be done, to bring along those who had to be engaged, to smooth down ruffled feathers, and to apply good old-fashioned integrity to the most difficult and challenging of situations.

It was not for nothing that Ike, himself one of the superb political talents in uniform, called on Goodpaster to organize and operate the apparatus in the White House that was needed to enable the president to be president in his commander-in-chief hat. It was not for nothing that Goodpaster was sent to Europe as supreme allied commander at a time when the allies needed reassurance that America was truly "over here" and the rock-solid provider of security for Europe. It was not for nothing that he was called to straighten out unfortunate goings-on at the U.S. Military Academy, and that, in his semiretirement, he was called upon to make something of the Atlantic Council of the United States—and while there saw the glimmerings of possibilities in working with the Soviet Union; not just in containing it, but in building new relationships in security that have, indeed, stood the test of time through the period of the USSR's collapse and some new and hopeful—though as yet unfulfilled—prospects in a NATO-Russia relations.

Some of America's premier leaders, in and out of uniform, have believed that they have had to raise their voices in order to be heard, much less to be obeyed. Andy Goodpaster was the opposite. He always carried with him a "zone of quiet" that was infectious in calming the most troubled spirits and the most difficult circumstances. He spoke under the turmoil, not over it, with his precise, understated logic, taking apart the complexities of argument and then reassembling the key elements with clarity and coherence; and he was listened to, always.

In the process, he never stood on ceremony, or invoked his rank, or traded on his comprehensive array of people known or jobs held or results achieved (while making sure that the credit got spread around, himself avoiding the limelight rather than trying to hog it). He always had time for those whom the world might regard as unimportant but in whom Andy would see potential, who could and should be nurtured, and who would make a signal contribution to the nation's well-being, if not today, still being so junior, surely tomorrow.

Isaac Newton said, "If I have seen further it is by standing on the shoulders of giants." Andy Goodpaster did often "see further," but never claimed the credit for doing so. But unimpeachable is the fact that he was surely in the company of those "giants" with unassuming but strong shoulders that helped others to see what had to be done and have the courage to do it. And he set a style and lived a life of character that may have too much faded of late, but still forms the bedrock of the best that is in the American soul, always has been, and always will be if this great nation is to persevere and prosper.

We are all better off that the newly minted Army second lieutenant Andrew J. Goodpaster took the oath on the plain at West Point in 1939 and then served, and served, and served his nation and the Western Alliance for so long and so well. Those of us who had the chance to know and work with him and to benefit from his unforced, unpretentious wisdom have gained an "increased devotion" to do those things that matter most because of the trust, and kindness, and counsel, and friendship of this good man, this great American.

Ambassador Robert E. Hunter
U.S. Permanent Representative to the North Atlantic Council
The RAND Corporation

Appendix

Contributions to Public and Voluntary Service

I. Voluntary Service: St. Mary's College*

General Andrew Goodpaster was appointed to the St. Mary's College of Maryland Board of Trustees in 1987. He was reappointed in 1992, serving for a total of twelve years. He served as Vice Chair of the Board of Trustees and Chair of the Academic Affairs Committee, as a member of the Committee on Historic St. Mary's City, and as Chair of the Task Force on St. Mary's Programs of Study Abroad in the aftermath of an attack on students and faculty in a College sponsored study tour to Guatemala in January 1998. The Task Force worked in parallel with a criminal suit brought by the College against perpetrators of the crime in Guatemala.

As Chair of the Task Force, General Goodpaster oversaw a comprehensive appraisal of the College's programs, reviewing in particular the policies and procedures safeguarding students' health and safety. The membership of the Task Force included faculty, staff, students and trustees of the College, as well as the parents of the students attacked.

The Task Force began its work in March 1998 and completed its report to the Board of Trustees and the St. Mary's Community the following May, recommending several changes to improve safeguards. The Task Force advanced the community's confidence in study abroad programs and underscored the College's willingness to review and revise procedures to anticipate and meet risks.

As Chair of the Academic Affairs Committee, he established the system for faculty compensation based on reaching the mid-point of salaries for a select group of peer institutions. The system also is applied to staff salaries as well. The application of this method has created an expectation of fairness for compensation and, although disputes arise from time to time, discussions are rooted in objective criteria and focused on data that is collected, analyzed, and distributed regularly.

The College's faculty leave of absence program was also a product of the Academic Affairs Committee during General Goodpaster's tenure, and

---

* Prepared for C. Richard Nelson by St. Mary's president Margaret O'Brien, dated 2 June 2010. Used with permission.

this program has been particularly important to the scholarship opportunities awarded to St. Mary's faculty for career development and renewal.

As Vice Chair of the Board, he chaired the Presidential search of 1996, which attracted Dr. Jane Margaret O'Brien to the College. Under her leadership, the College rose in national rankings to within the first tier liberal arts colleges, and a period of student, residential and academic expansion was undertaken that included the development of a new General Education curriculum with international programs available for students in England, Italy, Gambia, Thailand, Vietnam and China.

During the College's $40 million Heritage Campaign, the College developed a close relationship with neighboring Historic St. Mary's City. General Goodpaster served with Ben Bradlee, Vice President at large of the *Washington Post* and Chair of the Historic St. Mary's City Commissioners, to resurrect interest in the shared missions of the College and St. Mary's City and to encourage cooperation and collaboration. Governor Parris Glendening and the Maryland General Assembly subsequently committed $60 million to the Maryland Heritage Project in support of the College's and the City's joint planning initiatives. The Heritage Project enabled the College to reorganize its residential and academic campus, which led to the spatial restructuring of the historic campus to accommodate a new visitor's complex on land adjoining and including a portion of Historic St. Mary's City.

The College gained national attention as a public honors college largely due to the courage and prescience of the Board of Trustees, which in 1992 proposed St. Mary's College as Maryland's Public Honors College. General Goodpaster, Johns Hopkins University President Emeritus Steven Muller, Senator Benjamin Cardin, Ambassador Paul Nitze, Terry Meyerhoff Rubenstein, Ben Bradlee, Harry Weitzel, Tom Waring and Governor William Donald Schaefer were among the key Trustees leading the College's initiative to create this unique public-private model of higher education that has been a model for many other States.

In 1998, the College established the Andrew J. Goodpaster Endowed Leadership and Honor Lecture Series in General Goodpaster's honor. The first lecturer was General Goodpaster's close friend and fellow Presidential advisor, Lt. General Brent Scowcroft, who said in his opening remarks what many at the College also felt, that General Goodpaster was his hero. This sentiment was deeply felt by all who served alongside General Goodpaster as Trustees. He inspired the Board to do its best and the College flourished in many ways under his gentle guidance and careful direction.

Before his death in 2005, the Trustees announced that the new academic building would be named in his honor. He was deeply appreciative of the honor. The Andrew J. Goodpaster building at St. Mary's College houses psychology, education and several important lecture halls. It was dedicated a year after General Goodpaster's death, with Lt. General Scowcroft serving as the invited speaker for the dedicatory remarks.

General Goodpaster's granddaughter Sarah Nesnow was exceptionally helpful in providing for the Heritagescapes story that graces the grand foyer and tells the story of General Goodpaster's dedication to his country, to West Point, and to the College he helped launch in to its finest hours as a public honors college for the State of Maryland.

In summary, General Goodpaster was the undisputed conscience of the Board during his tenure and helped to assure the College's rise in stature as it sought to define a new level of achievement for a model of public-private partnership in higher education.

II. Public Policy Participant: The Atlantic Council[*]
Chair, 1985–1997

The two areas of foreign policy that Goodpaster cared most about—his own "blue chips"—were nuclear weapons and Russia. It was in these areas that he made his greatest contribution during the final two decades of his life.

On Nuclear Weapons

Goodpaster thought that it was not helpful to lump nuclear, chemical, and biological weapons in the same category as "weapons of mass destruction" because each posed quite different threats and called for different responses. Deterring conventional, biological, or even chemical attacks should be left to other, non-nuclear means, while the main function of nuclear weapons still was to deter the use of nuclear weapons by others. Such deterrence had to rely on a credible capacity for instant, devastating response.

His thinking on nuclear weapons was based on personal experience in more than a dozen high-level strategic, policy, and command positions spanning most of the Cold War. For Goodpaster, thinking about nuclear weapons was not merely an intellectual exercise; he was often faced with thinking through the consequences of their use in a wide variety of specific situations, from the time he served with Eisenhower when nuclear weapons became the definitive dimension of the Cold War, to his own tenure as Supreme Allied Commander in the early 1970s, when he had several thousand such weapons under his command.

It once was common to think of nuclear weaponry as just one more tool in the arsenal of modern warfare. But it became increasingly clear to Goodpaster, and to his boss Eisenhower, that the tremendous destructive power of such weapons, particularly with the advent of thermonuclear weapons, made it very difficult to conceive of using nuclear weapons as a rational instrument for the pursuit of any national objectives other than survival.

Setting Goodpaster apart from many other military thinkers was his ability to place problems in a global and longer-term context. He often found himself arguing against more simplistic thinking that more weapons are better, especially if they were enhanced with the latest technology. Using this logic, there would never be enough, given the dynamics of Cold

---

*   This is adapted and edited from a larger tribute to General Goodpaster, written shortly after his death in 2006, by C. Richard Nelson and Kenneth Weisbrode, who were associated with him at the Atlantic Council. Used with permission.

War competition.[1] By contrast, Goodpaster persistently pressed the issue of clearly defining the proper roles and limitations for nuclear weaponry.

Goodpaster continued to insist after the collapse of the Soviet Union that nuclear weapons were not useful in war-fighting and that the existing inventories could be safely reduced. The challenge was to determine by how much and how fast this could happen.

Much of his thinking in this area was presented in a series of Atlantic Council Papers known collectively as the *Further Reins on Nuclear Arms* series. In these papers, Goodpaster developed the criteria that would be necessary to reduce safely nuclear inventories of the United States and Russia to successively lower levels. He said that he could not foresee for the indefinite future ever reducing beyond a few hundred weapons, because this would require such a radically different and safer security environment, one inconceivable in his lifetime. Nevertheless, he encouraged analyses that addressed the requisites of a nuclear weapons–free world, because this remained the desired objective of the international community.[2]

In addressing the prospects for a "zero level" of nuclear weapons, Goodpaster took a middle road between the nuclear "abolitionists"—whose ultimate goals he shared—and the skeptics, whose prudence he respected. He concluded that the international stability and confidence required for abolition to work had to be built and sustained before the levels of stockpiles reached zero. Drawing down arsenals on a pragmatic, negotiated, multilateral basis could go a long way toward building that trust, while hedging against the possible breakout by one or more nations.

Goodpaster never denied that states could reconstitute nuclear weapons capabilities rather easily.[3] In order to counter that likelihood, and to take advantage of a once in a lifetime opportunity presented by the end of the Cold War, Goodpaster advocated a five-power nuclear agreement to reduce stockpiles down to the lowest acceptable levels. He feared that, absent such an agreement, Cold War–era restraints on nuclear proliferation would give way to new strategic arms races in volatile regions, notably the Middle East and East Asia.

Goodpaster would probably say that it is not too late to stem the tide again. Indeed, he kept working on this issue up to the very end of his life.

On Post-Soviet Russia

Goodpaster knew several of the Soviet military leaders personally from his tenure as NATO SACEUR, and he continued those associations after the Cold War. He was also one of the first Americans to take seriously the changes proposed by Mikhail Gorbachev and was instrumental in convincing the Reagan administration to embrace them. He later believed that it was essential for the United States to understand the problems facing Russia, and to accord its leaders proper respect at a time when cooperation with the United States was highly controversial. In particular, he was concerned about the Russian military and with transforming *its* thinking about NATO.

Five years before the collapse of the Soviet Union, Goodpaster initiated a series of semiannual meetings between Atlantic Council representatives and leading Soviet strategic thinkers. This exchange was expanded to include Ukraine after 1991. These dialogues were useful in assuaging the feelings of isolation and humiliation of many former Soviet leaders. The exchanges addressed nuclear weapons, missile defense, conventional forces in Europe, and other issues that were important in promoting a more stable, peaceful environment. They treated security in a broad sense, including creating a more favorable climate for foreign investment, tax reform, fighting corruption, commercial codes, intellectual property, privatization, and other issues. Their efforts forged new ties in the direction of greater prosperity, democracy, and peaceful relations.

Early in these exchanges, Goodpaster noted that while Russia still had the rights of a Great Power, it also had responsibilities. (To a lesser extent, this was true of Ukraine as well, and the Goodpaster meetings contributed directly to the Ukrainian government's decision to remove its nuclear warheads to Russia.) He urged Russians to participate in NATO's Partnership for Peace (PfP, a program he helped to originate), so that Russia's voice would be heard within as well as outside NATO. This was a difficult case to argue because many Russian leaders still saw NATO as the great enemy. To help make his case, Goodpaster sought to establish an "overarching framework" of friendship and cooperation between the United States, NATO, and Russia.

Although Partnership for Peace was eclipsed by NATO enlargement and the interventions in Bosnia and Kosovo—actions that produced in Goodpaster feelings that were mixed, to say the least—it nevertheless laid the groundwork for a post–Cold War European security system that showed every sign of succeeding in the long run.

On Public Service

One of Goodpaster's favorite quotations was one he attributed to his former boss, General Marshall, "You'd be amazed to see how much a man gets done if he doesn't seek credit."[4] Goodpaster probably envisioned himself as a conveyor or facilitator of ideas rather than as the emblematic "soldier-intellectual." He would urge his staff to forgo labeling this or that idea, saying, "The important thing is just to get it out there." Goodpaster sought results over posturing. For him, ideas were not sufficient unless they were translated into actions.

To the unfamiliar observer, Goodpaster's writings and thoughts may sound rather conventional or dry. With the exception of his public call in 1996 for the elimination of nuclear weapons, few made headlines or sent shock waves through the bureaucracy. This was the secret of their success. His was a form of constructive, independent thinking for action. As a result, he moved the debate forward on many key issues with a steady, yet subtle, persistence. His impact was measured in decades, not news cycles.

Notes

1. Goodpaster noted that just after World War II, military leaders thought a handful of nuclear weapons would be sufficient.
2. See Andrew J. Goodpaster, *Further Reins on Nuclear Arms: Next Steps for the Major Nuclear Powers.* Atlantic Council Policy Paper, Consultation Paper Series, August 1993.
3. Ibid., p. 21.
4. The quotation has also been attributed to Dwight Morrow and Jean Monnet.

III. International Public Policy: The International Institute for Strategic Studies (IISS)*

An Appreciation from Abroad

I came to know General Goodpaster through the International Institute for Strategic Studies (IISS), of which we were both members. He, of course, was a very senior member of the Institute and I, a generation younger, had yet to make my mark. But the Institute had a broad span of members, not only in international terms—some eighty countries were represented in its membership in the late 1970s—but also in terms of age and profession. These were great strengths, and they helped to propel the Institute from very humble beginnings as a British research and discussion group in 1958 to one which, by the mid-1960s, spanned the NATO membership but also included several other closely associated countries, such as my own Australia.

The Institute was well suited to the kind of discussions in which General Goodpaster shone. There was no doubting his professional standing as a man with a distinguished record of military service during the Second World War and the Cold War. Moreover, he had what many of his contemporaries lacked at that time: serious intellectual credentials in the form of a PhD from Princeton.

He was used to the cut and thrust of debate that challenged basic assumptions, such as the utility of nuclear weapons for the defense of Western Europe. He did not tighten up when under challenge from his juniors, or rely on his seniority to buttress a point that others did not hold. He was well-informed, not behind the times in terms of what was appearing in leading journals, books and newspapers. He was skeptical about much of what others claimed to be the right approach to this issue or that. Furthermore, he respected the rights of others to be skeptical about positions that he held, or had to defend publicly because of the official position he held as Supreme Allied Commander, Europe (SACEUR). Continuous study was part of his life and had been for decades.

There can be no doubt that Goodpaster's impact on others was reinforced by his appearance and his engaged but relaxed nature. His height and figure revealed a man who kept himself physically fit. His penchant for wearing tartan trousers certainly won him favorable attention from those of us of Scottish descent. And in conversation he displayed a ready sense of

---

* Written by Dr. Robert O'Neill, Chichele Professor of the History of War, Emeritus, All Souls College, Oxford University; former Director, International Institute for Strategic Studies (London).

156

humor and was quick to appreciate a lighter point made by others to whom he was talking.

As I came to know the views of other generals of other NATO countries I could see that several, but far from all, of them were basically skeptical about the pillars on which western security rested in the middle and later decades of the Cold War. And of course later, as we know, General Goodpaster came out publicly in advocating the elimination of nuclear weapons. One wonders how early he came to espouse this view, and whether the kind of fundamental debates that sometimes were held by the IISS at its conferences had contributed to this direction in his thinking?

Certainly, he advocated the development of strong conventional forces by NATO members as the best way to maintain security against any possible Warsaw Pact move against the West. In doing this he recognized that several NATO governments would resist his arguments to make a greater contribution of conventional forces for the common good. Nonetheless, he sustained his beliefs and policies, even when in discussion with allies whom he regarded as free-riders. For myself, having been a Captain in an Australian infantry battalion in the Vietnam War, I found his emphasis on conventional force development and operational methods very welcome. The Vietnam War at least had some good effect in giving a wide range of U.S. and allied soldiers cause to lift their standards both in terms of operating against an enemy and in the delicate process of relating with a civil population over which the war was being fought.

I did not know much about General Goodpaster while I was in Vietnam because our periods of service there did not overlap. Also, he was too far above me, while not in the public eye in the way that Generals Westmoreland and Abrams were. Nonetheless, it was apparent that, by the early 1970s when I first had contact with him *via* the IISS, Goodpaster was not happy with some of the approaches to counter-insurgency taken by the Johnson Administration. He felt that Johnson was trying too hard to perform a political juggling act and was thereby failing to devote sufficient resources to winning the war.

Goodpaster was a maximalist rather than a "light-touch" counter-insurgent. At the same time, he could see that it had become very difficult for the U.S. to provide a massive increase in its forces on the ground in Vietnam because of the needs of other theatres, especially Europe. He seemed to be glad that his period in Vietnam as General Abrams' deputy was only a year. The top military post in NATO was much more to his taste than fighting the Vietnam War.

After his first retirement in 1974, Goodpaster was able to utilize the links with the university and think-tank community that he had begun to build up while he was SACEUR. My former mentor and friend Norman Gibbs at Oxford spoke highly of Goodpaster's contributions to the annual NATO conference that Gibbs and others at Oxford ran each spring or summer. He was a frequent participant in the major research institute conferences on international security on both sides of the Atlantic. By the late 1970s, there were many security intellectuals in Europe and North America who thought that a general with a PhD was a great asset and that there should be more of them! General Goodpaster set a career example for many of us in the security analysis business, both military and otherwise. Briefly put, he did the standing of the United States in this community a great power of good.

In 1981, General Goodpaster was elected a Vice-President of the IISS, and he attended Council meetings until he stepped down at his own request in March 1989. I was the Director of the Institute from 1982 to 1987, and was very grateful to have had the General's advice and encouragement throughout this period. He made a remarkable contribution in so many ways to rational thinking on international security questions for over fifty years.[1]

Notes

1. General Goodpaster was also affiliated at times and in various ways with the George C. Marshall Foundation, the Woodrow Wilson International Center for Scholars, The Citadel, The Institute for Defense Analyses, and the Center for Strategic and International Studies. There is also the Andrew J. Goodpaster Prize and Lecture awarded by the American Veterans Center, and the Andrew J. Goodpaster Award of the George C. Marshall Foundation.

Notes

Foreword

1. A. J. Goodpaster, "Oral History of the Superintendency of Gen. A. J. Goodpaster, USA (Ret.)," interviewed by Lt. Col. James M. Johnson, USA (Ret.), Department of History, U.S. Military Academy (USMA), n.d., p. 93.
2. Floyd W. Matson, *The Broken Image: Man, Science, and Society* (New York: Anchor Books, 1966), p. 236.

Preface

1. William B. Pickett, "General Andrew Jackson Goodpaster: Managing National Security," in *The Human Tradition in America since 1945*, ed. David L. Anderson (Wilmington, DE: Scholarly Books, 2003), p. 26.

Chapter 1. The Professional Foundation

1. Stephen E. Ambrose, *Ike's Spies: Eisenhower and the Espionage Establishment* (Jackson, MS: University Press of Mississippi, 1999), p. 307.
2. Stephen Hess, *Presidents and the Presidency* (Washington, DC: The Brookings Institution, 1996), pp. 17–18.
3. Hans Gerth and C. Wright Mills, *Character and Social Structure: The Psychology of Social Institutions* (New York: Harcourt, Brace and World, 1953), p. 412.
4. Andrew J. Goodpaster, Oral History interview, by Dr. Maclyn P. Burg, 20 August 1976, Eisenhower Presidential Library, p. 23.
5. Wallace Stegner, "The Writer and the Concept of Adulthood," in *Adulthood*, ed. Erik H. Erikson (New York: W. W. Norton, 1978), p. 227.
6. Andrew J. Goodpaster, transcript of filmed interview by Ken Mandel and James McCall, Great Projects Film Company, Atlantic Council, 31 July–1 August 2001; 15–16 January 2002; 11–12 February 2004, George C. Marshall Foundation.
7. Ibid.
8. Stephen E. Ambrose, *Rise to Globalism: American Foreign Policy, 1938–1980*, 2nd rev. ed. (New York: Penguin Books, 1980), p. 13. There were U.S. troops in overseas dependencies, such as Alaska, Hawaii, and the Philippines.
9. *Howitzer* (USMA Yearbook), 1939, p. 339.

10. See Edwin A. Deagle, "General George A. Lincoln: Architect of American National Security" unpublished manuscript. Used with permission.

11. Goodpaster, Mandel and McCall interview.

12. Edgar P. Dean, Secretary of Study Groups, Council on Foreign Relations, to Lt. Col. Herman Beukema, USMA, 23 February 1939, George C. Marshall Foundation Research Library, Lexington, VA.

13. During his post-Army years, they maintained a townhouse in Alexandria, Virginia, and a weekend home at Swan Point, Maryland. He tried to divide his time and energies thus: one-third employment, one-third pro-bono activities, and one-third recreation (which included salmon fishing in Labrador each year). I am grateful for the cooperation of Susan Goodpaster Sullivan and granddaughter Sarah Nesnow.

14. Quoted from the paper "Concept for Duty Development," which was transmitted in a memorandum of 16 April 1981, signed by Lieutenant General Goodpaster as superintendent.

15. Ibid. For an interesting background summary of life at West Point over the years, see Edward Cox, *Grey Eminence: Fox Conner and the Art of Mentorship* (Stillwater, OK: New Forums Press, 2011).

16. Simone de Beauvoir, *The Mandarins* (New York: The World Publishing Co., 1956), p. 275.

17. Quoted in David Dimbleby and David Reynolds, *An Ocean Apart: The Relationship between Britain and America in the Twentieth Century* (New York: Random House, 1988), p. 133.

18. Gordon L. Rottman, *U.S. Combat Engineer, 1941–45* (Long Island City, NY: Osprey Publishers, 2010), pp. 38–50. As an illustration of the state of the Army's unpreparedness for global combat, consider: "In mid-1939, the U.S. Army Corps of Engineers numbered less than 800 officers and 6,000 enlisted men in active Regular Army service."

19. Michael Matloff, "The American Approach to War, 1919–1945," in *The Theory and Practice of War*, ed. Michael Howard (London: Cassell, 1965), p. 221.

20. Goodpaster, Mandel and McCall interview.

21. Matloff, "The American Approach to War 1919–1945."

22. Ibid.

23. Ibid.

24. Joseph P. Hobbs, *Dear General: Eisenhower's Wartime Letters to Marshall* (Baltimore: The Johns Hopkins University Press, 1971), pp. 84–85. Marshall was meticulous in his dealings with his professional colleagues, as the following anecdote illustrates. "Then, on January 30 [1944] Eisenhower referred to a rug he had given to Mrs. Marshall: 'So far as I can recall I have never before in my service given a personal present to my superior

or to a member of his family, and I assure you that I regard this as a real privilege.' He discussed the present again on June 26 because Marshall had given the rug to Mrs. Eisenhower as a present from her husband."

25. Stewart W. Husted, *George C. Marshall: Rubrics of Leadership* (Carlisle Barracks, PA: Army War College Foundation, 2006), p. 13. This inclusion was both undated and without a citation, but Husted attributes it to Marshall and it serves as the subtitle to his very readable biography.

26. Goodpaster, Mandel and McCall interview. It is worth noting that these engineers helped build the famed Burma Road. It was part of the 48th Engineer Combat Regiment, which was activated on 25 July 1942 at Camp Gruber.

27. Goodpaster, Mandel and McCall interview, p. 14.

28. Ibid.

29. Capt. Mark Reardon, CE, *The Battalions: History of the 1108th Engineer Combat Group* (publisher unknown, 1945), p. 29. "Demolitions and minefields blocked every avenue of approach; machine gun and mortar positions were well-dug-in—many blasted out of solid rock—and camouflaged to disappear into the rugged scenery. German artillery had registered on all roads, trails, and possible sites for bivouac and assembly area." See also Fifth Army Historical Section, *From the Volturno to the Winter Line 6 October–15 November 1943*, American Forces in Action series (Washington, DC: U.S. Army Center of Military History, 1990), CMH Pub 100–8.

30. Goodpaster, Mandel and McCall interview.

31. Mark Perry, *Partners in Command: George Marshall and Dwight Eisenhower in War and Peace* (New York: The Penguin Press, 2007), p. 231.

32. One of the most fascinating accounts of this operation, as told from the German side, is *Neither Fear nor Hope: The Wartime Career of General Frido Von Senger Und Etterlin, Defender of Cassino*, trans. George Malcolm (London: MacDonald, 1963).

33. Rick Atkinson, *The Day of Battle: The War in Sicily and Italy, 1943–1944* (New York: Henry Holt, 2007), p. 348. This is a dramatic recounting of the entire Rapido operation, in which Goodpaster was deeply involved.

34. For a description of the multiplicity of functions for combat engineers, see Rottman, *U.S. Combat Engineer, 1941–45*, pp. 38–50.

35. Goodpaster, Mandel and McCall interview.

36. Ibid., pp. 17–20. Goodpaster was serving as both the commander of the 48th Division and the 1108th Group. The author has done minor editing of the literal oral interview text. The Fifth Army had initially attacked across the Volturno River on the night of 12 October. The Germans skillfully used the terrain, which was favorable for defense, and retreated to

the next line north (the Barbara Line), which the Allies reached by 2 November.

37. Lt. Col. Andrew J. Goodpaster, "A Message to the Men of the 48th Engineer Combat Battalion," 23 December 1943.

38. Dwight D. Eisenhower, *Crusade in Europe* (Garden City, NY: Doubleday, 1948), p. 210.

39. Reardon, *The Battalions*, p. 31.

40. U.S. Army, Headquarter II Corps, 2210.5/193-SS (AG).

Chapter 2. Professional Planning

1. Andrew J. Goodpaster, interview by Ed Edwin, 25 April 1967, Eisenhower Presidential Library.

2. Goodpaster, Mandel and McCall interview, 15 January 2002, pp. 5–6.

3. Deagle, "General George A. Lincoln," ch. 14, p. 1. Portions of this section, slightly revised, are drawn with permission.

4. Lincoln remained in Washington until 1947, when he became deputy head of West Point's soon-to-be-renamed Department of Social Sciences. In order to return to West Point, he had to accept a two-rank demotion to colonel (having been promoted to major general), which he willingly did. As recalled: "Lincoln's friend and mentor, Colonel Herman Beukema, convinced him that the powerful strategy for intervening in the education of general officers was to equip them for handling political and military high command matters at West Point—not at the military war colleges." Beukema had been head of the department when Goodpaster was a student.

5. Deagle, "General George A. Lincoln."

6. See Ray S. Cline, *United States Army in World War II, The War Department, Washington Command Post: The Operations Division* (Washington, DC: Center of Military History, U.S. Army, 1951), p. 309.

7. Niall Ferguson, Charles S. Maier, Erez Manela, and Daniel J. Sargent, *The 1970s in Perspective* (Cambridge, MA: The Belknap Press of Harvard University Press, 2010), p. 13.

8. See Robert S. Jordan, "The Influence of the British Secretariat Tradition on the Formation of the League of Nations," in *International Administration: Its Evolution and Contemporary Applications*, ed. Robert S. Jordan (New York: Oxford University Press, 1971), pp. 27–50. This same tradition, first introduced into the League of Nations (under Sir Eric Drummond), was incorporated into the NATO International Staff/Secretariat under the leadership of the first secretary-general, Lord Ismay.

9. Andrew Roberts, *Masters and Commanders: How Four Titans Won the War in the West, 1941–1945* (New York: HarperCollins, 2009), p. 114.

10. Cline, *United States Army in World War II*, pp. 94–95.

11. Maj. Jeffrey J. Tierney, USA, "Campaign Planning: A Missing Piece in the Joint Planning Process," Executive Summary, *GlobalSecurity.org*, 1992, http://www.globalsecurity.org/military/library/report/1992/TJJ.htm.

12. Cline, *United States Army in World War II*, p. 337. With the atomic bombing of Hiroshima and Nagasaki, war-fighting planning speedily gave way to postwar planning, including the JWPC: "Only the existence of the State-War-Navy Coordinating Committee and the experience of staff like Colonel Bonesteel's political-military group in the Policy Section made such speed possible" (Ibid., p. 350).

13. Ibid., p. 17.

14. Gen. Andrew Goodpaster, interview by Dr. Thomas Soapes, Oral Historian, 11 October 1977, Eisenhower Presidential Library, p. 63.

15. Ibid.

16. "Information Sheet on the Joint Advanced Study Committee, Office," Joint Chiefs of Staff. The committee was expected to engage in "intensive analysis." See also Memorandum No. 10–15–1, "Advanced Study Group, Plans and Operations Division," War Department General Staff, dated 1 May 1947.

17. Untitled JASC memorandum, 29 November 1950, p. 1.

18. Andrew J. Goodpaster, "Basic Considerations," JASC memorandum, 30 November 1950, p. 1ff.

19. Ibid.

20. Ibid., p. 2; Goodpaster to Col. R. W. Porter, 7 November 1950. Goodpaster also observed: "Because atomic explosives are due, before long, to become a factor in nearly every kind and phase of military activity, some penetrating influences are going to be felt on such matters as balance of forces, 'strategic' vs. 'tactical' courses of action, etc., extending to dispersion of troops on the battlefield, and problems of communications and control, as well as concentration."

21. For a thorough analysis of this dilemma, see the Rockefeller Panel Report, *Prospect for America: The Problems and Opportunities Confronting American Democracy—in Foreign Policy, in Military Preparedness, in Education, in Social and Economic Affairs* (New York: Doubleday and Co., Inc., 1961). Goodpaster's mentor, Abe Lincoln, served on the panel. Goodpaster was assigned to serve as an aide to the vice resident.

22. Goodpaster to Lincoln, p. 4. Goodpaster also noted, wryly: "I am beginning to have some impressions about the military establishment. I can perhaps express them best by stating the extremes, which bound the range within which the truth probably lies. The most striking features to me are the 'diffuseness' . . . and the low current level of intellectual honesty in the sense of willingness and freedom to re-open basic questions."

23. Ibid., p. 3. The British military historian John Keegan termed it "post-heroic" leadership.

24. Goodpaster to Professor Harold Sprout, 8 November 1950.

25. JCS Memorandum: Efficiency Report (Letter), Lt. Col. Andrew J. Goodpaster Jr., o 21739, CE [Corps of Engineers], period 24 June 1950 to 4 January 1951.

26. Goodpaster, Mandel and McCall interview, 31 July–1 August 2001.

27. Goodpaster to Brodie, 7 January 1947.

28. Goodpaster, Mandel and McCall interview, 31 July–1 August 2001.

29. For example, even though the author had not taken a seminar from him, when it came time to choose where to write his doctoral dissertation— Harvard or Oxford—Professor Sprout stepped forward with an introduction to two key Oxonians, Professor Norman Gibbs of All Souls College, and Sir William Deakin, the warden of St. Antony's College. The author became a member of St. Antony's College, and Professor Gibbs became his dissertation adviser, and later, with the intervention of Professor Max Beloff of All Souls College, the Oxford University Press published the dissertation.

30. Goodpaster may have noted that the warden of Princeton's Graduate College had stones from the garden walls of both Cambridge and Oxford Universities embedded in the wall of his private garden. Also, when he would "dine in," Goodpaster would have worn the black commoner's gown similar to those worn at these two venerable British universities.

31. Letter, Sprout to Goodpaster, 20 March 1955, and reply, Goodpaster to Sprout, 28 March 1955. It took only this one week to get the policy changed.

32. The author was president of APGA at that time, and so conveyed to Goodpaster his medal.

33. Andrew J. Goodpaster, "National Technology and International Politics" (unpublished doctoral dissertation, Department of Politics, Princeton University, May 1950), pp. 1–9.

34. Robert Heilbroner has stated it in similar terms: "Technological determinism is peculiarly a product of a certain historic epoch . . . in which the forces of technical change have been unleashed, but when the agencies for the control or guidance of technology are still rudimentary." Quoted in Charles W. Yost, *History and Memory: A Statesman's Perceptions of the Twentieth Century* (New York: W. W. Norton, 1980), p. 199.

35. Goodpaster, "National Technology and International Politics," pp. 1–9.

36. Ibid.

37. Ibid.

38. Ibid., pp. 376–377. This conclusion also shows how Goodpaster could combine his engineering work while at Princeton with his increasing interest in international and national security affairs and the social sciences generally.

39. Goodpaster to Lt. Col. James L. Cantrell, 20 September 1950, p. 2.
40. Ibid., p. 1.

Chapter 3. Goodpaster and the Creation of NATO/SHAPE

1. See, for example, Robert S. Jordan, *The NATO International Staff/ Secretariat, 1952–1957: A Study in International Administration* (London: Oxford University Press, 1967).

2. For a general background, see Kenneth Weisbrode, *The Atlantic Century: Four Generations of Extraordinary Diplomats Who Forged America's Vital Alliance with Europe* (Cambridge, MA: Da Capo Press, 2009). For a more NATO focus, see Gustav Schmidt, ed., *A History of NATO: The First Fifty Years*, vol. 1 (New York: Palgrave, 2001).

3. Lawrence S. Kaplan, *NATO Divided, NATO United: The Evolution of an Alliance* (Westport, CT: Praeger, 2004), p. 9. Dr. Kaplan's numerous writings on the alliance have become an informal NATO library.

4. Stephen E. Ambrose, *Eisenhower: Soldier, General of the Army, President-Elect, 1890–1952* (New York: Simon & Schuster, 1983), 1:506.

5. John V. Wahlfeld, *Eisenhower and the Second Crusade in Europe* (master's thesis, University of North Carolina, 1975), p.11n12.

6. Timothy P. Ireland, *Creating the Entangling Alliance: The Origins of the North Atlantic Treaty Organization* (Westport, CT: Greenwood Press, 1981), p. 183.

7. Goodpaster, Mandel and McCall interview.

8. Ibid.

9. Gregory W. Pedlow, "The Politics of NATO Command, 1950–1965," in *U.S. Military Forces in Europe: The Early Years, 1945–1970*, ed. Simon W. Duke and Wolfgang Krieger (Boulder, CO: Westview Press, 1993), p. 18.

10. Andrew J. Goodpaster, "The Development of SHAPE: 1950–1953," in *Generals in International Politics: NATO's Supreme Allied Commander, Europe*, ed. Robert S. Jordan (Lexington, KY: The University Press of Kentucky, 1987), p. 1. On 18–19 December, the North Atlantic Council formally requested that Eisenhower be appointed SACEUR.

11. Ibid., p. 2.

12. Memorandum for Admiral Davis from Lieutenant General Gruenther, 15 December 1950.

13. Jordan, *Generals in International Politics*, p. 122. On 2 April 1951, Eisenhower signed the activation order for ACE and SHAPE. On the same day, ACE's subordinate headquarters in Northern and Central Europe were activated, with the Southern Region following in June. In July, SHAPE moved to Rocquencourt.

14. Goodpaster, "The Development of SHAPE: 1950–1953."

15. Ibid. Goodpaster's specific responsibilities in the planning groups were monitoring the creation of the plans and operations, the training, and the intelligence headquarters units. He also recognized early on the importance of establishing an historical section to chronicle the evolution of this new multinational military entity.

16. *The Papers of Dwight David Eisenhower*, ed. by Louis Galambos et al., vol. 12, *NATO and the Campaign of 1952* (Baltimore, MD: The Johns Hopkins University Press, 1989), p. 663.

17. Gen. A. M. Gruenther, "The Mission of SHAPE and NATO in Furthering the Security of the Free World" (speech at West Point, 21 April 1952, p. 6).

18. Goodpaster, Soapes interview. Also see Galambos et al., *The Papers of Dwight David Eisenhower*, p. 594: In a letter to his son John, in regard to John's joining SHAPE, Eisenhower commented: "Some time ago, I casually asked General Gruenther whether there was a place in his General Staff for a man of your qualifications, giving as my reason that I thought you would have a great experience to work with a group of young American officers we have, all of them really brilliant. They are men named . . . Goodpaster."

19. Jordan, *Generals in International Politics*, pp. xiv–xviii. By the mid-1950s the two "hats" were accompanied by a third "hat," called Live Oak, which involved the SACEUR in the planning for the use of nuclear weapons in Europe. For more, see Robert S. Jordan, *Norstad: Cold War NATO Supreme Commander, Airman, Strategist, Diplomat* (New York: St. Martin's Press, 2000), chap. 7. See also George C. Mitchell, *Matthew B. Ridgway, Soldier, Statesman, Scholar, Citizen* (Mechanicsburg, PA: Stackpole Books, 2002).

20. Jordan, *Staff/Secretariat*, p. 26.

21. Robert S. Jordan, *Political Leadership in NATO: A Study in Multinational Diplomacy* (Boulder, CO: Westview Press, 1979), p. 13.

22. For a thorough description of the methods employed and the results obtained, see Jordan, *Staff/Secretariat*, pp. 202ff.

23. Goodpaster, Mandel and McCall interview.

24. Jordan, *Staff/Secretariat*, pp. 204–205.

25. Goodpaster, Mandel and McCall interview.

26. Harriman to Eisenhower, 18 December 1951. Goodpaster's friend and mentor Abe Lincoln was in Paris representing Secretary of Defense Lovett to the TCC's "Three Wise Men," which would have pleased Goodpaster.

27. Goodpaster to Col. G. A. Lincoln, 14 January 1952.

28. Goodpaster to William Burnham, 15 February 1952.

29. Gruenther to Goodpaster, 21 December 1951.

30. Goodpaster to H. Igor Ansoff, 17 July 1952. His particular letter ran to four typewritten, single-spaced pages. He also was coauthor of an article

in the August issue of the academic journal *International Organization* and speculated at length on coalition theory.

31. Gen. Andrew J. Goodpaster, "SHAPE and Allied Command Europe: Twenty Years in the Service of Peace and Security, 1951–1971," *NATO's Fifteen Nations Magazine*, April 1971, pp. 11–12.

32. Quoted in Jordan, *Generals in International Politics*, p. 122.

33. Goodpaster to Flood, 25 April 1951.

34. Andrew J. Goodpaster, memoranda for Mr. William J. Hopkins; and Mr. Ralph Dungan, 21 January 1961.

35. Andrew J. Goodpaster, "George Marshall's World, and Ours," *New York Times*, 11 December 2003.

36. Quoted in Husted, *George C. Marshall, Rubrics of Leadership*, p. 1.

37. Forrest C. Pogue, *George C. Marshall: Statesman 1945–1959* (New York: Penguin Books, 1987), p. 505.

38. Quoted in Hobbs, *Dear General*, p. 104.

Chapter 4. Solarium: The Articulation of a National Posture

1. George F. Kennan, ("X"), "The Sources of Soviet Conduct," *Foreign Affairs*, July 1947. Kennan wrote his famous "X" article in the journal *Foreign Affairs* in 1947, suggesting that pressure applied consistently, over time, would result in the Soviet system collapsing from within.

2. Campbell Craig and Sergey Radchenko, *The Atomic Bomb and the Origins of the Cold War* (New Haven, CT: Yale University Press, 2008), p. 131.

3. David J. Rothkopf, *Running the World: The Inside Story of the National Security Council and the Architects of American Power* (New York: Public Affairs, 2005), p. 69.

4. Tyler Notting, *Once and Future Policy Planning: Solarium for Today* (Washington, DC: The Eisenhower Institute, January 1993), p. 1.

5. Quoted in Donald F. Bletz, *The Role of the Military Professional in U.S. Foreign Policy* (New York: Praeger Publishers, 1972), p. 42.

6. Theodore Zeldin, *An Intimate History of Humanity* (New York: Harper Perennial, 1996), p. 14.

7. John Foster Dulles Centennial Conference (also called "'Project Solarium': A Collective Oral History"), "The Challenge of Leadership in Foreign Affairs," Princeton University, 27 February 1988, pp. 18–19. Hereafter referred to as Princeton Conference.

8. Steven L. Rearden, *The Evolution of American Strategic Doctrine: Paul H. Nitze and the Soviet Challenge* (Washington, DC: Westview Press, 1984), p. 423.

9. Ernest R. May, *American Cold War Strategy: Interpreting NSC 68* (New York: Bedford/St. Martin's, 1993), pp. 1–2.

10. Andrew J. Goodpaster Jr., transcript of oral history interview by Malcolm S. McDonald, 10 April 1982, Eisenhower Presidential Library, p. 2.

11. Princeton Conference, p. 19.

12. Ibid., p. 23.

13. Nonetheless, Goodpaster remained a "hawk" vis-à-vis the Soviet threat throughout his post-Army career, cochairing, for example, the Committee on the Present Danger in 1974.

14. Barton Gellman, *Contending with Kennan: Toward a Philosophy of American Power* (New York: Praeger, 1984), p. 131.

15. Quoted in Paul Kennedy, ed., *Grand Strategies in War and Peace* (New Haven, CT: Yale University Press, 1991), p. 2.

16. Robert R. Bowie and Richard H. Immerman, *Waging Peace: How Eisenhower Shaped an Enduring Cold War Strategy* (New York: Oxford University Press, 1998), p. 124.

17. Ibid.

18. Ibid., pp. 126–127. The authors are quoting from the original documents. See also Meena Bose, *Shaping and Signaling Presidential Policy: The National Security Making of Eisenhower and Kennedy* (College Station, TX: Texas A&M University Press, 1998), pp. 29–41.

19. Goodpaster, McDonald interview.

20. Robert Cutler, *No Time for Rest* (Boston: Little, Brown and Co., 1966), p. 309.

21. Quoted in Rothkopf, *Running the World*, p. 70.

22. Princeton Conference, pp. 9–10.

23. Quoted in Lewis Sorley, *Honorable Warrior: General Harold K. Johnson and the Ethics of Command* (Lawrence, KS: University Press of Kansas, 1998), p. 112.

24. Ibid.

25. For more on this point, see Bowie and Immerman, *Waging Peace*, pp. 123–138.

26. Ibid.

27. Ibid., p. 137. Much of this aspect of the Cold War is chronicled in David Caute, *The Dancer Defects: The Struggle for Cultural Supremacy during the Cold War* (Oxford: Oxford University Press, 2003).

28. James Marchio, "The Planning Coordination Group: Bureaucratic Casualty in the Cold War Campaign to Exploit Soviet-Bloc Vulnerabilities," *Journal of Cold War Studies* 4, no. 4 (2002): 28. As it was described: "The violent suppression of the popular rebellion in Hungary in November 1956 convinced the president and his top advisers [which would have included Goodpaster] of the dangers of political war. . . . The bloodshed in the streets of Budapest helped force the Eisenhower administration to abandon its

strategy of 'conflicting approaches.'" See also Kenneth A. Osgood, "Hearts and Minds: The Unconventional Cold War [review essay]," *Journal of Cold War Studies* 4, no. 2 (Spring 2002): 85–107.

29. Andrew J. Goodpaster, interview by Ed Edwin, 25 April 1967, Eisenhower Presidential Library.

30. In an aside, during the Princeton Conference, Kennan commented: "Foster Dulles sat at my feet and was thus instructed on what the policy ought to be toward the Soviet Union. Since it was only three months since he had fired me from the Foreign Service, this gave me a certain satisfaction. I could talk, and he had to listen, for about a half an hour." (Princeton Conference, pp. 5–6.) In this respect, the following comment is apt: "Kennan gave modern meaning to a role for intellectuals in high politics." (Bruce Kuklick, *Blind Oracles: Intellectuals and War from Kennan to Kissinger* [Princeton, NJ: Princeton University Press, 2006], p. 41.)

31. Bose, *Shaping and Signaling Presidential Policy*, p. 41.

32. Kenneth Weisbrode, "A Tale of Three Cold Warriors," *NATO Review* (Spring 2006).

Chapter 5. The "New Look"

1. Steven L. Rearden, *The Formative Years, 1947–1950* (Washington, DC: Office of the Secretary of Defense, 1984), p. 36.

2. Quoted in Dale R. Herspring, *The Pentagon and the Presidency: Civil-Military Relations from FDR to George W. Bush* (Lawrence, KS: University Press of Kansas, 2005), p. 93.

3. Goodpaster, Soapes interview, p. 104.

4. This is in reference to NSC-68.

5. Kenneth W. Thompson and Steven L. Rearden, eds., *Paul H. Nitze on National Security and Arms Control* (New York: University Press of America for the Miller Center of the University of Virginia, 1990), p. 5n.

6. Marc Trachtenberg, *History and Strategy* (Princeton, NJ: Princeton University Press, 1991), p. 138. Trachtenberg observed: "His thinking was right out of the first few pages of Clausewitz: war has an innate tendency to become absolute. 'In such a war,' [Eisenhower] said, 'the United States would be applying a force so terrible that one simply could not be meticulous as to the methods by which the force was brought to bear.'"

7. David Callahan, *Dangerous Capabilities: Paul Nitze and the Cold War* (New York: HarperCollins, 1990), p. 176.

8. There are several variations of this paradoxical thought in the literature of the time.

9. Gordon A. Craig and Alexander L. George, *Force and Statecraft: Diplomatic Problems of Our Time* (New York: Oxford University Press, 1995), pp. 259–260.

10. Contained in White House Office of the Staff Secretary, 1952–61, Eisenhower Presidential Library, Box No. 24, p. 4.

11. Ibid.

12. Princeton Conference, p. 13.

13. Goodpaster, McDonald interview, p. 3.

14. Neil Sheehan, *A Fiery Peace in a Cold War: Bernard Schriever and the Ultimate Weapon* (New York: Random House, 2009), p. 273. Sheehan discusses through the lens of Schriever's career the full scope of the government's efforts at reconciling these new technologies with the more traditional roles-and-missions posture of the three services.

15. National Reconnaissance Office, "A National Imperative (1945–1955)," http://www.nrojr.gov/teamrecon/res_his-NationalImp.html.

16. David Haight to Robert S. Jordan (n.d.).

17. This observation is attributable to Steven Rearden in a private, undated memorandum.

18. Andrew J. Goodpaster, *For the Common Defense* (Lexington, MA: Lexington Books, 1977), pp. 62–63.

19. Goodpaster, McDonald interview, p. 5.

20. Princeton Conference, p. 7.

21. Michael R. Beschloss, *Mayday: Eisenhower, Khrushchev and the U-2 Affair* (Boston: Faber and Faber, 1986), p. 6n.

22. Ibid., p. 23.

23. Walter LaFeber, *America, Russia, and the Cold War, 1945–1966* (New York: John Wiley and Sons, Inc., 1968), p. 151.

24. See, for example, Francis Stonor Saunders, *The Cultural Cold War: The CIA and the World of Arts and Letters* (New York: The New Press, 2001); also Cord Meyer, *Facing Reality: From World Federalism to the CIA* (New York: Harper and Row, 1980).

25. Goodpaster, McDonald interview, p. 10.

26. Craig and George, *Force and Statecraft*, p. 262.

27. Edgar O'Ballance, *Korea: 1950–1953* (Malabar, FL: Robert E. Krieger Pub. Co., 1985), p. 147.

28. Rearden, *The Evolution of American Strategic Doctrine*, p. 39.

29. Gen. Andrew J. Goodpaster, "Interests and Strategies in an Era of Détente: An Overview," Foreword to *National Security and Détente* (New York: Thomas Y. Crowell, 1976), pp. x–xiii. The policy of détente could only make sense, if a concession by one of the parties was "linked" to a related concession by the other party. A good example was the seemingly endless negotiations over Berlin.

30. Lord Ampthill, quoted in Graham Wallas, *Human Nature in Politics*, 4th ed. (London: Constable, 1948), p. 290.

31. David A. Nichols, *Eisenhower 1956: The President's Year of Crisis—Suez and the Brink of War* (New York: Simon & Schuster, 2011), p. 278.

Chapter 6. Presidential Staff Secretary and Counselor

1. Stephen Hess, *Organizing the Presidency*, 3rd ed. (Washington, DC: Brookings Institution Press, 2002), p. 187.

2. Weisbrode, "A Tale of Three Cold Warriors."

3. Elmo Richardson, *The Presidency of Dwight D. Eisenhower* (Lawrence, KS: University Press of Kansas, 1979), p. 26.

4. Stephen E. Ambrose, *Nixon: The Education of a Politician, 1913–1962* (New York: Simon & Schuster, 1987), p. 611.

5. Ibid., p. 63.

6. Robert H. Ferrell, ed., *The Diary of James C. Hagerty: Eisenhower in Mid-Course, 1954–1955* (Bloomington, IN: Indiana University Press, 1983), p. 1131.

7. Phillip G. Henderson, *Managing the Presidency: The Eisenhower Legacy—From Kennedy to Reagan* (Boulder, CO: Westview Press, 1988), p. 115.

8. Dwight D. Eisenhower, *The White House Years: Mandate for Change, 1953–1956* (Garden City, NY: Doubleday, 1963), p. 117. According to Goodpaster, Eisenhower invented the title.

9. See memo for record, Robert Cutler, Special Assistant to the President for National Security Affairs, "Attendees at National Security Council Meetings," 30 November 1954.

10. Goodpaster, Mandel and McCall interview, 16 January 2002, pp. 5–6.

11. "President Eisenhower's Diary," Scope and Content Note, DDE Diaries, p. 1, http://www.ibiblio.org/lia/president/EisenhowerLibrary/finding_aids/DOE's_Diary.html.

12. Bradley H. Patterson Jr., *The Ring of Power: The White House Staff and Its Expanding Role in Government* (New York: Basic Books, 1988), pp. 298–299.

13. Piers Brendon, *Ike: His Life and Times* (New York: Harper and Row, 1986), p. 236.

14. Robert S. Jordan, "The Contribution of the British Civil Service and Cabinet Secretariat Tradition to International Prevention and Control of War," in *The Limitations of Military Power: Essays Presented to Professor Norman Gibbs on his Eightieth Birthday*, ed. John B. Hattendorf and Malcolm H. Murfett (New York: St. Martin's Press, 1990), pp. 99–100.

15. Brendon, *Ike*, p. 235.

16. Hattendorf and Murfett, *Limitations*, p. 100. Hankey kept extensive diaries, whereas Goodpaster did not, unfortunately for his biographer. See Stephen Roskill, *Hankey, Man of Secrets*, vol. 2, *1919–1931* (London: Collins, 1972). For more, see Ismay, Lord Hastings, *The Memoirs of General Lord Ismay* (New York: The Viking Press, 1960). Ismay was Hankey's deputy and later chief aide to prime minister Winston Churchill; later Ismay was the first secretary-general of NATO. In many ways, Ismay served at the highest level of government in a role similar to Goodpaster's: the self-effacing emissary and coordinator who was trusted by all parties.

17. Brendon, *Ike*, p. 235.

18. For an elaboration on this point, see Henderson, *Managing the Presidency*, ch. 2.

19. Great Projects, Oral Interview, 16 January 2002, pp. 5–6.

20. Quoted in Pickett, "General Andrew Jackson Goodpaster: Managing National Security," p. 29.

21. Allen Dulles to Goodpaster (with enclosure), 2 June 1959.

22. Goodpaster, Mandel and McCall interview, pp. 10–11.

23. Pickett, "General Andrew Jackson Goodpaster: Managing National Security," p. 25.

24. Douglas Kinnard, *President Eisenhower and Strategic Management: A Study in Defense Politics* (New York: Pergamon-Brassey's, 1989), p. 135.

25. For an authoritative discussion, see Margaret MacMillan, *Paris 1919: Six Months That Changed the World* (New York: Random House, 2001).

26. John Mason Brown, *The Worlds of Robert E. Sherwood: Mirror to His Times, 1896–1939* (New York: Harper and Row, 1965), pp. 385–386.

27. Robert E. Sherwood, *Roosevelt and Hopkins: An Intimate History* (New York: Harper and Row, 1948), p. 11.

28. Rothkopf, *Running the World*, p. 68.

29. This is a transposed version of a remark made in Colin Wilson, *Beyond the Outsider* (New York: Carroll and Graf, 1991), p. 213.

30. David Stout, "Andrew J. Goodpaster, 90, Soldier and Scholar, Dies," *New York Times*, 17 May 2005.

31. Eisenhower, *Mandate for Change*, p. 477.

32. Ibid., p. 478.

33. Dwight D. Eisenhower, *The White House Years, Waging Peace, 1956–1961* (Garden City, NY: Doubleday, 1965). Pages indicated.

34. In this respect, see Ibid., pp. 150–159.

35. Ibid., p. 247.

36. Leonard Mosley, *A Biography of Eleanor, Allen, and John Foster Dulles and Their Family Network* (New York: The Dial Press, 1978), pp. 406–407.

37. Ibid., p. 409.

38. For a readable account of Eisenhower's reactions at this time, with Goodpaster in the background, see Donald Neff, *Warriors at Suez: Eisenhower Takes America into the Middle East* (New York: Simon & Schuster, 1981).

39. Douglas Kinnard, *The Secretary of Defense* (Lexington, KY: The University Press of Kentucky, 1980), p. 46.

40. Gen. Maxwell D. Taylor to the Adjutant General, Department of the Army, "Promotion to Brigadier General." Taylor's enthusiastic language was tantamount to a direct order.

41. Great Projects, Oral Interview, 16 January 2002, p. 2.

42. Ibid., p. 6.

43. Stout, "Andrew J. Goodpaster, 90." It is also on the Arlington National Cemetery website, http://www.arlingtoncemetery.net/ajgoodpaster.htm.

44. David L. Anderson, *Trapped by Success: The Eisenhower Administration and Vietnam, 1953–1961* (New York: Columbia University Press, 1991), pp. 87–88.

45. Briefing Notes on OCB Activities of Possible Presidential Interest, 17 December 1954 [copy to Goodpaster].

46. Brendon, *Ike*, p. 308.

47. Ibid.

48. Roy L. Prosterman, *Surviving to 3000: An Introduction to the Study of Lethal Conflict* (Belmont, CA: Duxbury Press, 1972), p. 153.

49. Amos A. Jordan Jr., ed. *Issues of National Security in the 1970s* (New York: Praeger, 1967), p. 227–228.

50. Allen Dulles to Goodpaster, 18 July 1956, Doc. 76, "White House: Office of the Staff Secretary—International Series," p. 426.

51. Memorandum, Goodpaster to Calhoun, 26 May 1959, Doc. 99, "Papers as President (Anne Whitman Files)—Administration Series."

52. See Richard E. Neustadt, *Presidential Power: The Politics of Leadership* (New York: The Free Press, 1961), and Fred Greenstein, *The Hidden-Hand Presidency: Eisenhower as Leader* (Baltimore, MD: The Johns Hopkins University Press, 1994).

53. Recounted by Henderson, *Managing the Presidency*, p. 179.

54. John P. Burke and Fred I. Greenstein, *How Presidents Test Reality: Decisions on Vietnam, 1954 and 1965* (New York: Russell Sage Foundation, 1989), p. 11.

55. Hess, *Presidents and the Presidency*, p. 32.

56. Dwight D. Eisenhower, Enclosure to Efficiency Report on Colonel Andrew J. Goodpaster Jr., from 6/1/55 to 5/31/56, Item #10, Goodpaster Papers, Marshall Foundation.

57. Ferrell, *Hagerty*, p. 189.

58. *JCS Reform: Proceedings of the Conference* (Newport, RI: Naval War College, n.d.), p. 62.
59. Goodpaster, Soapes interview, pp. 92–93.
60. Saki Dockrill, *Eisenhower's New-Look National Security Policy, 1953–1961* (New York: St. Martin's Press, 1996), p. 23.
61. This is described at length in Michael D. Pearlman, *Warmaking and American Democracy: The Struggle over Military Strategy, 1700 to the Present* (Lawrence, KS: University Press of Kansas, 1999).
62. H. R. McMaster, *Dereliction of Duty: Lyndon Johnson, Robert McNamara, The Joint Chiefs of Staff, and the Lies That Led to Vietnam* (New York: Harper Perennial, 1997), pp. 54–55.
63. Dwight D. Eisenhower, Memorandum for the Secretary of the Army: Re: Brigadier General Andrew J. Goodpaster Jr., 3 June 1958, Goodpaster Papers, Box 18, Folder 14, Marshall Foundation Library. Also Cutler to Eisenhower, with copies to Army chief of staff and secretary of the Army, 10 July 1958: In 1958 Robert Cutler, when he was leaving the White House, sent a letter to Eisenhower in which he wrote: "I don't think I ever knew a fellow who could get to the heart of a subject quicker, retain so much of its substance in his mind, work at such top speed, and all the time keep his good humor and sense of proportion. To share the doing of a task with him was always a delight. His opinions and judgments are as sound as they are frank. The serenity of his intellectual processes is fortified by his integrity and courage."

Chapter 7. A Functional National Security System

1. Husted, *George C. Marshall: Rubrics of Leadership*, pp. 130–131.
2. Ibid.
3. Bletz, *The Role of the Military Professional in U.S. Foreign Policy*, p. 82. This is a quotation attributed to Samuel Huntington. See also Steven L. Rearden, *The Formative Years, 1947–1950* (Washington, DC: Office of the Secretary of Defense, 1984), pp. 125.
4. Jordan, *Issues of National Security in the 1970s*, p. 222.
5. Goodpaster, Mandel and McCall interview, 15 January 2002, pp. 14–15.
6. Ibid., p. 13.
7. Hobbs, *Dear General*, p. 9.
8. Ibid., p. 3.
9. Ed Cray, foreword to *General of the Army George C. Marshall, Soldier and Statesman* (New York: Cooper Square Press, 2000). Goodpaster claimed that Eisenhower regretted the incident, in which he did not defend Marshall from McCarthyite attacks on Marshall's patriotism while campaigning in Wisconsin. He said, "When I joined President Eisenhower in the fall of

1954 . . . I learned that this was a matter of deep chagrin to Eisenhower. He felt he had got himself mouse-trapped and . . . I think he took to his grave the regret that he had not done right by General Marshall. He told me one time, 'You keep your eye out for anything we can do that will show our respect and regard for General Marshall,' and we did." (Goodpaster, Mandel and McCall interview, 15 January 2002, p. 17.)

10. "National Security Council: The Truman and Eisenhower Years," in *Encyclopedia of the New American Nation*, ed. Paul Finkelman (Boston: Charles Scribner's Sons, 2005), p. 1.

11. Rudy Abramson, *Spanning the Century: The Life of W. Averell Harriman 1891–1986* (New York: William, Morrow and Co., Inc., 1992), p. 444.

12. Goodpaster to Frederick Tipson, Senate Foreign Relations Committee, 3 April 1980, in *Letters and Statements of Former Secretaries of State and White House Advisers* (Washington, DC: Government Printing Office), p. 315. See also Senate Foreign Relations Committee, "Comments on the National Security Advisor," article 31, in *Decisions of the Highest Order: Perspectives on the National Security Council*, ed. by Karl F. Inderfurth and Loch K. Johnson (Pacific Grove, CA: Brooks/Cole, 1988).

13. For a summary of the evolution of the NSC, see Patterson, chap. 7 in *The Ring of Power*.

14. Judson Knight, "NSC (National Security Council), History," *Encyclopedia of Espionage, Intelligence, and Security* (2004), http://www.encyclopedia.com/doc/1G2-3403300554.html.

15. See James S. Lay, *Organizational History of the National Security Council during the Truman and Eisenhower Administrations*, p. 26, for a detailed description/discussion of the NSC. In the postelectoral period, Robert Cutler had conducted a wide-ranging study of how national security affairs had been handled during the preceding Truman administration, with recommendations for changes.

16. For more about the OCB's "role and mission," see OCB, Memorandum to the Operations Coordinating Board, sub: "Recommendations to Improve the Effectiveness of the OCB—A Report from the Executive Officer of the Board," 3 January 1955.

17. This observation is attributable to Steven Rearden in a private, undated memorandum.

18. Lay, *Organizational History*, p. 176.

19. Ibid., p. 1198.

20. Jordan, *Issues of National Security in the 1970s*, p. 225.

21. Cutler, *No Time for Rest*, p. 366. Curiously, Cutler hardly mentions the nature and extent of his relationship to Goodpaster, although it was considerable, as the record shows.

22. Inderfurth and Johnson, *Decisions of the Highest Order*, p. 44.

23. Goodpaster, Soapes interview, p. 74. There was also William J. Jackson, in addition to Cutler and Gray. For an elaboration of the NSC adaptations, see Memorandum for the National Security Council: "The Structure and Functions of the National Security Council, 3 July 1957." Relevant is: "Many changes since [17 March 1953]—particularly the bringing within the NSC structure on July 1, 1957, of the Operations Coordinating Board—have required revision of the above-mentioned memorandum."

24. Ivo H. Daalder and I. M. Destler, *In the Shadow of the Oval Office* (New York: Simon & Schuster, 2009), p. 6. The person who came closest in the Truman administration in temperament and career development was George Elsey. See George McKee Elsey, *An Unplanned Life* (Columbia, MO: University of Missouri Press, 2005).

25. Greenstein, *The Hidden-Hand Presidency*, p. 134.

26. *The Papers of Dwight David Eisenhower*, ed. Louis Galambos et al., vol. 13, *NATO and the Campaign of 1952* (Baltimore, MD: The Johns Hopkins University Press, 1989), p. 2191.

27. David Eisenhower with Julie Nixon Eisenhower, *Going Home to Glory: A Memoir of Life with Dwight D. Eisenhower, 1961–1969* (New York: Simon & Schuster, 2010), pp.16–17.

28. Goodpaster, note (handwritten) for the record, 19 August 1957, Eisenhower Presidential Library.

29. John S. D. Eisenhower, interview by Carol Hegeman, Supervisory Park Ranger, 26 January 1984, pp. 2–3.

30. Goodpaster, Soapes interview, p. 77.

31. John S. D. Eisenhower, interview by Hegeman, p. 4. He also commented that on the frequent weekends when the president was at his Gettysburg home, "I was his 'eyes and ears' to the staff."

32. Goodpaster, Soapes interview, p. 74.

Chapter 8. National Defense Writ Large

1. Ferrell, *Hagerty*, p 133.

2. Lt. General Andrew J. Goodpaster, "The Role of the Joint Chiefs of Staff in the National Security Structure," in *Issues of National Security in the 1970s*, p. 226.

3. Ibid., p. 229.

4. JCS Reform, pp. 53–54.

5. Bletz, *The Role of the Military Professional in U.S. Foreign Policy*, p. 149.

6. John P. Burke and Fred I. Greenstein, *How Presidents Test Reality: Decisions on Vietnam, 1954 and 1965* (New York: Russell Sage Foundation, 1989), pp. 13 and 14.

7. Goodpaster, Burg interview, p. 99.
8. JCS Reform, pp. 12–13.
9. Ibid., pp. 36–37.
10. Paul L. Davies, "A Business Look at the Army," *Harvard Business Review*, July–August 1954, p. 56, as quoted in Paul Y. Hammond, *Organizing for Defense: The American Military Establishment in the Twentieth Century* (Princeton, NJ: Princeton University Press, 1961), p. 293.
11. Jordan, *Issues of National Security in the 1970s*, p. 230.
12. Herspring, *The Pentagon and the Presidency*, p. 89.
13. Similar, but even more bitter, feelings existed between Secretary of Defense McNamara and the JCS over how to analyze the progress (or lack thereof) in Vietnam and what to do about it. See, for example, Sorley, *Honorable Warrior*.
14. Cited in Sidney Warren, *The President as World Leader* (New York: J. B. Lippincott, 1964), p. 387.
15. Ibid., p. 388.
16. Barry R. Posen, *The Sources of Military Doctrine: France, Britain, and Germany between the World Wars* (Ithaca, NY: Cornell University Press, 1984), p. 71.
17. Colin S. Gray, ed., *Strategy and History: Essays on Theory and Practice* (New York: Routledge, 2006), pp. 76–77.
18. See Maxwell D. Taylor, *The Uncertain Trumpet* (New York: Harper and Co., 1960). See also Ivo Daalder, *The Nature and Practice of Flexible Response* (New York: Columbia University Press, 1991). The latter is a detailed discussion of the types of weaponry—including nuclear—and their efficacy as "bargaining tools" that was embraced in the notion of "flexible response." The bibliography is especially thorough.
19. Quoted in John M. Taylor, *An American Soldier: The Wars of General Maxwell Taylor* (Novato, CA: Presidio Press, 2001), p. 216. The author points out that these views were closer to those of Taylor, Kissinger, and Kennan (p. 215).
20. Andrew P. N. Erdmann, "The Intellectual and Bureaucratic Origins of Flexible Response: The Policy Planning Staff, 1953–1961," unpublished paper for private group, 25 June 1999, p. 5.
21. Christopher A. Preble, *John F. Kennedy and the Missile Gap* (DeKalb, IL: Northern Illinois University Press, 2004), p. 89.
22. Goodpaster, Burg interview, p. 99.
23. Ibid.
24. Eisenhower, *Waging Peace*, p. 483.
25. David A. Koplow, "Major Acts of Congress | Arms Control and Disarmament Act (1961) and Amendments," *E-Notes*, 21 March 2011, http://www

.enotes.com/arms-control-disarmament-act-1961-amendments-reference/
arms-control-disarmament-act-1961-amendments.

26. Ibid. In many respects, the act was a tremendous success. It led to an impressive array of legally binding arms control treaties, with ACDA in the lead role: the 1963 Limited Test Ban Treaty (prohibiting atmospheric nuclear weapons tests), the 1967 Outer Space Treaty (establishing the "rules of the road" for peaceful operations in space), the 1968 Non-Proliferation Treaty (restricting the spread of nuclear weapons capabilities), and the 1972 Biological Weapons Convention (banning the development and production of germ weapons) were early successes. They are still in force. SALT (Strategic Arms Limitation Talks) and START (Strategic Arms Reduction Talks) would not have been possible without ACDA, and all participants acknowledge the agency's leadership role on other such diverse subjects as chemical weapons and conventional forces. A reorganization of the foreign affairs bureaucracy merged ACDA into the State Department on 1 April 1999. The agency was abolished by statute, and its core functions and personnel were absorbed by State.

27. *The Papers of Dwight David Eisenhower*, ed. Louis Galambos and Daun Van Ee, vol. 21, *The Presidency: Keeping the Peace* (Baltimore: The Johns Hopkins University Press, 2001), p. 2190. Goodpaster remained with Kennedy until April 1961.

28. Ibid., pp. 2205–2206.

29. John Prados, *Presidents' Secret Wars: CIA and Pentagon Covert Operations from World War II through the Persian Gulf*, rev. ed. (New York: Ivan R. Dee/Elephant Paperbacks, 1996), p. 197.

30. Memorandum, J. Kenneth McDonald to Robert S. Jordan, n.d.

31. Prados, *Presidents' Secret Wars*, p. 175.

32. I. M. Destler, "The Presidency and National Security Organization," in *The National Security: Its Theory and Practice, 1945–1960*, ed. Norman A. Graebner (New York: Oxford University Press, 1986), pp. 238–239.

33. Don Paarlberg to Goodpaster, 26 January 1961.

34. Quoted in Patterson, *The Ring of Power*, p. 107.

Chapter 9. Eisenhower's Health Crises

1. Eisenhower, *Mandate for Change*, p. 537. Eisenhower termed the coronary occlusion a "coronary difficulty."

2. Memorandum, Eisenhower to Nixon, 1 October 1955, Eisenhower Presidential Library.

3. Chester J. Pach Jr. and Elmo Richardson, *The Presidency of Dwight D. Eisenhower*, rev. ed. (Lawrence, KS: The University Press of Kansas, 1991), p. 119.

4. Dockrill, *Eisenhower's New-Look National Security Policy, 1953–61*, p. 145.

5. Stephen E. Ambrose, *Eisenhower, Soldier and President* (New York: Simon & Schuster, 1990), pp. 396–397.

6. Whitman to Gruenther, n.d., Eisenhower Presidential Library.

7. Memorandum, Goodpaster to Adams, 14 December 1955, Eisenhower Presidential Library.

8. Goodpaster, Mandel and McCall interview, 16 January 2002, p. 16.

9. Kinnard, *President Eisenhower and Strategic Management*, pp. 40–41.

10. Goodpaster, Mandel and McCall interview, 16 January 2002, pp. 16–17.

11. Eisenhower, *Waging Peace*, p. 4.

12. John S. D. Eisenhower, *Strictly Personal* (Garden City, NY: Doubleday, 1974), pp. 185–187.

13. Sherman Adams, *First-Hand Report: The Story of the Eisenhower Administration* (New York: Harper and Bros., 1961), pp. 193–194.

14. Eisenhower, *Waging Peace*, pp. 9–10.

15. Geoffrey Perret, *Eisenhower* (New York: Random House, 1999), p. 388.

16. Ibid., p. 10n4.

17. Press Conference, 12 June 1956, Hagerty File, Eisenhower Presidential Library.

18. H. W. Brands, *Woodrow Wilson* (New York: Henry Holt, 2003), p. 123. Eisenhower's successor, Kennedy, put the final stamp to any notion that presidential health secrecy was politically or morally acceptable.

19. Memorandum, "Notes on Arrangements Incident to President's Illness," n.d., Eisenhower Presidential Library.

20. Memorandum (handwritten), signed by Goodpaster, 21 October 1955, Eisenhower Presidential Library. It specifically directed that the vice president should not take any specific action "with recognition of the incapacity of the President"(Memorandum, Goodpaster to Adams, 27 September 1955). Eisenhower also did not want the phrase "all indications point to a rapid recovery" used (Memorandum, Goodpaster to Adams, 29 November 1955).

21. John Eisenhower, *Strictly Personal*, p. 195.

22. Eisenhower, *Waging Peace*, pp. 227–228.

23. John Eisenhower, *Strictly Personal*, p. 195.

24. Ibid., pp. 196–197.

25. Eisenhower, *Waging Peace*, p. 229. Officially, he had "an occlusion of a small branch of a cerebral vessel which has produced a slight difficulty on occasion. There is no evidence of a cerebral hemorrhage or any serious lesion of the cerebral vessels." (Press Release, The White House, 26 November 1956.)

26. Goodpaster to Norstad, 26 November 1957, USNMR SHAPE, Norstad Papers, Eisenhower Presidential Library.

27. Eisenhower, *Waging Peace*, pp. 601–602.

28. Ibid., p. 407.

29. Ibid., p. 205.

30. David Eisenhower with Julie Nixon Eisenhower, *Going Home to Glory*, p. 273.

31. Ann Whitman to Goodpaster, undated, George C. Marshall Research Library.

Chapter 10. The U-2 and Overflights

1. Goodpaster, Mandel and McCall interview, 16 January 2002, p. 7.

2. Eisenhower, *Waging Peace*, p. 483. It is dubious that anyone in either the American or the Soviet governments took Open Skies seriously, given the closed society of the Soviet Union. Allen Dulles' successor at the CIA, John McCone, had a thorough memorandum on the history of the U-2 episode prepared for General Eisenhower after he had retired to Gettysburg, which was probably used in Eisenhower's memoirs.

3. Memorandum of Conference with the President, 24 November 1954.

4. Goodpaster, Mandel and McCall interview, 16 January 2002, p. 15. Another version is that the whole thing was a setup by the Americans in order to scuttle the Paris Conference—and hence détente; see James A. Nathan, "A Fragile Détente: The U-2 Incident Re-examined," *Military Affairs*, October 1975.

5. Memorandum, Rearden to Jordan, n.d. As Steven Rearden remarked: "Throughout his career, Goodpaster was intimately involved in off-the-books operations. Later, as Assistant to the Chairman of the Joint Chiefs, one of his major functions was to represent the JCS in these discussions."

6. Richard Immerman, ed., *John Foster Dulles and the Diplomacy of the Cold War* (Princeton, NJ: Princeton University Press, 1990), p. 13.

7. Richard H. Immerman, *John Foster Dulles: Piety, Pragmatism, and Power in U.S. Foreign Policy* (Wilmington, DE: Scholarly Resources, 1999), p. 47.

8. Quoted in David Haight to Robert Jordan, November 2011.

9. Goodpaster, interview by Soapes, p. 80.

10. Goodpaster, interview by Burg, pp. 15–16.

11. Eisenhower, *Waging Peace*, pp. 544–545.

12. Mosley, *Dulles*, p. 366.

13. Beschloss, *Mayday*, pp. 155–156. This is an exhaustive recounting of the U-2 crisis. Within two years after the program got under way, Bissell claimed that 90 percent of all hard intelligence coming into the CIA about the Soviet Union was "funneled through the lens of the U-2's aerial cameras."

14. See Richard Helms, with William Hood, *A Look over My Shoulder: A Life in the Central Intelligence Agency* (New York: Ballantine Books, 2003). See also Ambrose, *Ike's Spies*.

15. Joseph J. Trento, *The Secret History of the CIA* (New York: Carroll and Graf, 2001), p. 139.

16. Tim Weiner, *Legacy of Ashes: The History of the CIA* (New York: Anchor Books, 2008) p. 183.

17. Mosley, *Dulles*, pp. 367–368.

18. Richard M. Bissell, with Jonathan E. Lewis and Frances E. Pudlo, *Reflections of a Cold Warrior: From Yalta to the Bay of Pigs* (New Haven, CT: Yale University Press, 1996), p. 115.

19. Ibid., p. 176.

20. Ibid., p. 183.

21. Arthur Krock, *Memoirs: Sixty Years on the Firing Line* (New York: Funk and Wagnalls, 1968), p. 297.

22. Dino A. Brugioni, *Eyes in the Sky: Eisenhower, the CIA, and Cold War Aerial Espionage* (Annapolis, MD: Naval Institute Press, 2010), p. 193.

23. Gregory W. Pedlow and Donald E. Welzenbach, *The CIA and the U-2 Program, 1954–1974* (Washington, DC: History Staff, Center for the Study of Intelligence, Central Intelligence Agency, 1998), p. 187.

24. Ambrose, *Eisenhower, Soldier and President*, pp. 434–435.

25. Keith Eubank, *The Summit Conferences, 1919–1960* (Norman, OK: University of Oklahoma Press, 1966), pp. 191–192.

26. Bissell, Lewis, and Pudlo, *Reflections*, p. 123. This book is an excellent discussion, with historical references. See also Pedlow and Welzenbach, *The CIA and the U-2 Program, 1954–1974*, for an authoritative account.

27. Mosley, *Dulles*, p. 456.

28. John S. D. Eisenhower, interview by Carol Hegeman, 26 January 1984, Eisenhower Presidential Library, p. 10.

29. Eisenhower, *Waging Peace*, p. 550.

30. Ibid., p. 548.

31. Ibid., pp. 552 and 554.

32. Gregory F. Treverton, *Covert Action: The CIA and American Intervention in the Postwar World* (London: I. B. Tauris, 1987), p. 229.

33. James Bamford, *Body of Secrets: From the Cold War through the Dawn of a New Century* (New York: Doubleday, 2001), p. 50.

34. Paraphrased in ibid., p. 52.

35. Rebecca Burg, "Powers, U-2 Pilot Captured by Soviets, Awarded Silver Star," *Washington Post*, 16 June 2010. Powers himself, once captured, behaved according to the rules of war, revealing nothing during the course of his interrogations and public trial. He was posthumously awarded the Silver Star medal in 2010.

36. Bamford, *Body of Secrets*, pp. 54–55.

37. Goodpaster, Hegeman interview.

38. Quoted in Brugioni, *Eyes in the Sky*, p. 357.

39. Ibid., p. 358.

40. Memorandum for the President, "Measures to Obtain the Release of the RB-47 Officers, 10–11 November 1960," Eisenhower Presidential Library. On 14 November, Eisenhower wrote: "Approved as to Phase II; approved for planning purposes only as to Phase III."
41. Brugioni, *Eyes in the Sky*, pp. 358–359.
42. Eubank, *The Summit Conferences*, p. 205. Eubank commented further: "The feeling that the Cold War was merely the result of misunderstanding and that if Eisenhower could only charm Khrushchev all would be well, was as erroneous as some of Roosevelt's views regarding Stalin."
43. This observation is cited in several places, among which is Perret, *Eisenhower*, p. 584.

Chapter 11. Deputy Commander and Commander-Designate in Vietnam

1. Goodpaster, Johnson interview, p. 205. This interview is an exposition of the argument that if the nation's military had been left to fight the war without civilian interference and with what it considered adequate resources (including reinstituting the draft), the United States could have avoided the humiliating outcome that ensued.
2. Ibid.
3. David Eisenhower and Julie Nixon Eisenhower, *Going Home to Glory*, p. 167.
4. Ibid., pp. 165–166. President Johnson also telephoned frequently and invited Eisenhower to lunch at the White House periodically to discuss Vietnam and foreign policy.
5. McMaster, *Dereliction of Duty*, p. 63.
6. C. Richard Nelson and Kenneth Weisbrode, eds., *Reversing Relations with Former Adversaries: U.S. Foreign Policy after the Cold War* (Gainesville, FL: University Press of Florida, 1998), p. 84. This is a concise exposition of the twists and turns in American policy toward Vietnam prior to eventual formal diplomatic recognition and reconciliation.
7. John J. Mearsheimer, *The Tragedy of Great Power Politics* (New York: W. W. Norton, 2001), p. 60.
8. Lewis Sorley, *Thunderbolt: General Creighton Abrams and the Army of His Times* (Bloomington, IN: Indiana University Press, 2008), p. 251.
9. James Chace, *Acheson: The Secretary of State Who Created the American World* (Cambridge, MA: Harvard University Press, 1998), p. 426.
10. Ibid.
11. Col. Harry G. Summers Jr., *On Strategy: The Vietnam War in Context* (Carlisle Barracks, PA: Strategic Studies Institute), p. 80.
12. Chace, *Acheson*, pp. 8–9.
13. Lewis Sorley, *A Better War: The Unexamined Victories and Final Tragedy of America's Last Years in Vietnam* (New York: Harcourt, Inc., 1999), pp. 90–91.

14. Ibid.
15. Lewis Sorley, *Westmoreland: The General Who Lost Vietnam* (New York: Houghton Mifflin Harcourt, 2011), pp. 104–105. See also Michael D. Pearlman, *Warmaking and American Democracy: The Struggle over Military Strategy, 1700 to the Present* (Lawrence, KS: University Press of Kansas, 1999), p. 375.
16. For more on this, see Prados, *Presidents' Secret Wars*, pp. 268–290. This is a very readable and detailed account of the tortuous negotiations and the accompanying on-the-ground events over this period.
17. Sorley, *A Better War*, p. 217.
18. Paul Kennedy, *The Rise and Fall of the Great Powers: Economic Change and Military Conflict from 1500 to 2000* (New York: Vintage Books, 1989), pp. 405–406.
19. Quoted in ibid., p. 216.
20. Sorley, *Westmoreland*, p. 199.

Chapter 12. As NATO Supreme Allied Commander

1. For more on this, see Robert S. Jordan, *Norstad*.
2. Gruenther to Goodpaster, 23 October 1955, NATO Series, Eisenhower Presidential Library.
3. David D. Newsom, "The Allied Quarrel: Consultations Are No Panacea," *Christian Science Monitor*, 22 September 1982.
4. Ferguson et al., *The 1970s in Perspective*, p. 58.
5. Quoted in Lewis Sorley, "Goodpaster: Maintaining Deterrence during Détente," in *Generals in International Politics: NATO's Supreme Allied Commander, Europe*, ed. Robert S. Jordan (Lexington, KY: The University Press of Kentucky, 1987), p. 126.
6. Ibid.
7. Ibid., p. 124.
8. Goodpaster, Mandel and McCall interview, p. 12.
9. "Goodpaster's Warning," *Die Welt*, 22 October 1970. He was addressing the German Foreign Policy Society.
10. Robert Kennedy, "International Leadership in an Era of Détente," in *National Security and Détente* (New York: Thomas Y. Crowell Co., 1976, for the U.S. Army War College), p. 304.
11. Ibid., p. 17.
12. Goodpaster, Mandel and McCall interview, p. 20.
13. Earlier, during General Ridgway's short tenure as SACEUR, the fact that he came to NATO directly from Korea (where he had replaced Gen. Douglas MacArthur) and was pictured everywhere wearing his battle-dress, including a grenade attached to his shoulder, did not enhance his

prestige in Europe. This obviously did not hurt his standing at home, however, as he went on from NATO to become the Army chief of staff.

14. Remarks given to the Royal United Services Institute (RUSI), 16 December 1970, *RUSI Journal*, p. 31.

15. "Paying for Defense," reprinted in the *International Herald Tribune*, 4 November 1969.

16. Gen. Andrew J. Goodpaster, "New Challenges, New Problems, New Dangers," *The Atlantic Community Quarterly* (Winter 1972–1973): 458.

17. Goodpaster, "Remarks," *RUSI Journal*, p. 35.

18. Goodpaster, "New Challenges," p. 460.

19. Ibid.

20. Goodpaster, "Interests and Strategies," p. xi.

21. David Callahan, *Dangerous Capabilities: Paul Nitze and the Cold War* (New York: Harper/Collins, 1990), p. 334.

22. Goodpaster, "Interests and Strategies," pp. x–xi.

23. Ibid., pp. xii–xiii.

24. Goodpaster to Gruenther, 9 April 1974, Gruenther Papers, Eisenhower Presidential Library.

25. Ibid., p. 6.

26. Lawrence J. Korb, *The Joint Chiefs of Staff: The First Twenty-Five Years* (Bloomington, IN: Indiana University Press, 1976), p. 34.

27. Goodpaster, Mandel and McCall interview, pp. 20–21.

28. Ibid., p. 7.

29. Conversation between author and Lt. Gen. Brent Scowcroft, June 2010.

30. Daalder and Destler, *In the Shadow of the Oval Office*, p. 67.

31. Linda Charlton, "New West Point Superintendent," *New York Times*, 5 April 1977.

32. See photo insert, Jordan, *Generals*.

33. SHAPE Public Affairs Office, Press Cutting Distribution Sheet, Subject: Change of Command, Source: AP Night Tapes, dated 16 December 1974.

34. SACEUR Message to Chiefs of Defense, 16 September 1974. The author is grateful to Richard Nelson for supplying this information and the note above.

35. Reported in the *Washington Star-News*, 6 February 1975.

36. For a confirmation of this point, see Jordan, *Generals*, passim.

Chapter 13. Returning to West Point as Superintendent

1. While at the center, he wrote *For the Common Defense*. He identified himself as being at The Citadel when it was published.

2. Goodpaster, Mandel and McCall interview, 12 February 2004, p. 13.

3. Charlton, "New West Point Superintendent." The adjective "avuncular" was attached to him at this time.

4. Goodpaster to Professor G. A. Lincoln, 17 September 1951.
5. Goodpaster, Mandel and McCall interview, 4 February 2004, p. 3.
6. Lt. Richard P. Hansen, USN, "The Crisis of the West Point Honor Code," *Military Affairs* (April 1985), p. 57.
7. Goodpaster, Johnson interview, p. 27.
8. Letter from the Department of Social Sciences, "Brothers," 29 August 1951. A copy was sent to Lincoln's brother, which was five single-spaced typed pages in length, reflecting the seriousness of the matter. An official explanatory letter subsequently was sent by the Association of Graduates, USMA, 23 August 1951.
9. Quoted in Sorley, *Westmoreland*, p. 223. Westmoreland sent a copy to Goodpaster at West Point.
10. Ibid., p. 4.
11. Quoted in Lewis Sorley, *Honor Bright: History and Origins of the West Point Honor Code and System* (New York: McGraw-Hill Learning Solutions, 2009), p. 18. This small book summarizes the issues surrounding a code of honor that relies more on voluntary adherence than coercion.
12. Goodpaster, Mandel and McCall interview, p. 58.
13. Recounted in Cox, *Grey Eminence*, p. 13. See also: Russ Stayanoff, "Major General Fox Conner: Soldier, Mentor, Enigma: Operations Chief (G-3) of the AEF," *The Doughboy Center: American Expeditionary Forces, World War One*, http://www.worldwar1.com/dbc/foxconner.htm.
14. Charlton, "New West Point Superintendent."
15. Ibid.
16. Memorandum, Subject: "Concept for Duty Development," Office of the Superintendent, U.S. Military Academy, 1 April 1981.
17. Ibid., attachment.
18. Goodpaster, Johnson interview, p. 15.
19. Goodpaster to Joe Dalton, 21 May 1981.
20. Linda Charlton, "New West Point Superintendent: Andrew Jackson Goodpaster," New York Times, 5 April 1977. Also see "Goodpaster + Two: West Point Today," Army Journal, June 1979.
21. Ibid., p. 27.
22. Quoted in Sorley, *Honor Bright*, p. 138.
23. Ibid., pp. 138–139.

Conclusions

1. Husted, *George C. Marshall: Rubrics of Leadership*, p. 192.
2. Report to Congress, 12 January 1961, pp. 4 and 5, Office of the Staff Secretary, 1952–1961, Eisenhower Presidential Library.
3. Ironically, the more they disagreed with their commander-in-chief and former chief of staff, the more popular they were with their fellow Army colleagues.

4. Goodpaster's successor, McGeorge Bundy, had been a Harvard dean who did not have any prior experience in top-level national security policy-making. The fact that he was a Republican contributed to Kennedy's decision to bring him "on board."

5. Memorandum, Eisenhower to the Secretary of the Army, 26 May 1959, Goodpaster Papers, George Marshall Foundation Research Library.

6. Pickett, "General Andrew Jackson Goodpaster: Managing National Security," pp. 36–37.

7. McMaster, *Dereliction of Duty*, p. 215.

8. Paradoxically, the most famous "hawk" in regard to containing Communism, Paul Nitze, did not agree with his Democratic colleagues that Vietnam was a major threat. See Callahan, *Dangerous Capabilities*, p. 290: "He argued that Vietnam was the wrong place to take a stand against communist expansion. . . . Undesirable as a takeover of the whole of Vietnam surely was, it did not pose an immediate or direct threat to the safety of the United States."

9. Ibid., p. 217.

10. Ibid., pp. 259–260. This report was submitted in July 1965. The sad thing is that "the 1965 record is of a great swirl of policy recommendations and analyses, much of which simply floated past the president."

11. Gen. Andrew J. Goodpaster, Epilogue to *Evolution of the American Military Establishment since World War II*, ed. Paul R. Schratz (Lexington, VA: George C. Marshall Research Foundation, 1978), pp. 111–113.

12. Geoffrey Blainey, *The Causes of War* (New York: The Free Press, 1973), pp. 12–13.

13. I am grateful to C. Richard Nelson for suggesting this analysis.

14. Jere Clemens King, *Generals and Politicians* (Berkeley: University of California Press, 1951), p. 243.

15. Donald Kagan, *On the Origins of War and the Preservation of Peace* (New York: Doubleday, 1995), pp. 7–8.

16. Robert Conquest, *Reflections on a Ravaged Century* ((New York: W. W. Norton, 2000), p. 289.

Source Material

Selected Publications by Andrew J. Goodpaster

Books

America's National Interests. (With Rita Hauser.) Cambridge, MA: Commission on America's National Interests, Center for Science and International Affairs, Harvard University, 1996.

Civil-Military Relations. (With Samuel P. Huntington.) Washington, DC: American Enterprise Institute for Public Policy Research, 1977.

Concept for Duty Development. West Point, NY: U.S. Military Academy, 1981.

"The Development of SHAPE: 1950–1953." In *Generals in International Politics: NATO's Supreme Allied Commander Europe*, edited by Robert S. Jordan. Lexington, KY: The University Press of Kentucky, 1987.

Epilogue to *Evolution of the American Military Establishment since World War II*, edited by Paul R. Schratz, 111–113. Lexington, VA: George C. Marshall Research Foundation, 1978.

For the Common Defense. Lexington, MA: Lexington Books, 1977.

Greece's Pivotal Role in World War II and Its Importance to the U.S. Today. (With E. T. Rossides.) Washington, DC: American Hellenic Institute Foundation, 2005.

"Interests and Strategies in an Era of Détente: An Overview." Foreword to *National Security and Détente*, x–xiii. New York: Thomas Y. Crowell, 1976.

"The Role of the Joint Chiefs of Staff in the National Security Structure." In *Issues of National Security in the 1970s*, edited by Amos A. Jordan Jr., p. 226. New York: Praeger, 1967.

Strengthening Conventional Deterrence in Europe: A Program for the 1980s. Boulder, CO: Westview Special Studies in International Security, 1985.

Toward a More Effective Defense. Washington, DC: Center for Strategic and International Studies, 1985.

Foreword to *Waging Peace: How Eisenhower Shaped an Enduring Cold War Strategy*, by Robert R. Bowie and Richard H. Immerman. New York: Oxford University Press, 1998.

Periodicals

"Advice for the Next President," *Foreign Affairs*, September/October 2000.

"Born-Again Generals: Too Late for Moral Absolution." *Washington Post*, 4 December 1996.

"George Marshall's World, and Ours." *New York Times*, 11 December 2003.

"Moral Choices: Military Ethics and National Values in the 1980s." *Liberal Education* 65, no. 2 (Summer 1979): 249–258.

"NATO Strategy and Requirements 1975–1985." *Survival*, September–October 1975.

"SHAPE and Allied Command Europe: Twenty Years in the Service of Peace and Security, 1951–1981." *NATO's Fifteen Nations Magazine*, April 1971: 11–12.

Oral History Interviews (by Interviewer's Name)

Burg, Maclyn P. 20 August 1976. Eisenhower Presidential Library.

Edwin, Ed. 25 April 1967 (also part of the Eisenhower Project of the Columbia University Libraries); 2 August 1967; 8 September 1967. Eisenhower Presidential Library.

Haclo, Hugh, and Anna Nelson (includes Andrew Goodpaster, Ann Whitman, Raymond Saulnier, Elmer Staats, Arthur Burns, Gordon Gray). 11 June 1980. The National Academy of Public Administration, Eisenhower Presidential Library.

Hegeman, Carol. Supervisory Park Ranger. 7 November 1983. Eisenhower Presidential Library.

Johnson, Lt. Col. James M. "Oral History of the Superintendency of Gen. A. J. Goodpaster, USA (Ret.)" Department of History, United States Military Academy, n.d.

Mandel, Ken, and James McCall, Great Projects Film Company, Atlantic Council. Transcript of filmed interview, 31 July–1 August 2001; 15–16 January 2002; 11–12 February 2004. George C. Marshall Foundation.

McDonald, Malcolm S. 10 April 1982. Eisenhower Presidential Library.

Soapes, Thomas. 11 October 1977; 16 January 1978. Eisenhower Presidential Library.

Other Sources

After Afghanistan—The Long Haul: Safeguarding Security and Independence in the Third World. (With Harlan Cleveland.) The Atlantic Council Policy Papers, March 1980.

Change in Eastern Europe: Soviet Interests and Western Opportunities. Atlantic Council, April 1989.

Combatting International Terrorism: U.S.–Allied Cooperation and Political Will. Atlantic Council Working Groups on "Defending Peace and Freedom: Toward Strategic Stability in the Year 2000" and "U.S. International

Leadership for the 21st Century: Building a National Foreign Affairs Constituency." Report of the Joint Working Group, January 1987.

Defining a New Relationship: The Issue of U.S. Access to Facilities in Panama. Atlantic Council, August 1996.

Further Reins on Nuclear Arms: Next Steps for the Major Nuclear Powers. Atlantic Council Consultation Paper, Consultation Paper Series, August 1993.

The Future of Russian-American Relations in a Pluralistic World, Phase I and Phase II—Constructive Interaction, Joint Policy Statement, and Recommendations. The Atlantic Council and the Institute of World Economy and International Relations, 14 February 1992, 20 November 1992.

Gorbachev and the Future of East-West Security: A Response for the Mid-Term. The Atlantic Council Occasional Paper, April 1989.

The Growing Dimensions of Security. Atlantic Council, November 1977.

Joint Policy Statements with Joint Policy Recommendations on the Future of Ukrainian-American Relations and Russian-American Relations in a Pluralistic World. Atlantic Council Policy Papers, June–July 1995; December 1995; January 1996; September 1996; March–April 1997.

Letter to Gen. Lauris Norstad, 26 November 1957. USNMR SHAPE Norstad Papers, Eisenhower Presidential Library.

Letter to Professor Harold H. Sprout, 8 November 1950; letter and reply, 20–28 March 1955.

Letter to Frederick Tipson, Senate Foreign Relations Committee, 3 April 1980. In *Letters and Statements of Former Secretaries of State and White House Advisors*, p. 315. Washington, DC: Government Printing Office.

Memoranda for Mr. William J. Hopkins; and Mr. Ralph Dungan. Washington, DC, 21 January 1961. Eisenhower Presidential Library.

Memorandum to Calhoun. Papers as President (Ann Whitman Files)— Administration Series, 26 May 1959. Eisenhower Presidential Library.

"National Technology and International Politics." PhD diss., Department of Politics, Princeton University, May 1950.

NATO to the Year 2000: Challenges for Coalition Deterrence and Defense. Report of the Atlantic Council's Working Group on the Future of NATO, Andrew J. Goodpaster, Chairman. Atlantic Council, 1988.

New Patterns of Peace and Security: Implications for the U.S. Military. Atlantic Council Occasional Paper, December 1997.

New Priorities for U.S. Security: Military Needs and Tasks in a Time of Change. Atlantic Council, June 1991.

Nuclear Weapons and European Security. Atlantic Council, April 1996.

"Oil and Turmoil: Western Choices in the Middle East." ACUS's Special
Working Group on the Middle East, September 1979 (cochair with Brent
Scowcroft).

*A Positive Framework for U.S.–Russian Relations: A Possibility for the Next
Summit?* Atlantic Council, November 1995.

"Remarks." Royal United Services Institute (RUSI), London, England. *RUSI
Journal*, 16 December 1970.

"SACEUR Message to Chiefs of Defense," 16 September 1974.

Shaping the Nuclear Future: Toward a More Comprehensive Approach. Atlantic
Council Occasional Paper, January 1998.

Tighter Limits on Nuclear Arms: Issues and Opportunities for a New Era.
Atlantic Council Consultation Paper, Occasional Paper Series, May 1992.

Toward a Consensus on Military Service. Report of the Atlantic Council
Working Group on Military Service. Atlantic Council Policy Papers,
June 1982.

*The United States and Japan: Cooperative Leadership for Peace and Global
Prosperity.* A Report by a Committee of Six, Atlantic Council, The
Bretton Woods Committee, The Japan Center for International
Exchange, 25 April 1989.

*The United States, NATO, and Security Relations with Central and Eastern
Europe.* Atlantic Council Policy Paper Series, September 1993.

*U.S. International Leadership for the 21st Century: Building a National Foreign
Affairs Constituency.* Atlantic Council, January 1987.

*U.S. Policy toward the Soviet Union: A Long-Term Western Perspective, 1987–
2000.* Report of the Atlantic Council's Working Group on U.S.–Soviet
Policy. Lanham, MD: University Press of America, 1987. (Cochair with
Walter J. Stoessel.)

When Diplomacy Is Not Enough: Managing Multinational Military Interventions.
A Report to the Carnegie Commission on Preventing Deadly Conflict.
New York: Carnegie Corporation of New York, July 1996.

General Sources

Books

Acacia, John. *Clark Clifford: The Wise Man of Washington.* Lexington, KY:
The University Press of Kentucky, 2009.

Adams, Sherman. *First-Hand Report: The Story of the Eisenhower
Administration.* New York: Harper and Bros., 1961.

Adams, Valerie L. *Eisenhower's Fine Group of Fellows: Crafting a National
Security Policy to Uphold the Great Equation.* New York: Lexington
Books, 2006.

Ambrose, Stephen E. *Eisenhower, Soldier and President.* New York: Simon & Schuster, 1990.

———. *Eisenhower: Soldier, General of the Army, President-Elect, 1890–1952.* Vol. 1. New York: Simon & Schuster, 1983.

———. *Ike's Spies: Eisenhower and the Espionage Establishment.* Jackson, MS: University Press of Mississippi, 1999.

———. *Rise to Globalism: American Foreign Policy, 1938–1980.* 2nd rev. ed. New York: Penguin Books, 1980.

Anderson, David L. *Trapped by Success: The Eisenhower Administration and Vietnam, 1953–1961.* New York: Columbia University Press, 1991.

Astor, Gerald. *Presidents at War: From Truman to Bush: The Gathering of Military Power to Our Commanders in Chief.* Hoboken, NJ: John Wiley and Sons, 2006.

Atkinson, Rick. *The Day of Battle: The War in Sicily and Italy, 1943–1944.* New York: Henry Holt, 2007.

Bamford, James. *Body of Secrets: From the Cold War through the Dawn of a New Century.* New York: Doubleday, 2001.

Beauvoir, Simone de. *The Mandarins.* New York: The World Publishing Co., 1956.

Beschloss, Michael R. *Mayday: Eisenhower, Khrushchev, and the U-2 Affair.* Boston: Faber and Faber, 1986.

Bills, Scott L., and E. Timothy Smith, eds. *The Romance of History: Essays in Honor of Lawrence S. Kaplan.* Kent, OH: The Kent State University Press, 1997.

Binder, L. James. *Lemnitzer: A Soldier for His Time.* Washington, DC: Brassey's, 1997.

Bissell, Richard M., with Jonathan E. Lewis and Frances T. Pudlo. *Reflections of a Cold Warrior: From Yalta to the Bay of Pigs.* New Haven, CT: Yale University Press, 1996.

Blainey, Geoffrey. *The Causes of War.* New York: The Free Press, 1973.

Bletz, Donald F. *The Role of the Military Professional in U.S. Foreign Policy.* New York: Praeger Publishers, 1972.

Bohlen, Charles E. *Witness to History, 1929–1969.* New York: W. W. Norton, 1973.

Bose, Meena. *Shaping and Signaling Presidential Policy: The National Security Making of Eisenhower and Kennedy.* College Station, TX: Texas A&M University Press, 1998.

Bowie, Robert R., and Richard H. Immerman. *Waging Peace: How Eisenhower Shaped an Enduring Cold War Strategy.* New York: Oxford University Press, 1998.

Brands, H. W. *Traitor to His Class: The Privileged Life and Radical Presidency of Franklin Delano Roosevelt*. New York: Doubleday, 2008.

Brendon, Piers. *Ike: His Life and Times*. New York: Harper and Row, 1986.

Brodie, Barnard. *War and Politics*. New York: Macmillan Publishers, 1973.

Brown, John Mason. *The Worlds of Robert E. Sherwood: Mirror to His Times, 1896–1939*. New York: Harper and Row, 1965.

Brugioni, Dino A. *Eyes in the Sky: Eisenhower, the CIA, and the Cold War Aerial Espionage*. Annapolis, MD: Naval Institute Press, 2010.

Burke, John P., and Fred I. Greenstein. *How Presidents Test Reality: Decisions on Vietnam, 1954 and 1965*. New York: Russell Sage Foundation, 1989.

Bush, George H. W., and Brent Scowcroft. *A World Transformed*. New York: Vintage Books, 1999.

Caute, David. *The Dancer Defects: The Struggle for Cultural Supremacy during the Cold War*. Oxford: Oxford University Press, 2003.

Cline, Ray. *United States Army in World War II, The War Department, Washington Command Post: The Operations Division*. Washington, DC: Center of Military History, United States Army, 1985.

Conquest, Robert. *Reflections on a Ravaged Century*. New York: W. W. Norton, 2000.

Cox, Edward. *Grey Eminence: Fox Conner and the Art of Mentorship*. Stillwater, OK: New Forums Press, 2011.

Craig, Campbell, and Sergey Radchenko. *The Atomic Bomb and the Origins of the Cold War*. New Haven, CT: Yale University Press, 2008.

Craig, Gordon A., and Alexander L. George. *Force and Statecraft: Diplomatic Problems of Our Time*. New York: Oxford University Press, 1995.

Cray, Ed. *General of the Army George C. Marshall, Soldier and Statesman*. New York: Cooper Square Press, 2000.

Crosswell, D. K. R. *Beetle: The Life of General Walter Bedell Smith*. Lexington, KY: The University Press of Kentucky, 2010.

Cutler, Robert. *No Time for Rest*. Boston: Little, Brown, 1966.

Daalder, Ivo H. *The Nature and Practice of Flexible Response: NATO Strategy and Theater Nuclear Forces since 1967*. New York: Columbia University Press. 1991.

Daalder, Ivo H., and I. M. Destler. *In the Shadow of the Oval Office*. New York: Simon & Schuster, 2009.

Dallek, Robert. *Lyndon B. Johnson: Portrait of a President*. New York: Oxford University Press, 2004.

Department of State. *Foreign Relations of the United States*. Various volumes.

Destler, I. M. "The Presidency and National Security Organization." In *The National Security: Its Theory and Practice, 1945–1960*, edited by Norman A. Graebner. New York: Oxford University Press, 1986.

Dickson, Paul. *Sputnik: The Shock of the Century.* New York: Walker, 2007.

Dimbleby, David, and David Reynolds. *An Ocean Apart: The Relationship between Britain and America in the Twentieth Century.* New York: Random House, 1988.

Dockrill, Saki. *Eisenhower's New-Look National Security Policy, 1953–61.* New York: St. Martin's Press, 1996.

Ehrman, John. *Cabinet Government and War, 1890–1940.* Cambridge: Cambridge University Press, 1958.

Eisenhower, David, and Julie Nixon Eisenhower. *Going Home to Glory: A Memoir of Life with Dwight D. Eisenhower, 1961–1969.* New York: Simon & Schuster, 2010.

Eisenhower, Dwight D. *Crusade in Europe.* Garden City, NY: Doubleday, 1948.

———. *The White House Years: Mandate for Change, 1953–1956.* Garden City, NY: Doubleday, 1963.

———. *The White House Years: Waging Peace, 1956–1961.* Garden City, NY: Doubleday, 1965.

Eisenhower, John S. D. *Strictly Personal.* Garden City, NY: Doubleday, 1974.

Elsey, George. *An Unplanned Life.* Columbia, MO: The University of Missouri Press, 2005.

Eubank, Keith. *The Summit Conferences, 1919–1960.* Norman, OK: University of Oklahoma Press, 1966.

Falls, Cyril. *A Hundred Years of War.* London: Gerald Duckworth, 1953.

Ferguson, Niall, Charles S. Maier, Erez Manela, and Daniel J. Sargent. *The 1970s in Perspective.* Cambridge, MA: The Belknap Press of Harvard University Press, 2010.

Ferrell, James. *The Diary of James C. Hagerty: Eisenhower in Mid-Course, 1954–1955.* Bloomington, IN: Indiana University Press, 1983.

Finkelman, Paul. "National Security Council: The Truman and Eisenhower Years." In *Encyclopedia of the New American Nation.* New York: Charles Scribner's, 2005.

Fontaine, Andre. *History of the Cold War: From the Korean War to the Present.* New York: Random House/Pantheon Books, 1969.

Gaddis, John Lewis. *George Kennan: An American Life.* New York: The Penguin Press, 2011.

———. *We Now Know: Rethinking Cold War History.* New York: Oxford University Press, 1997.

Galambos, Louis, et al. *The Papers of Dwight David Eisenhower.* Vols. 12–13, *NATO and the Campaign of 1952.* Baltimore, MD: The Johns Hopkins University Press, 1989.

Galambos, Louis, and Daun Van Ee. *The Papers of Dwight David Eisenhower.* Vol. 21, *The Presidency: Keeping the Peace.* Baltimore, MD: The Johns Hopkins University Press, 2001.

Gartoff, Raymond L. *A Journey through the Cold War: A Memoir of Containment and Coexistence.* Washington, DC: Brookings Institution Press, 2001.

Gates, David. *Non-Offensive Defence: An Alternative Strategy for NATO?* New York: St. Martin's, 1991.

Gates, Robert M. *From the Shadows: The Ultimate Insider's Story of Five Presidents and How They Won the Cold War.* New York: Simon & Schuster, 1996.

Gellman, Barton. *Contending with Kennan: Toward a Philosophy of American Power.* New York: Praeger, 1984.

Gerth, Hans, and C. Wright Mills. *Character and Social Structure: The Psychology of Social Institutions.* New York: Harcourt, Brace and World, 1953.

Goldstein, Gordon M. *Lessons in Disaster: McGeorge Bundy and the Path to War in Vietnam.* New York: Henry Holt, Holt Paperbacks, 2008.

Graebner, Norman A., ed. *The National Security: Its Theory and Practices, 1945–1960.* New York: Oxford University Press, 1968.

Gray, Colin S. *Strategy and History: Essays on Theory and Practice.* New York: Routledge, 2006.

Greene, Graham. *The Lost Childhood and Other Essays.* London: Eyre and Spottiswoode, 1951.

Greenstein, Fred. *The Hidden-Hand Presidency: Eisenhower as Leader.* Baltimore, MD: The Johns Hopkins University Press, 1994.

Gunther, John. *Procession: Dominant Personalities of Four Decades as Seen by the Author of the Inside Books.* London: Hamish Hamilton, 1965.

Gutman, Amy, and Dennis Thompson. *Ethics and Politics: Cases and Comments.* 3rd ed. Chicago: Nelson-Hall Publishers, 1997.

Haapanen, Lawrence W. "The Missed Opportunity: The U-2 and Paris." In *Eisenhower's War of Words: Rhetoric and Leadership,* edited by Martin J. Medhurst. East Lansing, MI: Michigan State University Press, 1994.

Halberstam, David. *The Best and the Brightest.* New York: Ballantine Books, 1993.

Hammond, Paul Y. *Organizing for Defense: The American Military Establishment in the Twentieth Century.* Princeton, NJ: Princeton University Press, 1961.

Harlow, Giles, and C. Maerz, eds. *Measures Short of War: The George F. Kennan Lectures at the National War College, 1946–47.* Washington, DC: National Defense University Press 1991.

Haslam, Jonathan. *Russia's Cold War: From the October Revolution to the Fall of the Wall.* New Haven, CT: Yale University Press, 2011.

Henderson, Phillip G. *Managing the Presidency: The Eisenhower Legacy—From Kennedy to Reagan.* Boulder, CO: Westview Press, 1988.

Henry, David. "Eisenhower and Sputnik: The Irony of Failed Leadership." In *Eisenhower's War of Words: Rhetoric and Leadership,* edited by Martin J. Medhurst. East Lansing, MI: Michigan State University Press, 1994.

Herspring, Dale R. *The Pentagon and the Presidency: Civil-Military Relations from FDR to George W. Bush.* Lawrence, KS: University Press of Kansas, 2005.

Hess, Stephen. *Organizing the Presidency.* 3rd ed. Washington, DC: Brookings Institution Press, 2002.

———. *Presidents and the Presidency.* Washington, DC: Brookings Institution Press, 1996.

Heuser, Beatrice, and Robert O'Neill, eds. *Securing Peace in Europe, 1945–62: Thoughts for the Post-Cold War Era.* New York: St. Martin's, 1992.

Hixson, Walter L. *George F. Kennan: Cold War Iconoclast.* New York: Columbia University Press, 1989.

Hobbs, Joseph P. *Dear General: Eisenhower's Wartime Letters to Marshall.* Baltimore: The Johns Hopkins University Press, 1971.

"Howitzer." *USMA Yearbook.* West Point, NY: U.S. Military Academy, 1939.

Humphries, James F. *Through the Valley: Vietnam 1967–1968.* Boulder, CO: Lynne Rienner, 1999.

Huntley, James Robert. *An Architect of Democracy: Building a Mosaic of Peace.* Washington, DC: New Academia Publishing, 2006.

Husted, Stewart W. *George C. Marshall: Rubrics of Leadership.* Carlisle Barracks, PA: Army War College Foundation, 2006.

Huxley, Aldous. *Ends and Means: An Enquiry into the Nature of Ideals and into the Methods Employed for Their Realization.* London: Chatto and Windus, 1948.

Inderfurth, Karl F., and Loch K. Johnson, eds. *Decisions of the Highest Order: Perspectives on the National Security Council.* Pacific Grove, CA: Brooks/Cole, 1988.

Ireland, Timothy P. *Creating the Entangling Alliance: The Origins of the North Atlantic Treaty Organization.* Westport, CT: Greenwood Press, 1981.

Isaak, Robert A. *Individuals and World Politics.* North Scituate, MA: Duxbury Press, 1975.

Ismay, Lord Hastings. *The Memoirs of General Lord Ismay.* New York: The Viking Press, 1960.

James, P. D. *Time to Be Earnest: A Fragment of Autobiography.* New York: Ballantine Books, 1999.

James, Robert Rhodes. "The Evolving Concept of the International Civil Service." In *International Administration: Its Evolution and Contemporary Applications*, edited by Robert S. Jordan. New York: Oxford University Press, 1971.

Jordan, Amos A., ed. *Issues of National Security in the 1970s*. New York: Praeger, 1967.

Jordan, Ralph B. *Born to Fight: The Life of Admiral Halsey*. Philadelphia: David McKay, 1946.

Jordan, Robert S., ed. "The Contribution of the British Civil Service and Cabinet Secretariat Tradition to International Prevention and Control of War." In *The Limitations of Military Power: Essays Presented to Professor Norman Gibbs on His Eightieth Birthday*, edited by John B. Hattendorf and Malcolm H. Murfett. New York: St. Martin's, 1990.

———. *Generals in International Politics: NATO's Supreme Allied Commander, Europe*. Lexington, KY: The University Press of Kentucky, 1987.

———. "The Influence of the British Secretariat Tradition on the Formation of the League of Nations." In *International Administration: Its Evolution and Contemporary Applications*, edited by Robert S. Jordan, pp. 27–50. New York: Oxford University Press, 1971.

———. *The NATO International Staff/Secretariat, 1952–1957: A Study in International Administration*. London: Oxford University Press, 1967.

———. *Political Leadership in NATO: A Study in Multinational Diplomacy*. Boulder, CO: Westview Press, 1979.

Kagan, Donald. *On the Origins of War and the Preservation of Peace*. New York: Doubleday, 1995.

Kaplan, Lawrence S. *The Long Entanglement: NATO's First Fifty Years*. Westport, CT: Praeger, 1999.

———. *NATO Divided, NATO United: The Evolution of an Alliance*. Westport, CT: Praeger, 2004.

Kariel, Henry S. *In Search of Authority: Twentieth-Century Political Thought*. Glencoe, IL: Free Press of Glencoe, 1964.

Keegan, John. *The Mask of Command*. New York: Penguin Books, 1987.

Kennan, George F. *American Diplomacy, 1900–1950*. Chicago: University of Chicago Press, 1951.

———. *Russia, the Atom, and the West: BBC Reith Lectures 1957*. London: Oxford University Press, 1958.

Kennedy, David M. *Freedom from Fear: The American People in Depression and War, 1929–1945*. New York: Oxford University Press, 1999.

Kennedy, Paul. *Grand Strategies in War and Peace*. New Haven, CT: Yale University Press, 1991.

————. *The Rise and Fall of the Great Powers: Economic Change and Military Conflict from 1500 to 2000*. New York: Vintage Books, 1989.

Kennedy, Robert. "International Leadership in an Era of Détente." In *National Security and Detente*, p. 304. New York: Thomas Y. Crowell, 1976.

King, Jere Clemens. *Generals and Politicians*. Berkeley, CA: University of California Press, 1951.

Kinnard, Douglas. *Eisenhower: Soldier-Statesman of the American Century*. Washington, DC: Brassey's, 2002.

————. *President Eisenhower and Strategic Management: A Study in Defense Politics*. New York: Pergamon-Brassey's, 1989.

————. *The Secretary of Defense*. Lexington, KY: The University Press of Kentucky, 1980.

Korb, Lawrence J. *The Joint Chiefs of Staff: The First Twenty-Five Years*. Bloomington, IN: Indiana University Press, 1976.

Krock, Arthur. *Memoirs: Sixty Years on the Firing Line*. New York: Funk and Wagnall's, 1968.

Kuklick, Bruce. *Blind Oracles: Intellectuals and War from Kennan to Kissinger*. Princeton, NJ: Princeton University Press, 2006.

LaFeber, Walter. *America, Russia, and the Cold War, 1945–1966*. New York: John Wiley and Sons, 1968.

Lay, James S. *Organizational History of the National Security Council during the Truman and Eisenhower Administrations*. Ann Arbor, MI: University of Michigan Press, 1988.

Macmillan, Margaret. *Paris 1919: Six Months That Changed the World*. New York: Random House, 2001.

Marlantes, Karl. *What It Is Like to Go to War*. New York: Atlantic Monthly Press, 2011.

Matloff, Michael. "The American Approach to War, 1919–1945." In *The Theory and Practice of War*, edited by Michael Howard. London: Cassell, 1965.

Matson, Floyd W. *The Broken Image: Man, Science, and Society*. New York: Anchor Books, 1966.

May, Ernest R. *American Cold War Strategy: Interpreting NSC 68*. New York: Bedford/St. Martin's, 1993.

McMaster, H. R. *Dereliction of Duty: Lyndon Johnson, Robert McNamara, the Joint Chiefs of Staff, and the Lies That Led to Vietnam*. New York: Harper Perennial, 1997.

Mearsheimer, John J. *The Tragedy of Great Power Politics*. New York: W. W. Norton, 2001.

Medhurst, Martin J., and H. W. Brands, eds. *Critical Reflections on the Cold War: Linking Rhetoric and History.* College Station, TX: Texas A & M University Press, 2000.

Meyer, Cord, Jr. *Facing Reality: From World Federalism to the CIA.* New York: Harper and Row, 1980.

Miller, Merle. *Ike the Soldier as They Knew Him.* New York: G. P. Putnam's Sons, 1987.

Mosley, Leonard. *Dulles: A Biography of Eleanor, Allen, and John Foster Dulles and Their Family Network.* New York: The Dial Press, 1978.

Neff, Donald. *Warriors at Suez: Eisenhower Takes America into the Middle East.* New York: Simon & Schuster, 1981.

Nelson, C. Richard, and Kenneth Weisbrode, eds. *Reversing Relations with Former Adversaries: U.S. Foreign Policy after the Cold War.* Gainesville, FL: University Press of Florida, 1998.

Neustadt, Richard E. *Presidential Power: The Politics of Leadership.* New York: The Free Press, 1961.

Nichols, David A. *Eisenhower 1956: The President's Year of Crisis—Suez and the Brink of War.* New York: Simon & Schuster, 2011.

Notting, Tyler. *Once and Future Policy Planning: Solarium for Today.* Washington, DC: Eisenhower Institute, 1993.

O'Ballance, Edgar. *Korea: 1950–1953.* Malabar, FL: Robert E. Krieger, 1985.

Ogburn, William. *Social Change with Respect to Cultural and Original Nature.* New York: Dell, 1966.

Pach, Chester J., and Elmo Richardson. *The Presidency of Dwight D Eisenhower.* Rev. ed. Lawrence, KS: The University Press of Kansas, 1991.

Patterson, Bradley H., Jr. *The Ring of Power: The White House Staff and Its Expanding Role in Government.* New York: Basic Books, 1988.

———. *The White House Staff: Inside the West Wing and Beyond.* Washington, DC: Brookings Institution Press, 2000.

Patterson, James T. *Grand Expectations: The United States, 1945–1974.* New York: Oxford University Press, 1996.

Pearlman, Michael D. *Warmaking and American Democracy: The Struggle over Military Strategy, 1700 to the Present.* Lawrence, KS: University Press of Kansas, 1999.

Pedlow, Gregory W., and Donald E. Welzenbach. *The CIA and the U-2 Program, 1954–1974.* Washington, DC: History Staff, Center for the Study of Intelligence, Central Intelligence Agency, 1998.

———. "The Politics of NATO Command, 1950–1965." In *U.S. Military Forces in Europe: The Early Years, 1945–1970*, edited by Simon W. Duke and Wolfgang Krieger. Boulder, CO: Westview Press, 1993.

Perret, Geoffrey. *Eisenhower.* New York: Random House, 1999.

Perry, Mark. *Partners in Command: George Marshall and Dwight Eisenhower in War and Peace.* New York: The Penguin Press, 2007.

Pickett, William B. "General Andrew Jackson Goodpaster, Managing National Security." In *The Human Tradition in America since 1945*, edited by David L. Anderson, pp. 25–45. Wilmington, DE: Scholarly Books, 2003.

Pogue, Forest C. *George C. Marshall: Organizer of Victory, 1943–1945.* New York: The Viking Press, 1973.

———. *George C. Marshall, Statesman 1945–1959.* New York: Penguin Books, 1989.

Posen, Barry R. *The Sources of Military Doctrine: France, Britain, and Germany between the World Wars.* Ithaca, NY: Cornell University Press, 1984.

Prados, John. *Presidents' Secret Wars: CIA and Pentagon Covert Operations from World War II through the Persian Gulf.* Rev. ed. New York: Ivan R. Dee/ Elephant Paperbacks, 1996.

Preble, Christopher A. *John F. Kennedy and the Missile Gap.* DeKalb, IL: Northern Illinois University Press, 2004.

Prosterman, Roy L. *Surviving to 3000: An Introduction to the Study of Lethal Conflict.* Belmont, CA: Duxbury Press, 1972.

Reardon, Capt. Mark, CE. *The Battalions: History of the 1108th Engineer Combat Group.* Publisher unknown, 1945.

Rearden, Steven L. *The Evolution of American Strategic Doctrine: Paul H. Nitze and the Soviet Challenge.* Washington, DC: Westview Press, 1984.

———. *The Formative Years, 1947–1950.* Washington, DC: Office of the Secretary of Defense, 1984.

Reichard, Gary W. "The Domestic Politics of National Security." In *The National Security: Its Theory and Practice, 1945–1960*, edited by Norman A. Graebner. New York: Oxford University Press, 1986.

Richardson, Elmo. *The Presidency of Dwight D. Eisenhower.* Lawrence, KS: University Press of Kansas, 1979.

Roberts, Andrew. *Masters and Commanders: How Four Titans Won the War in the West, 1941–1945.* New York: HarperCollins, 2009.

Roberts, Chalmers M. *The Nuclear Years: The Arms Race and Arms Control, 1945–1970.* New York: Praeger Publishers, 1971.

Rockefeller Panel Report. *Prospect for America: The Problems and Opportunities Confronting American Democracy—in Foreign Policy, in Military Preparedness, in Education, in Social and Economic Affairs.* New York: Doubleday, 1961.

Roskill, Stephen. *Hankey, Man of Secrets.* London: Collins, 1972.

Rothkopf, David J. *Running the World: The Inside Story of the National Security Council and the Architects of American Power.* New York: Public Affairs, 2005.

Rottman, Gordon L. *U.S. Combat Engineer, 1941–45.* Long Island City, NY: Osprey Publishing, 2010.

Ruffner, Kevin C., ed. *CORONA: America's First Satellite Program.* Washington, DC: CIA History Staff, Center for the Study of Intelligence, 1995.

Saunders, Francis Stonor. *The Cultural Cold War: The CIA and the World of Arts and Letters.* New York: Harper and Row, 1980.

Schlesinger, Arthur M., Jr. *The Cycles of American History.* Boston: Houghton Mifflin, 1986.

Schmidt, Gustav, ed. *A History of NATO: The First Fifty Years.* Vol. 1. New York: Palgrave, 2001.

Schratz, Paul R., ed. *Evolution of the American Military Establishment since World War II.* Lexington, VA: George C. Marshall Research Foundation, 1978.

Senger und Etterlin, Frido von. *Neither Fear nor Hope: The Wartime Career of General Frido von Senger und Etterlin: Defender of Cassino.* Translated from the German by George Malcolm. London: MacDonald, 1960.

Sheehan, Neil. *A Fiery Peace in a Cold War: Bernard Schriever and the Ultimate Weapon.* New York: Random House, 2009.

Sherwood, Robert E. *Roosevelt and Hopkins: An Intimate History.* New York: Harper and Row, 1948.

Slessor, Sir John. *The Great Deterrent.* New York: Frederick A. Praeger, 1957.

Smith, Jean Edward. *Eisenhower in War and Peace.* New York: Random House, 2012.

Smith, Theresa C. *Trojan Peace: Some Deterrence Propositions Tested.* Denver, CO: University of Denver Graduate School of International Affairs, 1982.

Sorley, Lewis. *A Better War: The Unexamined Victories and Final Tragedy of America's Last Years in Vietnam.* New York: Harcourt, Inc., 1999.

———. "Goodpaster: Maintaining Deterrence during Détente." In *Generals in International Politics: NATO's Supreme Allied Commander, Europe,* edited by Robert S. Jordan, pp. 122–150. Lexington, KY: The University Press of Kentucky, 1987.

———. *Honor Bright: History and Origins of the West Point Honor Code and System.* New York: McGraw-Hill Learning Solutions, 2009.

———. *Honorable Warrior: General Harold K. Johnson and the Ethics of Command.* Lawrence, KS: University Press of Kansas, 1998.

———. *Thunderbolt: General Creighton Abrams and the Army of His Times.* Bloomington, IN: Indiana University Press, 2008.

———. *Westmoreland: The General Who Lost Vietnam.* New York: Houghton Mifflin Harcourt, 2011.

Stegner, Wallace. "The Writer and the Concept of Adulthood." In *Adulthood*, edited by Erik H. Erikson, p. 227. New York: W. W. Norton, 1978.

Stoler, Mark A. *George C. Marshall, Soldier-Statesman of the American Century*. New York: Twayne/Simon & Schuster, 1989.

Stromseth, Jane E. *The Origins of Flexible Response: NATO's Debate over Strategy in the 1960s*. New York: St. Martin's, 1988.

Summers, Col. Harry G., Jr. *On Strategy: The Vietnam War in Context*. Carlisle Barracks, PA: Strategic Studies Institute, U.S. Army War College, 1981.

Taubman, Philip. *Secret Empire: Eisenhower, The CIA, and the Hidden Story of America's Space Espionage*. New York: Simon & Schuster, 2003.

Taylor, John M. *An American Soldier: The Wars of General Taylor*. Novato, CA: Presidio Press, 2001.

Taylor, Maxwell D. *The Uncertain Trumpet*. New York: Harper, 1960.

Thomas, Evan. *Ike's Bluff: President Eisenhower's Secret Battle to Save the World*. New York: Little, Brown, 2012.

Thompson, Kenneth W., and Steven L. Rearden. *Paul H. Nitze on National Security and Arms Control*. New York: University Press of America, 1990.

Toma, Peter, and Andrew Gyorgy, with Robert S. Jordan, eds. *Basic Issues in International Relations*. Boston, MA: Allyn and Bacon, 1974.

Tonsetic, Robert L. *Days of Valor: An Inside Account of the Bloodiest Six Months of the Vietnam War*. Philadelphia: Casemate, 2007.

Trachtenberg, Marc. *A Constructed Peace: The Making of the European Settlement, 1945–1963*. Princeton, NJ: Princeton University Press, 1999.

———. *History and Strategy*. Princeton, NJ: Princeton University Press, 1991.

Trento, Joseph J. *The Secret History of the CIA*. New York: Carroll and Graf Publishers, 2001.

Treverton, Gregory F. *Covert Action: The CIA and American Intervention in the Postwar World*. London: I. B. Tauris, 1987.

Wahlfeld, John V. *Eisenhower and the Second Crusade in Europe*. Chapel Hill, NC: University of North Carolina, 1975.

Wallas, Graham. *Human Nature in Politics*. London: Constable, 1948.

Warren, Sidney. *The President as World Leader*. New York: J. B. Lippincott, 1964.

Weiner, Tim. *Legacy of Ashes: The History of the CIA*. New York: Anchor Books, 2008.

Weisberger, Bernard A. *Cold War, Cold Peace: The United States and Russia since 1945*. New York: American Heritage, 1985.

Weisbrode, Kenneth. *The Atlantic Century: Four Generations of Extraordinary Diplomats Who Forged American's Vital Alliance with Europe*. Cambridge, MA: Da Capo Press, 2009.

Westerfeld, H. Bradford, ed. *Inside CIA's Private World: Declassified Articles from the Agency's Internal Journal, 1955–1992*. New Haven, CT: Yale University Press, 1995.

Wilford, Hugh. *The Mighty Wurlitzer: How the CIA Played America.* Cambridge, MA: Harvard University Press, 2009.

Wilson, Colin. *Beyond the Outsider.* New York: Carroll and Graf, 1991.

———. *The Outsider.* New York: Penguin Putnam, 1967.

Yost, Charles W. *History and Memory: A Statesman's Perceptions of the Twentieth Century.* New York: W. W. Norton, 1980.

Zeldin, Theodore. *An Intimate History of Humanity.* New York: Harper Perennial, 1996.

Zuckerman, Sir Solly. *Monkeys, Men, and Missiles: An Autobiography 1946–88.* New York: W. W. Norton, 1989.

Periodicals

Charlton, Linda. "New West Point Superintendent." *New York Times*, 5 April 1977.

Cleveland, Harlan. "Crisis Diplomacy." *Foreign Affairs*, July 1963.

Davies, Paul L. "A Business Look at the Army." *Harvard Business Review*, July–August 1954.

Die Welt. "Goodpaster's Warning." October 22, 1970.

Hansen, Richard P. "The Crisis of the West Point Honor Code." *Military Affairs*, April 1985.

Kennan, George F. "America's Unstable Soviet Policy." *The Atlantic Monthly*, November 1982.

Marchio, James. "The Planning Coordination Group: Bureaucratic Casualty in the Cold War Campaign to Exploit Soviet-Bloc Vulnerabilities." *Journal of Cold War Studies* 4, no. 4 (Fall 2002).

Nathan, James A. "A Fragile Detente: The U-2 Incident Re-examined." *Military Affairs* 39 (October 1975): 97–104.

Osgood, Kenneth A. "Hearts and Minds: The Unconventional Cold War." *Journal of Cold War Studies* 4, no. 2 (Spring 2002): 85–107.

"Paying for Defense." Reprinted in the *International Herald Tribune*, 4 November 1969.

Shane, Scott. "Spotlight Again Falls on Web Tools and Change." *New York Times*, 29 January 2011.

Smiley, Jane. "Sherry Turkle's Meditations on Technology, 'Alone Together.'" *Washington Post*, 28 January 2011.

Stout, David. "Andrew J. Goodpaster, 90, Soldier and Scholar Dies." *New York Times*, 17 May 2005.

Weisbrode, Kenneth. "A Tale of Three Cold Warriors." *NATO Review*, Spring 2006.

Other Sources

"Activities of Possible Presidential Interest." *Operations Coordination Board Briefing Notes*. Washington, DC: National Security Council, 23 November 1954.

"AP Night Tapes." SHAPE Public Affairs Office, Press Cutting Distribution Sheet, 16 December 1974.

Burr, William, ed. "The Atomic Bomb and the End of World War II: A Collection of Primary Sources." National Security Archive Electronic Briefing Book No. 162. *The National Security Archive*. Posted 5 August 2005, updated 27 April 2007. http://www.gwu.edu/~nsarchiv/NSAEBB/NSAEBB162/index.htm.

"The Challenge of Leadership in Foreign Affairs—PROJECT SOLARIUM: A Collective Oral History." Paper presented at John Foster Dulles Centennial Conference, Princeton University, Princeton, NJ, 1988.

Deagle, Edwin A. "General George A. Lincoln: Architect of American National Security." Unpublished manuscript.

Dean, Edgar P., Secretary of Study Groups, Council on Foreign Relations, to Lt. Col. Herman Beukema. U.S. Military Academy, West Point, New York, 23 February 1939.

Dulles, Allen. "Letter from Allen Dulles to Goodpaster." Washington, DC: White House: Office of the Staff Secretary–International Series, 18 July 1956.

Eisenhower, Dwight D., to Goodpaster, 20 December 1960.

———. *Report to Congress*. Eisenhower Presidential Library, 1961.

Eisenhower, John S. D. Oral history interviews by Maclyn P. Burg. 10 March 1972; 20 August 1976. Eisenhower Presidential Library.

———. Interview by Carol Hegeman, Supervisory Park Ranger, 26 January 1984. Eisenhower Presidential Library.

Erdmann, Andrew P. N. "The Intellectual and Bureaucratic Origins of Flexible Response: The Policy Planning Staff, 1953–1961." Unpublished manuscript, 1999.

"JCS Reform, Proceedings of the Conference." Newport, RI: Naval War College, n.d.

Koplow, David A. "Major Acts of Congress | Arms Control and Disarmament Act (1961) and Amendments." *E-Notes*, 21 March 2011. http://www.enotes.com/arms-control-disarmament-act-1961-amendments-reference/arms-control-disarmament-act-1961-amendments.

Scowcroft, Brent, interview by Robert S. Jordan, June 2010.

———. Memorandum of conversation, 15 February 1973, Washington, DC.

Stayanoff, Russ. "Major General Fox Conner: Soldier, Mentor, Enigma: Operations Chief (G-3) of the AEF," *The Doughboy Center: American*

Expeditionary Forces, World War One, http://www.worldwar1.com/dbc/
foxconner.htm.

Tierney, Maj. Jeffrey J., USA, "Campaign Planning: A Missing Piece in the
Joint Planning Process." *Global Security.org*, 1992. http://www.globalsecu
rity.org/military/library/report/1992/TJJ.htm.

Wampler, Robert S. "NATO Strategic Planning and Nuclear Weapons, 1950–
1957," *Nuclear History Program, Occasional Paper 6*. College Park, MD:
Center for International Security Studies, University of Maryland, 1990.

Index

Abrams, Creighton, 119, 121, 122, 123, 131, 157
accomplishments when not seeking credit, 148, 154–55
Acheson, Dean, 122
Adams, Sherman, 55–56, 95–96, 99–100
adulthood behaviors and definition, 4–5
Advanced Research Projects Agency (ARPA), 48
Air Force, U.S.: interservice rivalries, 86–87; joint committees of the services, 14–15; lobbying of Congress by, 70; reconnaissance flights over Soviet Union, 108, 112–13
Alaska-Hawaii-Panama strategic triangle, 8
All Souls College, Oxford University, 164n29
Alliance Defense program, 127
Allied Command Europe (ACE): activation of, 26, 165n13; command structure organization, 24–29; deterrence, defense, and détente objectives of, 30–31; formation of, 24
Allied nations combined chiefs-of-staff committee, 14–15
ambition, politics, and careers, 141
American Veterans Center, Andrew J. Goodpaster Prize and Lecture, 158n1
Amory, Robert, 37
Anderson, Dillon, 78
Anderson, Dorothy. See Goodpaster, Dorothy "Dossy" Anderson
Andrew J. Goodpaster Award, George C. Marshall Foundation, ix, 158n1
Andrew J. Goodpaster Endowed Leadership and Honor Lecture Series, 150
Andrew J. Goodpaster Prize and Lecture, American Veterans Center, 158n1
arms control and disarmament, 66–68, 88–91
Arms Control and Disarmament Act, 90–91, 178n26
Arms Control and Disarmament Agency (ACDA), 90–91, 178n26

Army, U.S.: budget for, 5; commitment to Army career, 6–7, 141–42; Eighth Infantry Division command, 93; Eisenhower and interservice deliberations, 142, 185n3; force strength before World War II, 5; future of Army, study by young officers to shape, 16; Goodpaster as Chief of Staff, consideration for, 123, 130; interservice rivalries, 86–87; joint committees of the services, 14–15; lobbying of Congress by, 70; New Look policy and conventional forces, 43–44; officer corps class size increase to prepare for war, 5; warfighting doctrine, 8; Westmoreland as Chief of Staff, 123
Army Corps of Engineers, U.S.: Camp Claiborne assignment, 9; Camp Gruber assignment, 9, 161n26; Command and General Staff College course, 9; commission in, ix, 7; construction project specs, 9; infantry service as second mission for engineers, 10; number of officers and enlisted men pre–World War II, 160n18; Panama and Panama Canal assignment, 7–9
Association of Princeton Graduate Alumni (APGA), 20
Atlantic Council: meetings between Soviets and, 154; nuclear weapons policy, 152–53; role at, xii, 147; Soviet and Russian policy, 153–54

behavior, meaning of, ix
Beloff, Max, 164n29
Berry, Sidney, 137
Beukema, Herman, 162n4
Biological Weapons Convention, 178n26
Bissell, Richard, Jr.: CIA role, 105; Cuba and Bay of Pigs plans, 92; reconnaissance flights over Soviet Union, 104, 105–7, 108, 109–10, 180n13
Bosnia, 154

to, 23, 24; writings about, 165n3.
See also supreme allied commander,
Europe (SACEUR)
nuclear weapons: arms control and disarmament, 66–68, 88–91; decision-
making changes because of, 17–18;
deterrence and stockpile of, 45–47,
48–52, 169n8; effects on the conduct of
military activities, 17–18, 35, 83, 86–88,
152–53, 163n20; Eisenhower strategy on
use of, 45–47, 169n6; elimination of,
153, 155, 157; Goodpaster thoughts on,
152–53; grand strategy for, 87–88; JASC
study of, 17; Korea, tactical nuclear
weapons use in, 17; Live Oak role, 27;
massive retaliation, 43–44, 45–46, 83,
86, 87–88, 89; more weapons and ideal
number to have, 152–53, 155n11; New
Look policy and reliance on, 43–44;
planning for use of, 17–18; proliferation of in volatile regions, 153; psychological readiness to use, 17; reduction
in inventories of, 153; roles and limitations of, 153; Soviet detonation of,
34; Soviet surprise attack on U.S., 47;
stockpiling of, 17; strategic and tactical
use of, 17–18, 50–51; testing and verification, 107; threat from and preparing
to act on threat, 43–44; U.S. inventory
of, 45–47

O'Brien, Jane Margaret, 150
Okinawa, 62
Open Skies proposal, 66–67, 103, 180n2
Operations and Plans Division (OPD),
War Department: duties at, 13, 15;
General Marshall's Command Post, 13;
Japan invasion planning, 15–16, 163n12;
mandate and mission, 15; Pacific war-
time planning trip, 14; plans and stra-
tegic direction of military forces,
responsibility for, 15; principles to
guide dealings with overseas com-
mands, 14; recruitment to, 13; Strat-
egy and Policy Group chief, Lincoln
as, 13–14
Osmana, Sergio, 73
Outer Space Treaty, 178n26
Oxford University, 5, 14, 158, 164nn29–31

Panama and Panama Canal, 7–9
Paris Conference, 106, 109–12, 114, 180n4
Partnership for Peace (PfP) program, 154
Patton, George, 137
peace: détente policy and, 51–52; maintenance of, 32
Persons, Wilton "Jerry," 56, 62
Philippines, 8, 73
Plowden, Edwin, 28
Poland, 7, 65
Political-Military Survey Section, 16
politics: ambition, politics, and careers,
141; foreign policy and national security, political framework for, 84–86,
142–43, 145, 186n4; intellectuals, role
for in, 169n30; political war, dangers
of, 168–69n28
Powers, Francis Gary, 106, 108, 109–11,
114, 181n35
Princeton University, 16, 18–22, 164n30
psychological warfare and propaganda, 38,
40, 42
public service, 154–55

Quemoy and Matsu islands and Formosa
Strait crisis, 50–51, 62, 87

Radford, Arthur W., 43, 44, 77, 96, 108, 109
RAND Corporation, 30, 166–67n30
RB-47H aircraft, 113, 182n40
RB-57D aircraft, 108
retirement: policy interests after, xii; post-
Army activities, 160n13; SACEUR role
and request for, 131–33
Rhodes scholarship, 5, 13–14, 19
Ridgway, Matthew, xi, 27, 87, 183–84n13
Rogers, Bernard, 136, 137
Roosevelt, Franklin D., 7, 60–61, 73
Rotary scholarship, 19
Rowny, Edward L., 19
Rubenstein, Terry Meyerhoff, 150
Rusk, Dean, 37
Russia. *See* Soviet Union and Russia

St. Anthony's College, Oxford Univer-
sity, 164n29
St. Mary's City, 150
St. Mary's College: board member at, x,
xii, 149–51; Goodpaster Hall, ix, 151;
Heritage Project, 150; improvements to

About the Author

Robert S. Jordan, who holds doctorates from both Princeton and Oxford Universities, has taught advanced courses in national security and international organization at U.S. war colleges and at private and public universities in the United States, Europe, and Africa. He served as director of research for the United Nations Institute for Training and Research and has participated in research projects at the Battelle Memorial Institute, the Ford Foundation, the Lucius Littauer Foundation, the Rockefeller Foundation, and the Atlantic Council. He was Distinguished Professor and Fleet Professor for the U.S. Naval War College. He also was University Research Professor at the University of New Orleans. He has published widely on Cold War alliance policy, coalition maritime affairs, international administration, and military biography.